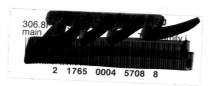
WITHDRAWN

The Family in Rural Society

Also of Interest

†*Rural Society: Issues for the 1980s,* edited by Don A. Dillman and Daryl S. Hobbs

†*Poverty in Rural America: A Case Study,* Janet M. Fitchen

Rural Education in Urbanized Nations: Issues and Innovations, edited by Jonathan P. Sher

The Myth of the Family Farm: Agribusiness Dominance of U.S. Agriculture, Ingolf Vogeler

Women and the Social Costs of Economic Development: Two Colorado Case Studies, Elizabeth Moen, Elise Boulding, Jane Lillydahl, and Risa Palm

†*Education in Rural America: A Reassessment of Conventional Wisdom,* edited by Jonathan P. Sher

The Family in Post-Industrial America: Some Fundamental Perceptions for Public Policy Development, edited by David Pearce Snyder

†*Violence and the Family,* edited by Maurice R. Green

Making of Child and Family Policy, edited by Harold C. Wallach and Lyn Chambers

†*Politics in Rural America: People, Parties, and Policy,* Frank M. Bryan

†Available in hardcover and paperback.

Westview Special Studies in Contemporary Social Issues

The Family in Rural Society
edited by Raymond T. Coward and William M. Smith, Jr.

Social and political attention often is focused on urban issues, neglecting the still-rural character of much of the United States. This volume of original papers provides a clear picture of present-day rural society, with special emphasis on the changing role and structure of the family. It describes demographic trends, discusses the family aspects of the new wave of inmigrants to small towns and rural communities, reviews the diversity of patterns and forms adopted by rural families, considers the plight of the rural aged, and explores the dynamics of intrafamily personal relationships. The book ends with speculations on future prospects and challenges facing rural families.

Dr. Raymond T. Coward is research associate professor at the Center for Rural Studies and associate professor in the College of Education and Social Services at the University of Vermont. **Dr. William M. Smith, Jr.,** is professor emeritus of rural sociology at the Pennsylvania State University. Both Dr. Coward and Dr. Smith are active members of the Rural Sociological Society.

The Family in Rural Society

edited by Raymond T. Coward
and William M. Smith, Jr.

Westview Press / Boulder, Colorado

Westview Special Studies in Contemporary Social Issues

Copyright © 1981 by Westview Press, Inc.

Published in 1981 in the United States of America by
Westview Press, Inc.
5500 Central Avenue
Boulder, Colorado 80301
Frederick A. Praeger, Publisher

Library of Congress Cataloging in Publication Data
Main entry under title:
The Family in rural society.
   (Westview special studies in contemporary social issues)
   Includes index.
   1. Rural families—United States—Addresses, essays, lectures. I. Coward, Raymond T.
II. Smith, William M. III. Series: Westview special studies in contemporary social issues.
HQ536.F369   306.8'0973   81-1769
ISBN 0-86531-121-8   AACR2

Printed and bound in the United States of America

TO THE FAMILIES OF RURAL AMERICA,
THEIR INNER STRENGTHS AND
THEIR CONTINUING RESOURCEFULNESS

CONTENTS

ix

Part 4
Prospects and Perspectives on Rural Families

TABLES AND FIGURES

Figures

PREFACE

The impetus for this volume emerged in 1975 from the Family Research Interest Group of the Rural Sociological Society. At their annual meeting, the family group agreed that there was a critical and growing need for a comprehensive volume focused exclusively on the family in rural society. Since no such volume existed, the group believed that such a collection could make a significant contribution to the better understanding and appreciation of rural family life among practitioners, researchers, and policymakers. Although the final form of this volume is considerably reduced in scale and scope from the original idea, it nevertheless is the initial tangible result of that collective effort. To acknowledge this origin, the authors and editors have assigned all royalties accrued from this volume to the Rural Sociological Society. It is the desire of the authors and editors that these monies be used to stimulate and facilitate continued debate and attention to the critical issues that are faced by families in rural society.

In preparing this volume, we created an outline covering what we felt were some of the most critical issues concerning families in rural society and invited selected individuals to prepare contributions. The advantage of this approach is that the authors are leaders in their respective fields of inquiry. The result, we believe, is that the individual contributions are more thoroughly documented and up-to-date than is possible when one or two authors attempt to review the pertinent literature on a wide range of topics. This does, however, mean that there is no single overarching conceptual framework imposed on the collection. Not all contributors agree with each other, nor do the editors agree with all contributors. We hope that this display of differences will only highlight the issues and serve as a useful contrast to the generally agreed-on main principles.

The creation of a collection of readings is a considerable undertaking and requires the collective support and commitment of many individuals. It would be impossible to list all those who have contributed their time and effort to the conceptualization, reformulation, preparation, and review of the chapters included in this volume. However, certain key individuals do need to be recognized.

First, and foremost, are the authors, who unselfishly devoted their time to this project. They were not paid for their individual contributions; rather, they felt the professional obligation and responsibility to share their experience, knowledge, and expertise. They represent, in our minds, some of the finest individuals with whom we have had the pleasure of working. Without their patience, tenacity, and professionalism this volume would not have become a reality.

In addition, the support and encouragement of colleagues is critical when projects are being formed, frameworks constructed, and advice sought. Many colleagues have contributed directly and indirectly to the making of this volume, but some deserve special mention and thanks: Charles R. Figley, Donald W. Felker, Russell A. Mullens, Robert W. Jackson, Richard K. Kerckhoff, Frederick E. Schmidt, F. Ivan Nye, Glenn R. Hawkes, Victor A. Christopherson, Katheryn A. Dietrich, and Jeanne Nolan.

It is always a pleasure, and sometimes a luxury, to work with a highly professional and competent publishing staff. In this regard, we have been very fortunate. Lynn S. Arts, Senior Editor at Westview Press, has provided enormous support and encouragement. From the beginning (and perhaps more importantly, until the end), she has been supportive, tolerant of delays, and professional. We are very pleased to have been able to work with her.

Finally, we have received capable secretarial support throughout the course of this project. In the beginning stages, Vicki E. Hogancamp (Purdue University) provided important assistance and input. In the latter stages, Cecile Fennell and Ann Briggs (The University of Vermont) assumed responsibility for the critical tasks of final preparation. Our appreciation is extended to each for her competence and patience during the development of this manuscript. Our sincere appreciation is also due Robert "Shamms" Mortier for his creative illustration and preparation of the tables and figures included in this volume.

As always, our warmest and deepest appreciation is reserved for our families. Their support, encouragement, and understanding are the foundation of this work.

Raymond T. Coward
William M. Smith, Jr.

Conway, Massachusetts

THE CONTRIBUTORS

EDWIN B. ALMIROL, Assistant Professor of Anthropology, Department of Applied Behavioral Sciences, University of California, Davis, California.

ROXANNE M. ANDERSON, Graduate Research Assistant, Family Social Science Department, University of Minnesota, St. Paul, Minnesota.

LINDA BESCHER-DONNELLY, Project Director, Chilton Research Services, Radnor, Pennsylvania.

STEPHAN R. BOLLMAN, Professor, Department of Family and Child Development; and Director, Family Training, Research and Resource Center, Kansas State University, Manhattan, Kansas.

DAVID L. BROWN, Sociologist, Economic Development Division, Economics and Statistics Service, U.S. Department of Agriculture, Washington, D.C.

MARGARET L. CASSIDY, Graduate Research Assistant, Department of Rural Sociology, Washington State University, Pullman, Washington.

VICTOR A. CHRISTOPHERSON, Professor, Department of Child Development and Family Relations, University of Arizona, Tucson, Arizona.

RAYMOND T. COWARD, Research Associate Professor, Center for Rural Studies, and Associate Professor, Department of Special Education, Social Work and Social Services, College of Education and Social Services, The University of Vermont, Burlington, Vermont.

WILLIS J. GOUDY, Professor, Department of Sociology and Anthropology, Iowa State University, Ames, Iowa.

DAVID L. HARVEY, Associate Professor of Sociology, University of Nevada, Reno, Nevada.

GLENN R. HAWKES, Professor of Human Development, Department of Applied Behavioral Sciences, University of California, Davis, California.

PETER L. HELLER, Associate Professor of Sociology, Texas Tech University, Lubbock, Texas.

PATRICIA M. KEITH, Professor, Department of Sociology and Anthropology, Iowa State University, Ames, Iowa.

NANCY G. KUTNER, Assistant Professor of Rehabilitation Medicine, Emory University, Atlanta, Georgia.

GARY R. LEE, Associate Professor of Sociology, Associate Rural Sociologist, and Associate Scientist, Social Research Center, Washington State University, Pullman, Washington.

LOUIS A. PLOCH, Professor of Rural Sociology, Department of Agricultural and Resource Economics, University of Maine, Orono, Maine.

EDWARD A. POWERS, Professor and Chairman, Department of Family Environment, Iowa State University, Ames, Iowa.

GUSTAVO M. QUESADA, Professor of Rural Extension and Agricultural Education, Universidade Federal de Santa Maria, Brazil.

PAUL C. ROSENBLATT, Professor, Family Social Science Department, University of Minnesota, St. Paul, Minnesota.

WALTER R. SCHUMM, Assistant Professor, Department of Family and Child Development, Kansas State University, Manhattan, Kansas.

LESLIE WHITENER SMITH, Sociologist, Economics and Statistics Service, U.S. Department of Agriculture, Washington, D.C.

WILLIAM M. SMITH, JR., Professor Emeritus of Rural Sociology, Pennsylvania State University, University Park, Pennsylvania.

DENA B. TARG, Assistant Professor and Extension Specialist, Department of Child Development and Family Studies, Purdue University, West Lafayette, Indiana.

LYLE G. WARNER, Associate Professor of Sociology, University of Nevada, Reno, Nevada.

MIRIAM J. WELLS, Assistant Professor of Anthropology, Department of Applied Behavioral Sciences, University of California, Davis, California.

EUGENE A. WILKENING, Professor, Department of Rural Sociology, University of Wisconsin, Madison, Wisconsin.

The Family in Rural Society

INTRODUCTION

Raymond T. Coward
and William M. Smith, Jr.

This collection of readings was created to focus attention on the dynamics of family life as it occurs in small towns and rural communities throughout the United States. By assembling "in one place" a collection that centered exclusively on the family in rural society, our intent was to create visibility for the research, policy, and programmatic concerns of this important segment of our society. It is our desire that this volume will serve as a catalyst to further promote, stimulate, and facilitate debate on these issues.

The chapters that follow will demonstrate repeatedly that the family in rural society has failed to attract the degree of academic or political attention that an objective review of its conditions would seem to warrant. Furthermore, much "traditional wisdom," or perhaps more accurately "traditional folklore," exists about the rural family. These mental images portray country living and family life as simple, pure, and wholesome; slow-paced; free from pressures and tensions; and surrounded by pastoral beauty and serenity. All families in rural settings are treated as if they were farm families. Unfortunately, there is often a stark distinction between such nostalgic and romantic images and the realities of rural family life. The chapters of this volume describe some of the positive and negative aspects of life in rural America. From these more accurate statements, scholars, social service providers, and policymakers should be able to develop a better understanding of, and thus be better able to respond to, families in rural society who are experiencing significant internal changes while adapting to a remarkably altered rural America.

The title of this book, *The Family in Rural Society,* was consciously chosen to reflect our conceptualization of the focus for the collection. For some it may seem a subtle message; yet, although we interchangeably use the phrases "rural families" and "families in rural society," it is our belief that the latter is more accurate. We are interested in the institution called "families" as they function and live under particular environmental conditions, namely, rurality. In our minds the functions and responsibilities of the family are relatively stable, but the day-to-day dynamics of family life are intimately entwined and mirror the changing environment in which families live. Indeed, there is nothing in the research literature that would lead us to believe that the major conceptual frameworks of family sociology are not applicable to studying families in rural society. We do believe, however, that the rural environment is sufficiently different from the urban environment—both in physical and social-psychological terms—to impose significant effects on certain aspects of family life. This renders generalizations from urban and suburban research highly tenuous for populations living in sparsely populated areas. We support the proposition that residence operates as an intervening variable or mediating influence. Thus, the importance of simple bivariate comparisons between rural and urban samples is reduced, and more attention must be directed at illuminating the antecedents, consequences, and interactions of particular variables under different categories and definitions of residence (see Lee and Lassey, 1980, for a more complete discussion of this perspective).

The debate over a precise definition of "rural" has been avoided in this collection. It is not that we fail to realize the importance of this issue; rather, we felt it more critical to begin the process of summarizing, synthesizing, and speculating on the major issues of rural families without being sidetracked into related problems. To paraphrase Atchley's (1975) discussion of the rural elderly—certainly there are rural areas in our country, and there are families who live in those areas, and, therefore, what is at debate is the boundaries of these categories, not their existence. As the study of the family in rural society continues and expands, these definitional problems will become more critical.

There are many important topics discussed in this volume—and there are just as many important topics that are not. The realities of time and cost necessitated our reduced focus. For example, the significant international literature on the rural family has not been reviewed herein. Similarly, although there is a chapter on "cultural islands," it was impossible to include all the many ethnic groups that lend vitality and pluralism to our rural countryside. Furthermore, the preeminent issues surrounding the development and delivery of social services to rural families have not been directly addressed in this collection. These issues, as well as others, are important in and of themselves and deserve in-depth and comprehensive coverage in other volumes. We hope that our colleagues will, in the near future, pursue these important aspects of the study of rural families.

Finally, we hope that this volume will help dispel the myth of homogeneity in rural society. In their zeal to characterize environmental similarities, academicians have too often made the mistake of overgeneralizing the concept of rurality. As a result, the diversity that exists in rural environments has been obliterated. We hope that readers of this collection will be left with a greater appreciation of the range of lifestyles, family structures, and patterns of family interaction that continue to exist in rural America.

Organization of the Collection

This volume is organized into four parts, with a total of twelve original chapters. The focus and contribution of each section are briefly reviewed below.

Part 1: Current Trends in the Family in Rural Society

The three chapters of this part are intended to provide a synopsis of the current state of the family in rural society. In the first chapter, David L. Brown reviews a wide range of trends and changes in family structure and process as they are reflected in sociodemographic data. Urban and rural trends are compared and contrasted on a variety of family indicators, including marriage rate, age at marriage, fertility, divorce, household size, and the labor force participation of women. In addition, the implications for the family of the important migration turnaround are explored.

In the second chapter, Eugene A. Wilkening examines the phenomenon of the declining number of family farms. Although now the majority of rural families are not directly engaged in farming, agriculture remains intimately intertwined with the fabric and nature of rural America. Wilkening examines a number of significant changes in the farm enterprise that have occurred in recent decades with special attention to the involvement of women on the farm and the growing employment of family members off the farm.

In the last chapter of this part, Louis A. Ploch discusses the "new wave" of inmigrants to rural communities. Through the use of case studies, Ploch illustrates the diversity of this population shift. He concentrates on the perceived positive family-related aspects of such moves and elaborates on the need for future monitoring of this important, and growing, segment of rural America.

Part 2: Patterns and Forms of Rural Families

The three chapters of this part are intended to illustrate the complexity and variety of patterns and forms reflected in families in rural society. The opening chapter by Gary R. Lee and Margaret L. Cassidy explores the relationship between residence and interaction with kin. In contrast to commonly held beliefs and sociological theory, the research on this topic is quite equivocal. This insightful analysis of the available research by Lee and Cassidy identifies some principles that are generalizable (for example, kinship interaction is diminished by migration and consequent separation from kin) while simultaneously challenging some popularly held beliefs (for example, empirical studies to date do not justify, either singly or collectively, the conclusion that urban residence destroys or seriously decreases the viability of kinship networks).

The next chapter, by Peter L. Heller, Gustavo M. Quesada, David L. Harvey, and Lyle G. Warner, presents a reconceptualization of the construct of familism. In contrast to approaches that have assumed family life to center on a set of activities and interactions located within the confines of the household, these authors argue that rural familism reflects at least two forms of kinship principles. They support this assertion with an analysis of interregional data and conclude their chapter with a discussion of the relevance of this reconceptualization for change agents working within diverse rural settings.

In the final chapter of this part, Glenn R. Hawkes has assembled four essays exploring the dynamics of family life within selected "cultural islands" in rural America. The first essay, by Nancy G. Kutner, reviews the circumstances of the rural Black family. The second, by Miriam J. Wells, discusses families of Mexican-American heritage. The third essay, by Victor A. Christopherson, explores the Navajo family in order to provide insight into the circumstances of rural Native Americans. And the last essay, by Edwin B. Almirol, presents a network of rights and obligations within the context of the Filipino-American rural family. Collectively these essays illustrate the diverse elements existing in small towns and rural communities and argue that the rural United States encompasses a polyglot culture in which the parts may be greater than the sum.

Part 3: Family Dynamics

The five chapters of Part 3 are devoted to exploring selected aspects of the internal dynamics of family life in small towns and rural communities. The opening chapter, by Walter R. Schumm and Stephan R. Bollman, is a comprehensive review of the literature available on key variables associated with marital and family relations in rural families. Specifically, their review focuses on the issues of family size and composition, satisfaction with family relationships, the quality of life and family satisfactions, parent-child relations, and marital satisfaction. Where appropriate, the authors have reported preliminary analysis of their statewide data base, which was collected as part of a larger multistate Department of Agriculture project.

In the second chapter of this section, Paul C. Rosenblatt and Roxanne M. Anderson discuss tension and stress in farm families. In contrast with the preceding empirically oriented chapter, the Rosenblatt and Anderson contribution is highly speculative and represents the "cutting edge" of thought on this important, but inadequately researched, area of inquiry. The shocking figures on mental health in nonmetropolitan areas have forced researchers and practitioners to reexamine the antecedents of stressors in rural environments. This piece will provide much fodder for the continuing debate.

The next chapter, by Linda Bescher-Donnelly and Leslie Whitener Smith, examines the increasing role diversity of rural women and focuses on their role behavior, functions, and responsibilities with respect to four major social institutions: the family, the economy, the educational system, and the political structure. The authors explore some of the ideological and structural conditions that restrict rural women from access to certain life sectors and conclude their chapter by suggesting ways to improve the status and lifestyle of rural women in the future.

The final chapters of this section examine two family phases of development that have only recently drawn attention from researchers, service providers, and policymakers. The first, by Dena B. Targ, reviews middle age in rural environments; the second, by Edward A. Powers, Patricia M. Keith, and Willis J. Goudy, examines the family relationships and friendships of the rural aged. Targ's chapter includes a summary of the extant research on men, women, and marriage in middle age and considers a number of factors associated with rural residence that might change or modify the experience of middle age. The chapter by Powers and his associates contains a comprehensive review of the literature on the rural aged with a special focus on family patterns of the older individual in rural settings. To illuminate and illustrate certain shifts in the social networks of older rural men, the authors present data from a comprehensive longitudinal study of rural Iowans.

Part 4: Prospects and Perspectives on Rural Families

In the concluding chapter the editors take a look into the "crystal ball" of the future. Given the foundations of the preceding chapters, we speculate on the prospects of the rural family entwined in a society characterized by both persistence and change. We conclude by proposing a research agenda for the next decade and arguing for the resources necessary to complete the task.

Closing

In preparing this volume the authors have attempted to review and digest a significant portion of the ever-expanding literature (both scholarly and popular) on the family, on life in small towns and rural communities, and on changes in the American rural society. The collection is not meant to be an exhaustive review of the literature; rather, it singles out those seminal resources that were most fruitful in understanding the topics under discussion. This process of selection was by nature subjective and by necessity reflects the authors' biases and understandings of the intricacies of rural family life.

Our volume is a combination of empirically derived generalizations and conceptually sound speculations. Because it is a mixture, it will frustrate some readers. Some empiricists may prematurely dismiss the speculations, and some practitioners may ignore the detail of data—both reactions are unfortunate. The complexity of our approach mirrors the state of the art in studying rural families. In certain areas of inquiry there is a wealth of information and a long-standing tradition of data collection—in other areas there is virtually nothing. Rather than ignore those areas where there is a paucity of data, we have chosen to include them because we feel that they present critical issues and because we believe that well-founded and logically sound speculations will prompt future investigators to advance our understanding. Our hope is that this volume will permit scholars, service providers, and policymakers to begin their inquiry of the family in rural society with a better understanding of the complexity and diversity of rural family life. To us, this is the *first* step, not the last.

References

Atchley, R. C. "Introduction." In R. C. Atchley and T. O. Byerts (eds.), *Rural Environments and Aging*. Washington, D.C.: The Gerontological Society, 1975.

Lee, G. R. and M. L. Lassey. "Rural-Urban Residence and Aging: Directions for Future Research." In W. R. Lassey, M. L. Lassey, G. R. Lee, and N. Lee (eds.), *Research and Public Service with the Rural Elderly*. Corvallis, Oregon: Western Rural Development Center, 1980, 77–88.

PART 1

CURRENT TRENDS IN THE FAMILY
IN RURAL SOCIETY

A QUARTER CENTURY OF TRENDS AND CHANGES IN THE DEMOGRAPHIC STRUCTURE OF AMERICAN FAMILIES

David L. Brown

The structure of American society has undergone rapid and pervasive change during the twentieth century, and few institutions have changed more than the family. The age at which persons marry has increased, the number of children they bear has reached a historical low, the average number of persons who live together in households has declined, and it has been estimated that over a quarter of women now in their 20s will end their first marriage in divorce (Glick, 1976).

This chapter takes a demographic perspective, one that has become increasingly popular among family researchers in recent years. Sweet (1977) identified four main reasons for this trend: (1) marriage and divorce are important demographic processes in their own right; (2) marital status and family composition are important dimensions of population composition; (3) each major demographic process (fertility, mortality, migration, and nuptiality) takes place in a familial context; and (4) demographic processes are causally linked with other familial processes.

The purpose of this chapter is to review trends and changes in particular dimensions of family structure and process as they are described by socio-demographic data. Family structure in urban and rural areas is compared and contrasted to determine the degree to which these trends and changes have permeated communities throughout U.S. society.

Slowdown in Marriage

Marriage Rate

Economic, political, and social conditions of the past 40 years have been accompanied by marked fluctuations in many aspects of marriage and the family. For example, the economic gloom of the Great Depression occurred simultaneously with extremely low rates of marriage and childbearing—a near record 9 percent of adult women during this period never married. The marriage rate began to rise early in World War II, declined somewhat during the war, increased substantially from 1946 through 1950—a time of relative stability in economic and political affairs—declined during the Korean War period, and then increased steadily from 1958 to 1972. In 1979, the marriage rate was 10.3 per 1,000 population, a significant decline from 11.0 in 1972, the peak rate of the 25-year period from 1951 to 1976.

This decline is more observable in a specific measure such as the marriage rate for unmarried women age 15–44. This rate dropped precipitously from 149.1 in 1969 to 113.4 in 1976, by far its lowest level in the past 20 years (U.S. National Center for Health Statistics, 1978).

Age at Marriage

Later age at marriage is a major determinant of the recent decline in the marriage rate. In 1979, the average age at marriage (males, 24.4 years; females, 22.1 years) was nearly 2 years higher than in the mid-1950s, and the proportion of women who remained single until they were 20 to 24 years old increased markedly to 49.4 percent over the 29 percent single at these ages in 1960 (U.S. Bureau of the Census, 1980a). This recent pattern could be associated with current conditions of economic uncertainty, but more importantly, perhaps, it may reflect increased opportunities for women's work outside of the home (Preston and Richards, 1975), improved availability of more effective contraception and increased accessibility of abortion (Bauman, Koch, Udry, and Freedman, 1975), higher educational attainment among women—that is, staying in school longer and thus being less available for marriage (Rindfuss and Sweet, 1975)—and the viability of alternatives to the traditional nuclear family for at least part of one's adult life.

Decline in Fertility

Trends in Birth Rate

In 1979, the birth rate was 15.3 live births per 1000 population, a decline of 15 percent from its level of 18.4 live births just 9 years earlier in 1970 (U.S. National Center for Health Statistics, 1980). This low birth rate is reflected in the relatively slow growth of the American population between 1970 and 1979, .9 percent per year (U.S. Bureau of the Census, 1980b). However, the potential for growth continues to exist. The number of persons in the prime childbearing ages is now quite large (a legacy of the baby boom), and recent surveys of birth expectations indicate that young women still expect to have at least two births each (U.S. Bureau of the Census, 1980b). Indeed, the birth rate has risen in recent years, from 14.7 in 1976, the lowest level ever recorded, to 15.3 in 1979. Hence, if persons actualize their birth expectations, we can expect the growth rate of the population to accelerate in the near future (as it already has between 1976 and 1979).

Determinants of Lower Fertility

The family is part of the institutional structure through which a society replaces its population. It is the unit in which reproduction is authorized and expected, and consequently, changes in the marriage rate and the age at first marriage affect a society's level of fertility. There is little question that recent declines in the marriage rate for young women in the United States have contributed to our low level of current fertility. In fact, Gibson (1976) has demonstrated that approximately one-fifth of the decline in period fertility between 1971 and 1975 can be attributed to changes in marital status. Four-fifths was due to lower rates of childbearing among married couples.

This decline in marital fertility is strongly associated with increased availability and efficacy of contraception. The 1970 National Fertility Survey (NFS) showed that by 1970, 52 percent of U.S. couples at risk of unintended conception were protected by highly effective, coitus-independent methods of contraception—the pill, surgical sterilization, or the IUD. This is an increase from one-third in 1965 and from less than 10 percent in 1960 (Westoff, 1975). The NFS also showed that women are initiating their use of contraception at increasingly younger ages. Among married women age 20–24, the percent adopting contraception before their first pregnancy rose from roughly two-fifths to three-fourths (Rindfuss and Westoff, 1974).

The future course of American fertility is uncertain, although as mentioned earlier, there is reason to expect that it will increase somewhat. Some economists predict that we are about to enter a new baby boom. They believe that children born during recent low fertility years will enjoy a competitive advantage for jobs and income because of their smaller numbers. Therefore, they are expected to marry earlier and have more children (Lee, 1976).

There is little empirical evidence for this thesis and some strong contradictory sociological reasoning that brings it into doubt. The theory does not take into account the changing status and role of women in our society—their increased opportunities for work and career and for other roles outside of the home. Later age at marriage, to the extent that it is a long-term change, and changes in the control of fertility also argue against a return to significantly higher rates of childbearing and larger families.

Upturn in Divorce

Trends in Divorce

Accompanying the recent downturn in marriage has been a continuation of the long-term trend of increased divorce. The number of divorces per 1,000 women under 45 years of age in the United States increased by two-thirds between the mid-1950s and 1970. Moreover, for the last 30 years, the proportion of women whose first marriage ended in divorce by a given period of life has gone up consistently. For example, the percent divorced by their early 30s more than doubled from 6.3 percent in 1950 to 15.8 percent in 1970. It has been estimated that between 25 and 29 percent of women in their late 20s will end their first marriage in divorce sometime during their life. This compares with only 12 percent for women in their late 60s (Glick and Norton, 1973).

The rising level of divorce in our society has been a cause for substantial concern. It is one of the statistics most often cited by those who fear a breakdown in the American family. However, this belief is not shared by numerous observers of family trends, many of whom believe that divorce is an appropriate method of resolving a poor marriage. Indeed, this latter position tends to be shared by large segments of our population. Consider the case of those in public life. Not many years ago, the stigma attached to divorce was a heavy liability for candidates for public office. Today, the stigma appears to have diminished, a fact that tends to be supported by the marital histories of many of our highest officials.

Determinants of Increased Divorce

What factors are associated with the upturn in divorce? All other factors considered, early age at first marriage appears to be a basic determinant. Those who marry before age 20 have substantially higher rates of marital disruption than those who marry when older.

What is it about younger marriages that make them so susceptible to divorce? To begin with, a significant number of early marriages are precipitated by premarital pregnancy. Also, many persons who marry young have a low level of formal education. However, recent research has shown that the lower stability of early marriages is not due simply to their association with low education or premarital pregnancy. Young age at marriage, in and of itself, has an independent effect on divorce. To the extent that role patterns are tentative in the late teens and tend to stabilize with increasing age, post-marriage divergence in the spouses' expectations may be more likely for young marriages (Bumpass and Sweet, 1972).

Homogamy, the similarity between spouses in significant social characteristics, has also been shown to affect the probability of divorce. Higher instability was found for couples divergent in age or religion, while only extreme differences in education were associated with marital disruption. The greater probability of success for homogamous marriage is usually attributed to the greater likelihood of value consensus between spouses in basic life goals and priorities and to a similarity of expectations for marital roles (Bumpass and Sweet, 1972).

In addition, recent increases in divorce appear to be associated with a number of societal conditions: (1) the large number of men who lived apart from their wives while on military duty during the Vietnam War, (2) the low fertility rate among women of reproductive age (to the extent that the presence of young children inhibits divorce), and (3) increased employment opportunities for women. Liberalized divorce laws have also been pointed to as a factor in increased divorce, although some recent research casts doubt on this explanation (Schoen, Greenblatt, and Mielke, 1975).

Decline in the Household Size

One of the most dramatic occurrences in American demographic history has been the decline in average household size—from 5.8 persons in 1790 to 2.81 persons in 1978 (U.S. Bureau of Census, 1979). What factors account for this decline? Changes in the demographic processes of fertility and mortality have had a major impact. For example, declines in fertility reduced the number of very large household units, while declines in mortality enlarged the number of very small units by increasing the time couples survive after their children have established their own households (the so-called "empty nest" stage in the family life cycle). As a result of these demographic processes, the proportion of small households (two to four persons) increased continuously from 1790 to 1950 from one-third to over two-thirds of all households. However, in 1950 the number of four-person households was still much greater than the proportion with only one member.

The continued fall in household size since 1950 is attributable to the growth of very small households (one to two persons). One-person households grew from 4–5 percent of all units in 1900 to 22 percent in 1978 (U.S. Bureau of the Census, 1979). Are demographic forces the main determinants behind recent declines in household size as they were in declines through 1950? For example, has the increase in primary individuals (one-person households) been greatest among the elderly, as one would predict knowing of the aging of the population that has characterized recent times? For males the answer is no. The total number of male primary individuals tripled between 1950 and 1974 while the number of young (20–34 years of age) primary individuals increased more than eightfold. Clearly, increases in living alone for men have come at an early stage in the life cycle and are associated with moving out of the parental home to college dormitories, military barracks, and, most dramatically, to bachelor quarters.

In contrast, the aging of the population and the differential in mortality, which tends to favor older women over men, has been a key factor in enlarging the number of women who live alone. Of the 4.6 million increase in female primary individuals between 1950 and 1974, 63 percent, or nearly 3 million women, were 55–74 years old (Kobrin, 1976).[1]

The data reviewed above suggest that the decline in household size has had a significant impact on the family as a social unit. The great increase in persons living separately from their families and the concentration of these people at the youngest and oldest stages of the adult life cycle indicate that living in family situations has become much less continuous over the life cycle. If current trends continue, perhaps we may see the time when less than a majority of adults will be living in families (73.5 percent lived in families in 1970). Kobrin (1976) has suggested that this change must necessarily affect the relationships between generations and life-cycle patterns of interaction generally.

Increased Labor Force Participation of Women

Trends in Women's Labor Force Activity

Between 1940 and 1979, the labor force participation rate of women age 20 and older increased from 27.9 percent to 48.7 percent, and the number of women in the labor force grew from 14.2 million to 37.4 million workers

(U.S. Department of Commerce, 1973, and U.S. Department of Labor, 1980a). Moreover, the relationships between female labor force participation and age and family life cycle have changed as well.

In 1900, if the average woman worked at all for pay during her lifetime, it was only for a short period before marriage and childbearing. By 1940, the rates showed some changes in the degree of labor force participation, but the pattern by age was similar to that of 1900. Since 1940, significant changes have occurred in the age and family life-cycle pattern of female employment. The 1950 census showed a sharp increase over the 1940 census in work rates for women aged 35 and over—those whose children, by and large, had reached school age (Oppenheimer, 1973). This pattern has persisted and by 1979 the participation rate of women between 16 and 55 years did not drop below 50 percent at any age (Oppenheimer, 1973; U.S. Department of Labor, 1980a).

Along with the general rise in women's labor force participation there has been a marked increase in the proportion of families with two or more workers. In 1900, only about 5 percent of all wives were gainfully employed. From 1900 to 1920, the proportion increased to 9 percent, and by 1950 it had reached 36 percent. In 1979, more than one half (59.6 percent) of all husband-wife families had two workers or more, and 57 percent of husband-wife families with two or more workers had children under 18 years of age (U.S. Department of Labor, 1980b).

Factors Associated with Women's Labor Force Participation

Recent studies indicate that the likelihood of a wife working is increased by family economic pressure (as indexed by husband's income), by wife's level of employability (as indexed by educational attainment and/or by prior work experience), by women's status as the head of a household, and by a labor-market environment that provides equal opportunities regardless of sex (Cain, 1966).

Family composition has also been shown to affect the labor force participation of married women. It has been demonstrated that employment status is associated with the number and ages of children and with the presence of other adults (besides parents) in the household. Sweet (1970) explained that family status constrains employment in the following ways: (1) the older the youngest child, the lower the probability that a mother will regard her employment as an inappropriate activity; (2) the younger the youngest child, and the more children there are, the more housework that needs to be performed; and (3) the younger the youngest child, the greater the probability that child care will be expensive and reduce the net economic benefit from employment. The presence of another adult (especially a relative) in the household is likely to moderate the inhibiting effects of child status on mother's work by facilitating reliable and inexpensive child-care arrangements and by helping with household maintenance.

Although there has been a marked decrease over time in the inhibiting effects of young children on mothers' work activity, the number and ages of

children are still of extreme importance. Moreover, numerous studies show
that family size expectations are tied to expectations for career and other
nonfamilial activities. Women who plan to hold paid employment plan to
have smaller families than women who have no plans to enter the labor force
(Waite and Stolzenberg, 1976).

Implications for the Family

Women's labor force participation is an important issue in and of itself,
but it is also important because of its impact on aspects of family structure
and function. Increased opportunity for gainful employment of women has
been shown to be a key determining factor in later age at first marriage (Preston and Richards, 1975). Working women accumulate seniority, make friends
on the job, and increase their standard of living. For many women economic
activity is a major source of ego gratification and a link to the women's
movement, with which they identify and sympathize. Glick (1976) has
drawn a parallel between postponed marriage and postponed fertility. He
points out that the child deficit is seldom made up, and likewise he feels that
many young people who delay marriage may actually never marry.

Social scientists have been deeply involved in specifying the relationship
between women's work activity and fertility. While there is almost unanimous
consensus that women's labor force activity and fertility are negatively
associated, there is substantial disagreement on the nature of the relationship
between these two factors. The basic question is whether the level of fertility determines the probability of participation in the labor force or vice
versa. Bumpass and Westoff (1970, p. 1170) stated this dilemma clearly when
they asked: "Do women limit their fertility in order to have time to pursue
their non-familial activities, or do women work if their fertility permits them
to do so?" Recent research suggests that a simultaneous relationship exists
between the two factors. That is, women's labor force participation is both a
determinant and a consequence of the level of fertility. A study by Waite
and Stolzenberg (1976) indicated that young women develop their labor
force participation plans and their fertility expectations simultaneously and
interdependently. They demonstrated that women who plan to participate in
the labor force plan to have fewer children than women who do not value
paid employment so highly. They also showed that the number of children
a woman plans to bear affects her plans for participation in the labor force,
but this relationship is much weaker.

There has also been a basic change in the pattern by which families derive
their economic support. Not only have wives and mothers increased their
labor force activity, but their contribution to total family income has grown
as well. Between 1950 and 1970, the median annual income of families with
working wives more than doubled, compared with an increase of only 80 percent among families where the wife was not gainfully employed. In 1979,
the median weekly earnings of husband-wife families with two or more wage
earners ($477) was $81 greater than that of families where only one person
worked ($396) (U.S. Department of Labor, 1980a).

A woman's contribution to total family income is especially important if she is the household head. In 1978, 8.2 million women were heads of their households, an increase of 4.2 million over 1955. Also, a larger proportion than ever before of children under 18 years of age lived with their mother only; in 1979, over two-thirds of female-headed households included at least one child under 18 (U.S. Bureau of the Census, 1979). The data indicate that these children are economically better off if their mothers work. For 8.3 million children in fatherless families, the median income in 1972 was $5,750 if the mother worked and only $3,495 if she was not in the labor force (Waldman and Whitmore, 1974).

Urban-Rural Comparisons

How pervasive are the trends and changes described above? Have they permeated communities in both urban and rural America?

Recent analysis of opinion data from the Gallup Poll shows marked urban-rural differentiation in moral issues associated with marriage and the family. Rural people are more likely to feel that divorce should be more difficult to obtain, that premarital sex is wrong, and that birth control pills should *not* be available to teenage girls. They are less likely to favor making birth control information available to anyone who wants it or legalizing abortion (Larson, 1978).

Whether urban-rural differences are as large as in the past is difficult to say. Comparative cross-sectional data are only available on one item—premarital sex. However, here and on questions relating to public nudity, rural persons appear to have weakened their commitment to puritanical ethical standards. The proportion of rural persons who feel that premarital sex is wrong declined from 80 percent in 1969 to 61 percent in 1973. Corresponding figures for the largest cities are 56 percent and 34 percent, respectively (Larson, 1978). Thus, attitudinal data seem to suggest a persistence of rural-urban differentiation as well as a continuity of change.

Comparative Profile of Family Indicators

As early as 1958, Bertrand (p. 7) commented that "the rural family has quickened its tempo of acceptance of change, and the indications are that it will be more like the urban family in the future." He went on to add that it was impossible to distinguish different trends in rural and urban family changes.

The data presented in Table 1.1 show a comparative profile of family characteristics in rural and urban areas from 1950 to 1970. They allow us to ascertain, for selected indicators, whether Bertrand's expectations were accurate, that is, whether rural-urban differences in family structure have diminished and whether the direction of change in family structure has been similar in rural and urban areas. These data indicate a continuance of urban-rural differences in family structure. Rural people marry earlier than their urban counterparts, have more children, and live in larger households. Labor

Table 1.1: Profile of Household and Family Characteristics by Urban-Rural Residence, 1950-1970.

——— Urban   •••••••••• Rural

Item and Residence	Year		
	1950	1960	1970
Pct. of Women single, 20-24 Years	36.0	30.9	39.1
	24.0	21.3	25.7
Child-Women Ratio [1]	711.9	783.4	579.6
	490.5	653.9	500.6
Children ever born [2]	2981	3127	3427
	1978	2436	3027
Persons per household	3.7	3.6	3.3
	3.2	3.2	3.0
Pct. Divorced	2.6	2.9	3.8
	1.4	1.6	2.2
Female Labor Force Participation [3]	33.2	37.3	41.3
	20.6	27.3	32.7

1/ Population less than 5 yrs. divided by Women 20-44 yrs. x 1000.
2/ Children ever born per 1000 ever married women 35-44 yrs.
3/ Population 14 or more years; 1950 and 1970 civilian labor force—1960 total labor force which includes 28,000 military.

Source: U.S. Census of Population 1950, 1960, 1970: PC (1) - 1, U.S. Summary

force participation continues to be lower among rural women, and a smaller proportion of rural marriages end in divorce.

However, these data also show that changes affecting urban families have affected rural families as well. Regardless of residence, the age of marriage has increased, current fertility has declined, household size has diminished, the divorce rate has increased, and the labor force participation rate of women has grown.

A More Detailed Look

Demographic research has not focused on rural-urban differences in many of the important aspects of marriage and the family. Two areas, however, have received some detailed analyses: residential patterns in fertility and female labor force participation.

Beale (1978) has provided an illuminating summary of the comparative levels of urban and rural fertility in America from prerevolutionary times to the present. His major conclusions are: (1) rural birthrates have always exceeded those of urban areas; and (2) rural births have always contributed proportionately more than their share to national population growth. This latter point is particularly important. Even during the periods of lowest fertility in our history—the Great Depression of the 1930s and the postbaby-boom era of the 1970s—rural fertility significantly exceeded ultimate needs for generational replacement while urban fertility did not. Thus, even during periods of extremely low fertility, the rural birthrate has exerted pressure for job growth in small towns or for outmigration.

Why is fertility higher in rural areas? Recent research suggests that rural-urban fertility differentials are more associated with certain characteristics of the women living in these areas and not with the influence of the city or the rural hinterland. For example, Slesinger (1974) reported that urban dominance explained very little variation in the number of children born to women interviewed in the 1970 National Fertility Survey once the effects of race, duration of marriage, religion, and education were taken into account. The real question is, then, why does a disproportionately large number of women whose social characteristics are associated with higher-than-average fertility live in rural areas?

On the second issue, labor force activity, the data in Table 1.1 demonstrate that regardless of residence, work has become an important and continuing part of women's lives, not just before they marry and start raising children. (Figure 1.1 indicates that this holds true for both rural and urban women.) In 1970, the rate of labor force participation among rural women did not fall below 40 percent at any age between 20 and 59, and the pattern of high participation rates before and after childbearing was characteristic of both urban and rural residence categories.[2]

What kind of jobs are rural women obtaining? Data from the census show that the number of rural women increased in most categories of occupation and industry. The largest numerical growth was in clerical pursuits. Substantial growth also occurred in professional occupations and in operative

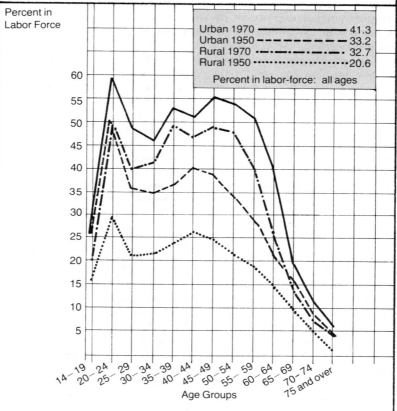

Figure 1.1: Percent of Women in the Labor Force by Age for Urban and Rural Residence, 1950-1970.

Urban 1970 ———————	41.3
Urban 1950 – – – – – – –	33.2
Rural 1970 ·—·—·—·—·	32.7
Rural 1950 ··················	20.6

Percent in labor-force: all ages

Source U.S. Census

Percent in Labor Force				
Age Group	Rural	Rural	Urban	Urban
	1950	1970	1950	1970
14-19	16	20	26	26
20-24	28	49	50	58
25-29	21	40	36	48
30-34	22	41	35	46
35-39	24	49	37	53
40-44	26	47	40	51
45-49	25	48	39	55
50-54	22	47	34	54
55-59	19	40	29	51
60-64	15	26	22	40
65-69	10	14	16	19
70-74	5	7	7	11
75+	2	4	4	6

and service blue collar jobs. Large percentage gains were registered in skilled crafts positions, but the base of employment in 1950 in this category was small, so percentage gains tend to exaggerate actual growth. Farm-related employment declined substantially.

Regarding industrial structure of employment, rural women made large gains in manufacturing, retail trade, and professional services. Large percentage gains were registered in other industrial categories, but once again these gains were calculated on a small employment base in 1950 (see Figure 1.2).

These employment changes present a mixed picture of economic opportunity for rural women. Jobs have been created where heretofore few existed, but a large proportion of new jobs are in low-wage occupations (clerical, operative, and services) and industries (nondurable manufacturing). In contrast, women's employment in urban areas is substantially less concentrated in these low wage pursuits (U.S. Bureau of the Census, 1979).[3]

Implications of the Nonmetro Migration Turnaround

The rural United States has undergone important demographic changes that have direct implications for the rural family. The recent turnaround in the relative rate of population growth between metropolitan (SMSA—Standard Metropolitan Statistical Area) and nonmetropolitan areas has affected the size and composition of the nonmetropolitan population. After two-thirds of a century of uninterrupted transfer of population, activities, and economic resources from smaller to larger places, population and employment are enjoying renewed vitality in nonmetropolitan areas. Between 1970 and 1978, nonmetropolitan counties grew in population by 10.5 percent, compared with only 6.1 percent in metropolitan areas (Brown and Beale, 1980). The effect of this renewed growth on the age composition of the population is especially important, because age is a prime factor in family formation and childbearing, household size and living arrangements, and marital dissolution.

If migration rates by age had continued from the 1960s into the 1970s, nonmetropolitan areas would have experienced significant losses at the young family ages (20–29 years) and only slight gains among children and older adults. Figure 1.3 indicates, however, that the young ages (5–14 years) middle family ages (35–44 years) and retirement age (65+ years) categories showed large nonmetropolitan gains over 1965–70 expectations (Bowles, 1978; Zuiches and Brown, 1978).

To the extent that these recent trends are indicative of the future, we can expect growth in the nonmetropolitan population at the ages where family formation and childbearing are most likely, and at the retirement ages. These are crucial age groups because young families and the elderly tend to need and demand various goods and services that are not always available in sufficient quantity in rural communities. Young families require additional housing units, child-care services, and educational programs; the elderly may need income maintenance, transportation, and various community, health, and social services.

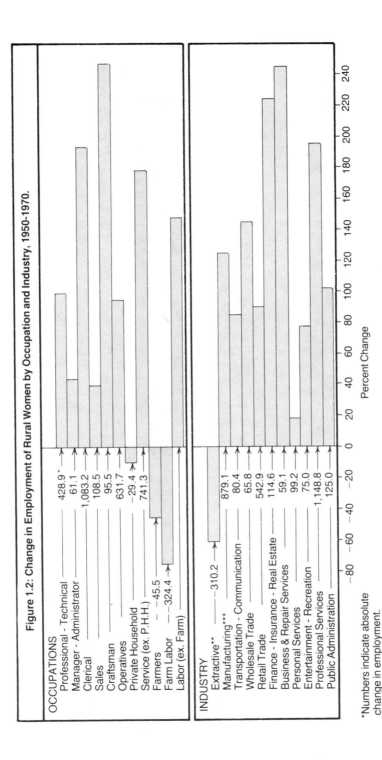

Figure 1.2: Change in Employment of Rural Women by Occupation and Industry, 1950-1970.

OCCUPATIONS

Professional - Technical — 428.9 *
Manager - Administrator — 61.1
Clerical — 1,083.2
Sales — 108.5
Craftsman — 95.5
Operatives — 631.7
Private Household — −29.4
Service (ex. P.H.H.) — 741.3
Farmers — −45.5
Farm Labor — −324.4
Labor (ex. Farm)

INDUSTRY

Extractive** — −310.2
Manufacturing*** — 879.1
Transportation - Communication — 80.4
Wholesale Trade — 65.8
Retail Trade — 542.9
Finance - Insurance - Real Estate — 114.6
Business & Repair Services — 59.1
Personal Services — 99.2
Entertainment - Recreation — 75.0
Professional Services — 1,148.8
Public Administration — 125.0

Percent Change

−80 −60 −40 −20 0 20 40 60 80 100 120 140 160 180 200 220 240

*Numbers indicate absolute
change in employment.
(Expressed in thousands)
**Agriculture, forestry, fisheries, mining
***Durable and non durable

Source: U.S. Census of Population

Figure 13: Expected and Actual Net Migration By Age for Metropolitan and Nonmetropolitan Areas, 1970-75.

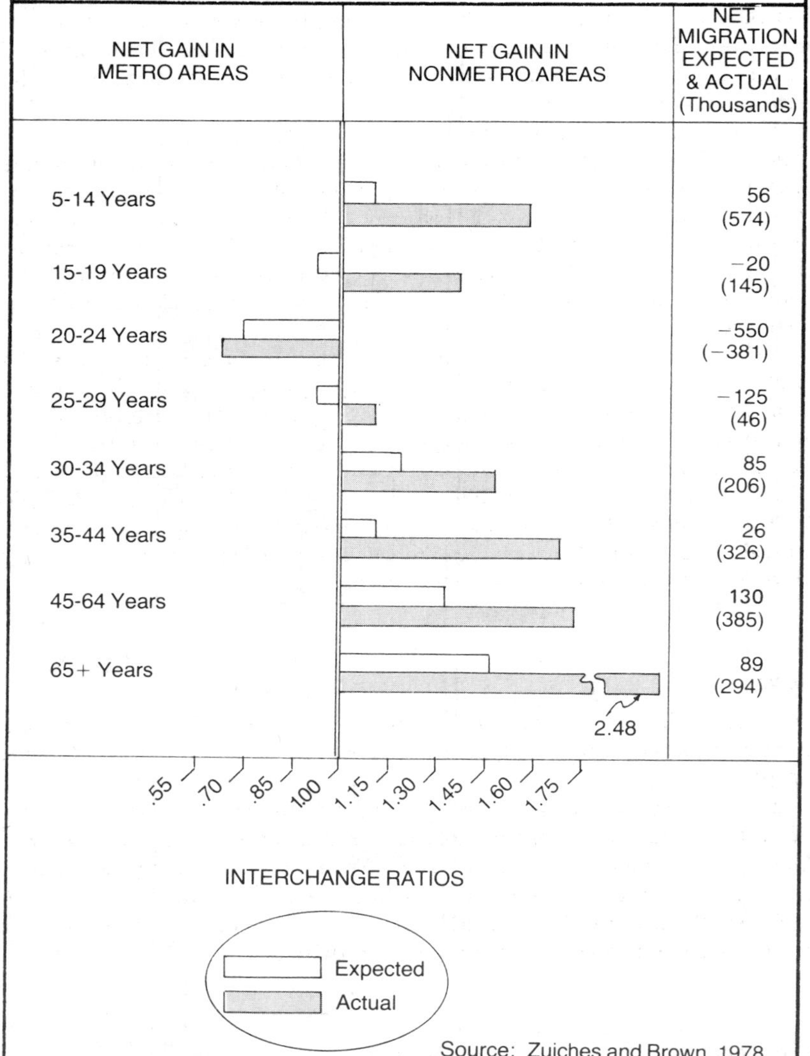

NET GAIN IN METRO AREAS	NET GAIN IN NONMETRO AREAS	NET MIGRATION EXPECTED & ACTUAL (Thousands)
5-14 Years		56 (574)
15-19 Years		−20 (145)
20-24 Years		−550 (−381)
25-29 Years		−125 (46)
30-34 Years		85 (206)
35-44 Years		26 (326)
45-64 Years		130 (385)
65+ Years		89 (294)

2.48

.55 .70 .85 1.00 1.15 1.30 1.45 1.60 1.75

INTERCHANGE RATIOS

☐ Expected
▨ Actual

Source: Zuiches and Brown, 1978.

Conclusions

Socioeconomic indicators have been used above to describe changes in structure and function of the American family during the latter half of the twentieth century. These changes have been pervasive, far-reaching, and interrelated with one another. Decline in the marriage rate, for example, is a basic determinant of lower fertility, which in turn, is associated with women's labor force activity, the recent upturn in divorce, and the decline in the size of the American household. Moreover, it was shown that these changes have permeated the urban hierarchy.

If one inference can be drawn from these sociodemographic indicators, it is that family roles and patterns of family interaction have been modified substantially during recent decades. Nonfamilial activities appear to be of greater importance than in the past; the proportion of the life cycle spent outside of a family unit has increased significantly; child care is increasingly the responsibility of third parties; and the husband-wife relationship has become more egalitarian. Yet, with all this change, there appears to be permanence.

Young people today may want some different things from marriage and family life, but there is evidence that marrying and having children continue to be nearly universal aspirations of young people entering adulthood (Taeuber and Sweet, 1976). Indeed, viability of the family is even suggested in statistics on divorce. According to the latest information available, about four out of every five of those who obtain a divorce will eventually remarry (Glick, 1976). Thus, the demographic trends presented in this paper do not suggest a breakdown of the American family, but rather point to significant changes in its structure and function in contemporary society.

Notes

1. There has been a substantial increase in young adults of both sexes living alone since Kobrin's article was written in 1976 (U.S. Bureau of Census, 1979).

2. However, regardless of residence, the dominant pattern for racial minority women is to work continuously through the family life cycle, while Anglo women tend to withdraw from the labor force during their 20s and return to it when their children reach school age (Brown and O'Leary, 1979).

3. See Brown and O'Leary (1979) for a detailed discussion of recent trends in women's labor force activity in nonmetropolitan areas.

References

Bauman, K. E., G. G. Koch, J. R. Udry, and J. L. Freedman. "The Relationship Between Legal Abortion and Marriage." *Social Biology*, 1975, 22, 117–124.

Beale, C. L. "Internal Migration in the U.S. Since 1970." Statement before the House Select Committee on Population, 95th Congress, 2nd Session, 1978.

Bertrand, A. L. *Rural Sociology: An Analysis of Contemporary Rural Life.* New York: McGraw-Hill, 1958.

Bowles, G. K. "Contributions of Recent Metro/Nonmetro Migrants to the Nonmetro Population and Labor Force." *Agriculture Economics Research,* 1978, 30 (4), 15–22.

Brown, D. L. and C. L. Beale. "The Sociodemographic Context of Land Use Change in Nonmetropolitan Areas in the 1970's." Paper presented at the Conference on Land Use Issues in Nonmetropolitan America, College Park, Maryland, June 24–25, 1980.

Brown, D. L. and J. M. O'Leary. "Labor Force Activity of Metropolitan and Non-metropolitan Women." *Rural Development Research Reports,* No. 15. Washington, D.C.: U.S. Department of Agriculture, 1979.

Bumpass, L. L. and J. A. Sweet. "Differentials in Marital Instability: 1970." *American Sociological Review,* 1972, 37 (6), 754–765.

Bumpass, L. L. and C. Westoff. "The Perfect Contraceptive Population." *Science,* 1970, 169, 1177–1182.

Cain, G. G. *Married Women in the Labor Force.* Chicago: University of Illinois Press, 1966.

Gibson, C. "The U.S. Fertility Decline, 1961–1975: The Contribution of Changes in Marital Status and Marital Fertility." *Family Planning Perspectives,* 1976, 8 (5), 249–250.

Glick, P. C. "Some Recent Changes in American Families." *Current Population Reports,* Series P-23, No. 52. Washington, D.C.: U.S. Bureau of the Census, 1976.

Glick, P. C. and A. J. Norton. "Perspectives on the Recent Upturn in Divorce and Remarriage." *Demography,* 1973, 10 (3), 301–314.

Kobrin, F. "The Fall of Household Size and the Rise of the Primary Individual in the United States." *Demography,* 1976, 13 (1), 127–138.

Larson, O. F. "Values and Beliefs of Rural People." In T. R. Ford (ed.), *Rural America: Persistence and Change.* Ames, Iowa: Iowa State University Press, 1978.

Lee, R. D. "Demographic Forecasting and the Easterlin Hypothesis." *Population and Development Review,* 1976, 2, 459.

Oppenheimer, V. K. "Demographic Influence on Female Employment and the Status of Women." *American Journal of Sociology,* 1973, 78 (4), 946–961.

Preston, S. and A. T. Richards. "The Influence of Women's Work Opportunities on Marriage Rates." *Demography,* 1975, 12 (2), 209–222.

Rindfuss, R. and J. A. Sweet. "The Pervasiveness of Postwar Fertility Trends in the United States." *D.E.C. Working Paper 75-25.* Madison, Wisconsin: Center for Demography and Ecology, University of Wisconsin, 1975.

Rindfuss, R. and C. Westoff. "The Initiation of Contraception." *Demography,* 1974, 12 (1), 75–87.

Schoen, R., H. N. Greenblatt, and R. Mielke. "California's Experience with Non-Adversary Divorce." *Demography,* 1975, 12 (2) 223–244.

Slesinger, D. P. "The Relationship of Fertility to Measures of Metropolitan Dominance." *Rural Sociology,* 1974, 39 (3) 350–361.
Sweet, J. A. "Demography and the Family." *Annual Review of Sociology,* 1977, 3, 363–405.
____. "Family Composition and Labor Force Activity of American Wives." *Demography,* 1970, 7 (2), 195–209.
Taeuber, K. E. and J. A. Sweet. "Family and Work: The Social Life Cycle of Women." In J. Kreps (ed.), *Women in the American Economy: A Look at the 1980's.* New York: The American Assembly–Columbia University, 1976.
U.S. Bureau of the Census. "Households and Families by Type: March 1978." *Current Population Reports,* Series P-20, No. 345. Washington, D.C.: U.S. Government Printing Office, 1979.
____. "Marital Status and Living Arrangements: March, 1979." *Current Population Reports,* Series P-20, No. 349. Washington, D.C.: U.S. Government Printing Office, 1980 (a).
____. "Population Profile of the United States: 1979." *Current Population Reports,* Series P-20, No. 350, Washington, D.C.: U.S. Government Printing Office, 1980 (b).
U.S. Department of Commerce, Bureau of Economic Analysis. *Long-Term Economic Growth, 1860–1970.* Washington, D.C.: U.S. Government Printing Office, 1973.
U.S. Department of Labor, Bureau of Labor Statistics. *Monthly Labor Review,* May 1980, 103 (5). Washington, D.C.: U.S. Government Printing Office 1980 (a).
____. *Employment in Perspective: Working Women,* Report 611, July 1980 (b).
____. *Perspectives on Working Women,* June 1980 (c).
U.S. National Center for Health Statistics. "Final Marriage Statistics, 1976." *Monthly Vital Statistics Reports,* 27 (6). Washington, D.C.: U.S. Department of Health, Education and Welfare, 1978.
____. "Provisional Statistics (Births, Marriages, Divorces and Deaths for October 1976)." *Monthly Vital Statistics Reports,* 9 (3). Washington, D.C.: U.S. Department of Health, Education and Welfare, 1980.
Waite, L. J. and R. M. Stolzenberg. "Intended Childbearing and Labor Force Participation of Young Women: Insights from Nonrecursive Models." *American Sociological Review,* 1976, 41 (2), 235–252.
Waldman, E. and R. Whitmore. "Children of Working Mothers, 1973." *Monthly Labor Review,* May 1974, 50–58.
Westoff, C. "The Yield of the Imperfect: The 1970 National Fertility Study." *Demography,* 1975, 12 (4), 573–580.
Zuiches, J. J. and D. L. Brown. "The Changing Character of the Nonmetropolitan Population, 1950–1975." In T. R. Ford (ed.), *Rural America: Persistence and Change.* Ames, Iowa: Iowa State University Press, 1978, 55–72.

2
FARM FAMILIES AND FAMILY FARMING

Eugene A. Wilkening

In contrast to most other occupations, farming provides the physical, economic, and social conditions that coincide with the needs, interests, and biological processes of the family. Despite changes in the structure and processes of agriculture, it continues to be largely a family-operated activity in most parts of the United States and in most industrialized nations. Changes toward capitalism, socialism, or other systems in the structure of agricultural production have subordinated the family to economic and political interests, but the family continues to be more closely associated with the productive processes than in most other occupational pursuits.

In the United States farming has grown out of historical conditions supported by an ideology that placed a high value upon family ownership and control of the land. For the early settlers, land was plentiful and families were encouraged to acquire land and produce for the market as well as for home consumption. Success in farming depended upon family assistance in the chores and field work. The needs of the farm for labor and for capital frequently took precedence over family needs. Hence, while the farm was family owned and operated in most regions of the United States, it became increasingly dependent upon the market system for many of its resources and for the disposal of its products. Thus, the size and type of farm enterprise has increasingly responded to market forces instead of to family factors. But exceptions to this trend are found among individual families in all countries and especially among certain ethnic groups that place higher value upon the integration of the farm with the natural environment and with the personal family and community systems affected by farming.

The purpose of this chapter is to show: (1) what changes in the farm enterprise have occurred in recent decades that have significance for the farm family, (2) how the farm family has become involved in work off the farm as an adaptation to these changing economic forces, (3) the definitions and characteristics of the family farm, (4) the involvement of women in the farm enterprise and changes in attitudes toward men's and women's roles, and (5) some suggestions for further research pertaining to the relationship of farm and family.

Changes in the Farm Enterprise

The trends in farm numbers, size, labor, and capital place the problem of the changes in farming in perspective. From a peak of 6.8 million farms in 1935, the number has declined to 2.7 million in 1977, with the most dramatic decline in absolute numbers in the 1950s and 1960s. In the meantime, farm acreages have increased from an average of 157 acres in 1930 to 383 in 1977, a gain of about 150 percent. This gain has been accentuated by the doubling of the acreage in farms of 1,000 acres or more from 1930 to 1974. While total labor input of both family and hired labor has decreased, the percentage of family labor of the total has increased. But due to improved farm technology, the output per worker has increased more than enough to offset the reduction in labor supply (Ball and Heady, 1971). This has meant that much of the increase in returns has gone to pay for the capital investment.

Capital used on farms increased even more than acreage in recent decades. The average value of land and buildings increased from $20,504 in 1920 to $147,838 in 1974. The increased capital investment needed to enter the farm enterprise has made it especially difficult for the beginning farmer. A longitudinal study of Wisconsin dairy farmers showed that personal savings were the most important source of funds for starting into farming before 1950, borrowing from the family was the most important source in the 1950s, and commercial sources became the most important source from 1961 to 1976. Inheritance was the dominant source for about 15 to 20 percent of the dairy farmers interviewed in 1976 (Dorner and Marquardt, 1978). The increased dependence upon commercial sources of credit to begin farming caused more sons to shift to other occupations. At the same time, more persons of nonfarm background have bought farmland for investment, operation, or residence and recreation. Research is just beginning to indicate the nature of this latter trend and its implications for rural life and farm families.

The increased size of farms and the capital investment needed to maintain them is at the root of the struggle of the farm family to stay in farming full time. When the family provided the major input to the farm, the size and nature of farm operations were determined to a great extent by family resources and interests. The size of farm operations varied, with the family cycle reaching a peak when the operator was 50 to 60 years of age, depending upon whether a son remained on the farm (Long and Parsons, 1950). Today, effective farm operations require more than "a strong back and the will to work." Additional expenses for modern equipment and new technology have required most farms to expand in order to remain competitive in the open market. Larger operations are able to guarantee sufficient income for both family and business needs.

Thus, while farming is no longer primarily a way of life, but more a business, certain conditions of agriculture provide a resistance to the shift to the industrial model of nonfarm enterprises. Farming still provides greater freedom of choice and independence than most other occupations. More study is needed, however, on how recent changes in the scale, the technology, and the integration of farming into commodity systems of production, processing, and marketing have affected the individuals, families, communities, and social structure of the larger society.

Off-farm Employment

The combining of off-farm work with farming was stimulated during the depression years, when nonfarm families returned to farming to provide subsistence and additional cash income. While off-farm work was regarded as a transition into or out of farming (Fuguitt, 1959), it has become a permanent pattern for an increasing percentage of farm families. In 1978, over half of the farm operators worked off the farm, with 44 percent working 100 days or more off the farm. This compares with only 16 percent in 1944 and 35 percent in 1974 who worked off the farm 100 days or more.

Off-farm work is pursued by those who wish to retain farming as their primary occupation but require additional income to pay farm debts or to add to family income. Dorner and Marquardt (1979) found that in dairy farms either the son or the father will likely work off the farm during the period of intergeneration transfer. Work off the farm is being encouraged by the location of industry and recreation in rural areas and by improved roads that make commuting up to 50 or 60 miles feasible. (Whether this will continue with the increasing cost of gasoline is uncertain.) So, as the returns from the farm have become insufficient to satisfy the income needs of the family, off-farm work has become an increasingly attractive alternative. Off-farm work also allows family members to pursue their individual interests and abilities and to have more leeway in their purchases for personal and family needs.

Off-farm work may be a way of keeping the farm and maintaining family income for many small farmers. But off-farm work is also becoming a pattern for an increasing percentage of large farmers. In a Wisconsin study (Wilkening and Ahrens, 1979) over half of the farm operators making less than $10,000 gross farm income worked off the farm, while about one-fourth of those making $40,000 or more worked off the farm, although not as many days per year. Off-farm work is more likely to be practiced by young farmers than older farmers, according to the 1969 U.S. Census of Agriculture. The surprising fact is that, since 1970, over half of the income of the farm population has come from nonfarm sources. This supports the notion that many persons involved in agriculture have primary employment interests other than farming.

Kada (1978) classified part-time farm families as "transitional" if they were first full-time farmers, "persistent" if they began as part-time farmers, as "U-turn" types if they left the farm for a period and returned, and as "entrants" if they entered farming without previous farm background. About one-fourth of the first two types have father-son partnerships, indicating that off-farm work may provide a means whereby two generations can earn sufficient income to continue as farmers. The latter two types consist mainly of nuclear families with small children and tend to have a higher level of education than the part-time farm operators who have never lived in the city. Farm families who have moved away from the city tend to be smaller in size, have smaller farm incomes, and engage in more extensive farm operations such as beef cattle raising. While the husband is more likely to be working off the farm, both husband and wife work off the farm about half as frequently and the wife only one-third as frequently as the husband only.

Since work off the farm is frequently done out of necessity rather than from preference, it is likely to produce conflict or stress in the family. Kada (1978) reported that 47 percent of the families with off-farm work indicated "some conflict." Conflict was reported more frequently by the operators less than 35 years of age. The economic need for dual job holding is greater for younger operators despite the conflicts that it produces, while for older operators dual job holding is more likely to become an accepted way of life without producing conflicts. Also, the amount of conflict in dual job holding is affected by the number of days worked off the farm and by the type of off-farm work. Those who worked fewer than 100 days off the farm saw no conflict, and few of those who held professional or white collar jobs off the farm were likely to report conflict with their farm work.

Off-farm work is likely to continue to be an option for members of the farm family. It provides an opportunity for the family to continue operating a farm without limiting their income to what the farm can provide. It also provides an opportunity for expanding the occupational interests of family members while retaining the advantages many see in country living. But these advantages must be measured against the costs of transportation, of conflicts between farm and nonfarm work within the family, and of the loss of status and independence for those who become wage workers. Most farmers who work off the farm become part of the working class, with few in the professional or managerial occupations (West, 1978). The extent to which this process of "proletarianization" enables the family to retain the advantages of rural living without too much exploitation and loss of freedom has yet to be determined in different social, economic, and geographical settings.

The Family Farm as the Basis of the Farm Family

Family-owned and operated farms continue to dominate in the United States, despite changes in their size and dependence upon nonfamily resources. According to Rodefeld (1978), 94 percent of all farms in 1969 (2,726,000) were operated by families. About three-fourths of the farm labor on all farms was provided by the families who owned or operated them. This has remained constant for the past 50 years (Nikolitch, 1972). But there have been considerable changes in the extent to which the farm enterprise is dependent upon the family for its land and capital resources, for technical information, and for various services associated with the production, harvesting, and marketing processes. While the percentage of tenant-operated farms in which the family does not own the land has declined following the high level of 43 percent in 1935, the percentage of rented farms has increased slightly in recent years. Of greater significance is the increase in the percentage of part-owned farms, in which the operator owns a portion of the land and rents the rest in order to expand his operations. One-fourth of the family-sized farms encompassed both owned and rented land in 1964, double the percentage in 1935. Hence the survival of the family farm has required expansion in the land resources beyond what is owned by the family.

The most dramatic change in family farms has been the increase in capital investment. This has meant that the family has had to go beyond inheritance and savings for the purchase of land, buildings, and equipment. These increases in capital costs have other effects on the family as well. To the extent that farmland is transferred between generations, the price tends to be kept below market value. The nature of the transfer and the share received by the son or daughter taking over the farm will affect the burden of the land investment (Salamon and Klein, 1979). Partnership arrangements with fathers or other persons are even more important in order for young farmers to get started in farming (Kowalski and Coughenour, 1975).

Owners of family farms in the future will find it more difficult to provide the resources needed for maintaining competitive operations, especially in those enterprises that require specialized production, handling, and marketing. This has already occurred in the fruit and vegetable farms of the West and to a lesser extent in many other areas. Contract farming, in which the processor provides the inputs and the scheduling of operations, can still be a family operation, although the family's contribution to the enterprise is limited to providing skilled labor, with fewer management decisions. Thus, the contract farmer becomes part of a much larger system of production, processing, and distribution that may exchange security for freedom to adapt to family, environmental, or community interests (Ploch, 1960).

The crux of the matter is that changes in the farm enterprise are encouraged by the larger immediate returns to capital inputs rather than by long-term returns to the land and labor. With a greater share of the returns going to land and capital investments, farm size must increase to maintain family income. One choice the family farmer can make is to reduce cash income and increase subsistence enterprises and alternative forms of production that require less capital outlay. The extent of such choices and the conditions under which they are made should be important topics for research that will influence future policies and programs concerned with the maintenance of family farms.

The Jeffersonian notion that the family-owned farm will make for a more democratic society seems largely irrelevant today. Family ownership of the land does not mean freedom from the control of the larger economic and political forces that affect the farm and the distribution of the returns from it. Yet attachment of the family to the land provides a basis for family continuity that is especially important for certain ethnic groups (Salamon and Klein, 1979). Furthermore, the commitment to farming as a more integrated way of life is receiving renewed attention as the costs and restraints upon energy and capital-intensive practices increase (Berry, 1977). The negative effects on the land of continuous cropping and chemical additives are increasingly recognized. Size and uniformity of operations lose some of their advantages when these factors and the variations of weather, soil, and infestations are taken into account. There is also evidence that smaller farms use less energy per unit of energy produced and can more easily adapt to the need for recycling plant and animal wastes.

Another consideration in farm size and structure is the problem of control over the distribution of benefits from the farm enterprise. This issue involves questions about the separation of land ownership, management, and labor that cannot be dealt with fully here. Since all three are combined in the family farm, the distribution of the returns to each area are seldom in question. But as ownership, management, and labor become separated, the problem of distributing the returns becomes quite complicated. Combining all three aspects in the same unit provides flexibility and continuity that is hard to come by when they are separately provided. The tenant and hired laborers are less interested in and committed to the enterprise than the owner who manages and works his own farm. Since operations cannot occur without the owner's consent, ownership conveys power and rights in the use and distribution of returns. Unless that ownership is earned through efforts contributed to the enterprise in the past or present, one basis of a stable and just social system is lacking. While community norms, public relations, and owner-tenant-worker agreements can offset these tensions, their potential must be recognized when alternatives to the family farm are considered.

Rodefeld (1978) provided a somewhat pessimistic view of farms owned, managed, and operated primarily by the family. He reported that in 1964 such family farms made up 78.6 percent of all farms and accounted for only 49.3 percent of all sales. Since that time these percentages have steadily declined, while the number of large farms of 1,000 acres or more and with produce sales of $100,000 or more have increased. These very large farms are increasing in all regions of the country, although the percentage increase is greater in the mountain and Pacific states, followed by the corn belt. This trend is being affected more by short-term economic considerations and by the structure of the market forces than by long-term rural and urban social, economic, and ecological considerations. Given the seriousness of the consequences of these changes in farming, the entire movement deserves far more study and attention than it has received to date.

Involvement of Wives in the Farm Enterprise

While it is assumed that the family is necessarily involved in the family farm, there has been relatively little study of the nature of that involvement. If the family farm is one in which the family assumes primary responsibility for the management and the labor of the enterprise, it is important to know how this responsibility is shared among family members and the consequence of this sharing for the farm and for the family. Furthermore, the effect of the changes discussed above on the involvement of the family has been only minimally studied.

Half a century ago studies (Beers, 1935) found that the wife could have a positive or a negative effect upon the farm enterprise, depending upon whether she provided help and support or was in conflict with the husband and created stress that affected financial matters. Straus (1958) found in the Columbia River basin that role specialization of husband and wife in farm and nonfarm matters was most characteristic of successful farms, with the farm operators making major farm decisions and the wives being supportive through their family and social roles. In a later study in Wisconsin, Straus (1960) found that the wives of high adopters of farm practices placed greater value upon efficiency and technical equipment in the home. In a separate investigation, Wilkening (1958) found joint decision making in the farm and family matters to be most characteristic of farm families in the middle income group.

These findings suggest that tendencies toward role specialization may be offset by other conditions affecting the involvement of women in the farm enterprise and involvement of men in family and household matters. While there is some evidence of specialization in work roles between husband and wife (Straus, 1960; Wilkening and Bharadwaj, 1967; Wilkening and Ahrens, 1979), this specialization occurs within the farm enterprise as well as between farm and family roles. Wilkening and Ahrens (1979) found that about two-thirds of the wives in 1978 had equal or major responsibility with their husbands for keeping farm records and paying the bills, compared with half with similar responsibility in 1962. The percentage with entire responsibility increases from 20 percent for the average farm to 30 percent for the farms with largest gross farm income. The involvement of wives in farm work is also more likely to lead to involvement in farm decisions for the larger farms. This suggests that the commitment of the wife to both work and management provides an opportunity for the expansion of the family farm.

A longitudinal study in Wisconsin also suggests the increased role of women in the farm enterprise (Dorner and Marquardt, 1977). While the labor input on the farms studied changed little during the period, the share of the wife's labor increased from 9.3 percent in 1950 to 16.4 percent in 1975, while the share of other family members declined slightly. Wives increased their labor input on farms with the largest dairy herds (Dorner and Marquardt, 1979). These findings indicate that many farm women see themselves as becoming more of a partner in the farm enterprise, with equal rights as well as equal responsibilities. A study of the productive time of farm wives on low-income farms in Iowa, North Carolina, and Oklahoma indicated that farm wives contribute about half as much as the husband to the farm work and that output produced by this effort is comparable to that of their nonfarm wage opportunities (Huffman, 1976).

The interest of farm women in the business side of farming is also indicated by attendance at Cooperative Extension meetings for women interested in farm management and in record keeping. This interest is also reflected in the activities of organizations such as the National Farm Women's Forum, American Agri-Women, and Wisconsin Women for Agriculture. But there is a lack of evidence of their participation as regular members of farmers' organizations and cooperatives and little information about how greater involvement in farm work and business affairs affects their involvement in other community organizations and activities.

The wife's involvement in the farm enterprise can be affected by the family cycle. Before having children, wives are more likely to be involved in fieldwork. They are less likely to be involved when there are young children under 6 years of age in the family (Wilkening and Ahrens, 1979). But of those involved in farm operations, just as many are likely to assume an equal share of the farm work with the husband. Involvement with chores and fieldwork tends to decline when there are children 12 years and over and when there are no children and the operator is 45 years or older.

The wife's work on the farm also tends to increase with the husband's work off the farm. There is a greater responsibility for the record keeping when the husband works 100 days or more off the farm, and the effect upon involvement in farm chores increases slightly (Wilkening and Ahrens, 1979). The increase of farm women's work off the farm is consistent with the increased labor force participation of women in general, as indicated in the opening chapter by David Brown. The more educated farm women are more likely to work off the farm. When the wife works off the farm, there is a decline in her involvement in farm work roles except for record keeping. While few of those working 100 days or more off the farm shared equally in the farm chores, about two-fifths still assisted with the fieldwork, and two-thirds shared equally with record keeping. When compared to women who do not work off the farm, those wives who do were more likely to obtain farm information from Cooperative Extension sources, indicating their continuing interest in farm matters. These findings indicate that farm women, as well as other women who work, are not relieved of their household and other commitments.

The wife's involvement in farm decisions is related to the involvement in farm work and in information seeking for the farms (Sawer, 1973; Wilkening and Bharadwaj, 1968). Involvement in farm decisions appears to be associated with the particular interests and aspirations of the wife more than with educational level, income, or family cycle (Wilkening and Guerrero, 1969). But the specific role of women in farm decision making is likely to depend upon whether she sees farm decisions as affecting family goals and upon whether she is accepted as a partner in the enterprise. No doubt the role of women affecting farm decisions varies by region and by type of farming. There is evidence among dairy farmers that involvement in decisions and in information-seeking related to the farm has an overall positive effect upon the adoption of those improved practices concerned with labor saving, as well as with production efficiency and maintenance of the land and livestock resources (Wilkening and Guerrero, 1969). This is likely to increase as more farm women are brought into agricultural training in high school, college, and Cooperative Extension courses. But research is needed on how such training affects the role of women in farming.

The extent of the interdependence between husband and wife in the farm family goes beyond the sharing of task roles and decision making. Family life and patterns are dependent upon the nature of the farm and its products and the patterns of work. While wives may share in the farm work and decision making in order to obtain things for the home, their satisfaction with the farm enterprise is related to the level of income and standard of living (Bharadwaj and Wilkening, 1974). The husband's satisfaction with the farm is affected by standard of living as well as by success in farming. These findings suggest that the way farm couples feel about their farm activities is affected by the way they feel it affects their goals and attainments in the home and family areas (Capener and Berkowitz, 1976). To this extent, success in farming is not judged as much by the profit produced as by how it affects family needs and interests. Is this changing as farming becomes more commercialized and farm and family enterprises become more distinct? In those regions where the family farm has been dominant, there is evidence that as farms increase in size the wife and other family members make a greater commitment to the work and management of the enterprise. The effect of this increased family commitment upon social, recreational, and community involvement needs to be studied.

Conclusion

Both the family farm and the farm family have changed considerably in the past two decades. The same economic and social forces affecting the larger society have affected the farm family. Although there is value placed upon the family farm and upon traditional family patterns, both have been affected by processes in the larger society. The close interdependence of family and farm has been replaced by greater dependence of each upon other systems and other relationships. Yet, more than other businesses farms are still a family enterprise, providing the basis for work patterns, leisure time, and social life. One set of questions relates to the viability of the farm enterprise. How does the relationship of the family to the farm affect its productivity, efficiency, and ability to survive adversity? Are family-operated farms more likely to provide the commitment needed for long-term productivity and continuity in the face of natural and economic adversity? Determining whether this is true requires a focus on the interrelationship of the structure and processes of the farm and family systems over time and how they support and limit their short- and long-term goals (see Bennett, 1967; and Kohl, 1976).

Another set of questions relates to the family as an institution that reproduces itself and has a set of dynamics that relate to the interest and well-being of its members and to the interests of the larger society. More study is needed of the internal relationships and processes of the farm family and how they are affected by the structures and processes of the environment. More intensive and longitudinal studies of farm families and of family farms under different geographic, political, and economic conditions are needed.

Farm and family will continue to affect each other, but the consequences for each and for the larger society will depend upon the patterns created. Much more knowledge of the nature of these patterns and the forces affecting them is needed in order to provide a basis for guiding our private interests and public policy.

References

Ball, A. G. and E. O. Heady. "Trends in Farm and Enterprise Size and Scale." In A. G. Ball and E. O. Heady (eds.), *Size and Structure and Future of Farms*. Ames, Iowa: Iowa State University Press, 1971.

Beers, H. W. *Measurements of Family Relationships in Farm Families of Central New York*. Memoir 183, Agricultural Experiment Station, Cornell University, Ithaca, New York, 1935.

Bennett, J. *Hutterite Brethren: The Agricultural Economy and Social Organization of a Communal People*. Palo Alto, California: Stanford University Press, 1967.

Berry, W. *The Unsettling of America: Culture and Agriculture*. New York: Avon Books, 1977.

Bharadwaj, L. and E. A. Wilkening. "Occupational Satisfaction of Farm Husbands and Wives." *Human Relations*, 1974, 26, 739–753.

Capener, H. and A. Berkowitz. "The Farm Family: A Unique Organization." *New York's Food and Life Sciences Quarterly*, 1976, 9, 8–11.

Dorner, P. and M. Marquardt. *Economic Changes in a Sample of Wisconsin Farms: 1950 to 1975*. Agricultural Economics Staff Paper Series, No. 135, University of Wisconsin–Madison, November 1977.

____. *Land Transfers and Funds Needed to Start Farming: A Sample of Wisconsin Farms 1950–1975*. Agricultural Economics Staff Paper Series, No. 148, University of Wisconsin–Madison, September 1978.

____. *The Family's Role in the Wisconsin Family Farm*. Agricultural Economics Staff Paper Series, No. 171, University of Wisconsin–Madison, 1979.

Fuguitt, G. V. "Part-time Farming and the Push-Pull Hypothesis." *American Journal of Sociology*, 1959, 64, 375–379.

Huffman, W. E. "The Value of Productive Time of Farm Wives: Iowa, North Carolina and Oklahoma." *American Journal of Agricultural Economics*, 1976, 58, 836–841.

Kada, R. "Off-farm Employment and Farm Adjustments: Microeconomic Study of the Part-time Farm Family in the United States and Japan." Unpublished Ph.D. dissertation, Department of Agricultural Economics, University of Wisconsin, 1978.

Kohl, S. B. *Working Together: Women and Family in Southwestern Saskatchewan*. Toronto: Holt, Rinehart and Winston of Canada, 1976.

Kowalski, G. S. and M. Coughenour. "Father-Son Decision Making in Joint Farming Arrangements." Paper presented at the Annual Meetings of the

Rural Sociological Society, San Francisco, California, 1975.

Long, E. J. and K. H. Parsons. *How Family Labor Affects Wisconsin Farming*. Madison, Wisconsin: Wisconsin Agricultural Experiment Station, Bulletin 167, 1950.

Nikolitch, R. "The Individual and the Family Farm." In A. G. Ball and E. O. Heady (eds.), *Size, Structure and Future of Farms*. Ames, Iowa: Iowa State University Press, 1972, 248-269.

Ploch, L. A. *Social and Family Characteristics of Maine Contract Broiler Growers*. Orono, Maine: Maine Agricultural Experiment Station, Bulletin 596, 1960.

Rodefeld, R. D. "Trends in U.S. Farm Organizational Structure and Type." In Rodefeld, R. D., et al. (eds.), *Change in Rural America: Causes, Consequences and Alternatives*. St. Louis: C. V. Mosby Co., 1978.

Salamon, S. and A. Mackey Klein. "Land Ownership and Women's Power in a Midwestern Farming Community." *Journal of Marriage and the Family*, 1979, 41, 109-119.

Sawer, B. J. "Predictors of Farm Wife's Involvement in General Management and Adoption Decisions." *Rural Sociology*, 1973, 38, 412-426.

Straus, M. A. "The Role of the Wife in the Settlement of the Columbia Basin Project." *Marriage and Family Living*, 1958, 20, 59-64.

____. Family Role Differentiation and Technological Change in Farming." *Rural Sociology*, 1960, 25, 219-228.

Wilkening, E. A. "Joint Decision-making in Farm Families as a Function of Status and Role." *American Sociological Review*, 1958, 23, 187-192.

Wilkening, E. A. and N. Ahrens. "Farm Work and Business Roles as Related to Farm and Family Characteristics." Paper presented at Annual Meetings of the Rural Sociological Society, Burlington, Vermont, 1979.

Wilkening, E. A. and L. Bharadwaj. "Aspirations and Task Involvement as Related to Decision-making among Farm Husbands and Wives." *Rural Sociology*, 1968, 33, 30-45.

____."Dimensions of Aspirations, Work Roles and Decision-making of Farm Husbands and Wives in Wisconsin." *Journal of Marriage and the Family*, 1967, 29, 703-711.

Wilkening, E. A. and S. Guerrero. "Consensus in Aspirations for Farm Improvement and Adoption of Farm Practices." *Rural Sociology*, 1969, 34, 182-196.

West, J. G. *Small Farms in Missouri: The Characteristics and Their Problems*. Washington, D.C.: The National Rural Center, Report No. 9, 1978.

3
FAMILY ASPECTS OF THE
NEW WAVE OF INMIGRANTS
TO RURAL COMMUNITIES

Louis A. Ploch

"Despite the massive magnitude of residential mobility, there has been relatively little research on post-movement adjustments of individuals and families" (Burchinal and Bauder, 1965, p. 197). The conclusion of Burchinal and Bauder pertained largely to the predominant rural-urban migration stream of the 1960s. Unfortunately it applies all too well to the so-called turnaround migration of the 1970s. It is not that information on the new wave of inmigrants to rural areas is lacking. On the contrary, turnaround migration has produced a prodigious amount of interest, both professional and popular.[1]

Perhaps the major reason for the lack of focus on the family aspects of turnaround migration is professional specialization. Turnaround migration is essentially a population movement, and, therefore, it has tended to attract the attention primarily of demographers and geographers. In addition to their normal preoccupation with numbers and trends, it is probable that the demographers, particularly, have not concerned themselves with the family aspects of turnaround migration because of its complexities (Ploch, 1976). As will be more fully commented upon below, there is no single modal family type migrating from urban to rural areas. Migrants range from the young rebels who are attempting to escape from self-perceived inequities of modern urban society to the urbane, upper-middle-class professional who wishes to retire early and enjoy the supposed serenities of rural life. In essence they range from the scruffy to the near baronial. Their family orientations appear to vary as widely, as do their economic and social philosophies.

Because of the lack of data, it will not be possible for me to fill completely the gaps that exist in our knowledge of the social and family characteristics of recent urban-to-rural migrants. I will attempt, however, to synthesize present information. In addition, I would like to put forward a number of hypotheses and assumptions that I hope can be tested in future research and study efforts.

Despite the known diversity among the rural inmigrants, there is increasing evidence of a trend toward homogeneity. Quoting a Lew Harris poll, Tweeten (1978, p. 18) states that "new residents compared to established residents in rural areas are wealthier (median income $13,500 versus $12,700 for established residents), higher in occupational status (24 percent in the professional occupation category), and concerned about inadequate community services." My own data pertaining to a representative sample of migrants to Maine in the 1970–1975 period corroborate the public poll information (Ploch, 1978).

Although in this chapter I will not ignore the presence among the new rural inmigrants of persons at the extremes of the continuum—hippies and/or upper-middle-class urban escapees—the major focus will be on the middle of the distribution. As indicated in the Tweeten quote, the majority of inmigrant families tend to be relatively young and highly educated. They also tend to be experienced in or qualified for white collar occupations, particularly those constituting the professional, entrepreneurial, and managerial fields.

It seems logical to conclude that the family interrelationships of the rural inmigrants would be affected by the norms and values of their new communities (England, Gibbons, and Johnson, 1979). It also seems logical to conclude that the norms and values of the settled families (native and longtime residents) would be affected by the presence of the new families. No detailed research data are presently available to test the validity of these assumptions. However, inferential data included in a number of sources tend to validate this position. For example, in a study conducted in a small town in the Northwest, definite distinctions were found between the loggers (primarily longtime settlers) and the Forest Service families (primarily short-time residents). Nevertheless, the authors report that "the boundary between these two ways of life is a fuzzy one. Some families straddle it; a woman may divorce a logger, marry a man in the Forest Service, and maintain her commitment to the way of life associated with logging" (Colfer and Colfer, 1978, p. 207).

Hennigh, in a study of what he describes as a taxpayers' revolt in a small Oregon community, describes how traditional leaders reacted to the thrust and presence of new people, many of whom were recent inmigrants from metropolitan areas.

> Observations indicated that traditional leaders of nonschool institutions adapted rather rapidly to changing social requirements. In 1977 traditional leaders often described themselves as coordinators, rather than as overseers of public policy, and as resources for anyone, even strangers, who chose to seek advice or information. Traditional leaders certainly spent much time listening to the sort of advice they would have been giving a few years earlier. They often commented on the increasing problem of having to deal with people they did not know personally, but they were likely to describe the changes in positive terms (Hennigh, 1978, p. 186).

Our research and observations in Maine indicate that processes like those described by Hennigh are by no means rare. A major component of the various examples of accommodation appears to be the fact that even though the inmigrants do differ in many ways from settled residents, the majority of them represent a middle ground. They are neither hippies nor avant-garde urbanites. Although a kind of middle-class central tendency does seem to exist among the inmigrants to rural areas, it would be a mistake to over-emphasize the homogeneity of the migration turnaround.

Indeed, despite the preponderance among them of highly educated persons with white collar experiences or potentials, these new entrants into rural life are not necessarily homogeneous in their motivations for migration nor in their goals and values. It is variation in goals and values that leads to variation in lifestyle preferences. Differences in lifestyle preferences are, in turn, intimately related to the structure and functioning of the new rural families. Case study examples will be presented below to illustrate this assumption.

Based largely on my empirical and observational research in Maine, but also based on a search of the literature, both popular and professional, and on discussions with other researchers, there appear to be at least three modal types of families or households among the urban-to-rural inmigrants. Our research would indicate that of the types listed below, the middle group is the most common:

- *Back-to-the-land social isolates.* While not classical hippies, they want to live in at least a semiisolated area, grow most if not all of their food needs, and be as independent as possible from community and society. Most of the adults are relatively young—under 35 years of age.
- *Rural pragmatists.* Generally they blend pragmatic economic and social/political points of view with a desire to share in the presumed amenities of rural or small-town life. They include the new store owners who restore a rural aura to their business and the professional who conducts his business according to his or her definition of traditional rural norms. They are often environmentally oriented.
- *The middle aged and other urbanites turned rural romanticists.* Many are relatively young retirees. Many are, by local standards, well off. They tend to see glories in rural life that natives, particularly those who live at relatively low economic levels, cannot. Many rural returnees are included in this group.

These short characterizations do not fully describe the range of family types. There are too many variations and subtleties among the families for any paradigm to be fully satisfactory. The variations are presented not as ideal types but as modalities.

Table 3.1 is an attempt to classify the three modal family types according to a number of variables. In some families, one of the attributes may be significantly more important than the others. The specific combination of the attributes can be an important factor in a family's ability to adjust to a new rural setting. It can also be a major force in the acceptance of the family at the community level.

Despite the lack of fully ascertainable differences between family types among the urban-to-rural inmigrants, they share one distinction at the local community level. They are newcomers, strangers. While attitudes toward newcomers will, of course, vary from cultural area to cultural area and from community to community, inmigrants to rural areas generally are not readily accepted. In a sense they must "prove" themselves. This type of attitude is particularly prevalent in Appalachia and in rural northern New England, which maintains many Appalachian attributes.

In areas like rural northern New England and Appalachia, where net outmigration had been the norm for approximately a century, a kind of stable equilibrium had been reached at both the community and family levels. New people were often perceived as a threat to that balance. And when the most conspicuous segment of the inmigrants (in characteristics, but generally not in numbers) is composed, by local definition, of hippies or other seeming nonconformists, the flags of local suspicion go up. All new families, whether or not they conform to the hippie mold, are suspect at first. Thus, whatever the intentions of the new families may be, whatever their actions are, they are subject to the gemeinschaft-like screening of local scrutiny. It is highly likely that this aura of testing and evaluation conditions the reactions of inmigrants toward the community and its residents. It is also likely that within the inmigrant families, tensions and frustrations are created that have intra- and interfamily as well as community consequences. Giordino and Levine (1977, p. 50) note that "overwhelmingly, the research shows that the forces of [family] disorganization primarily come not from within the family but from forces which impact on the family over which they have no control."

Oddly enough, the segment of the rural population that appears to be most receptive to the newcomers from urban areas is the older generation. In many instances a chemistry appears to be generated between the two groups. The inmigrants, particularly those with a back-to-the-land, subsistence-farm perspective, recognize older persons, particularly farmers or retired farmers, as valuable reference sources. Older persons tend to welcome the opportunity to once again assume important roles in the lives of younger persons. In many cases their own children either have left the community or tend to spurn farming and gardening for other pursuits.

No definitive data have been published on this phenomenon, but my research in Maine and contacts with researchers and rural residents in several states confirm that it is fairly widespread. There are probably several consequences of this pattern of relationships. An obvious one is the function it has of helping to integrate the new residents into the community social structure. It provides them with a sense of local identity. It might also have the negative effect of further alienating elderly parents from their children who remain in the community and who might resent the inmigration of new people. On the positive side, close relationships between relatively young

	TABLE 3.1 Life Style Status		
Inmigrant Family Characteristics	Back-To-Land/ Social Isolates	Rural Pragmatists	Rural Romanticists/ Retirees
Age	Young	Young to Middle Age	Middle Age, Older
Education	Mostly Some College or with Degree	Some College, or Degree	Varied--High School to College Degree
Present Income Level	Low, Generally by Choice	Medium Low to Medium High	Wide Variation
Community Involvement Level	Low or Highly Specific; Varied Potential	Medium to High; High Potential	Wide Variation; Potential in Larger Community Area
Occupation Before Migration	Student, Entry Level White Collar, Sub Professional	Skilled Blue Collar, Low to Medium White Collar, Professional	Wide Variation: Blue Collar to High Level Managerial, Professional
Occupation, Present	Not Working, or Working Part Time, Farming, Blue Collar, Crafts, Largely Self Employed	Wide Variation: Managerial, Professional, General White Collar	Retired or Part Time. Board Memberships, Consulting
Land Use for Sustenance	High	Low to Medium	Low
Environmental Orientation	Great Concern	Medium to High Concern	Great Variation
Isolation of residence	High	Low/Medium	Low with Variation
Housing Condition	Low, Lack of Conveniences, Functional	Medium/High	Medium/High

inmigrant parents and older rural residents may provide surrogate grandparents—or "aunts" and "uncles"—for children whose older natural relatives have been left behind in the urban area. Contacts with these older
persons could prove to be stabilizing forces in the lives of the inmigrant
children.

The Inmigrants—Three Examples

Before drawing further conclusions about inmigrant families, I'd like
to present profiles of three urban-to-rural migrant families in Maine. The
profiled families are not neatly illustrative of the inmigrant family types
presented in the paradigm. Nor do they represent all of the kinds of
families who have chosen to leave a more urban environment for life in
rural or small-town Maine. They do, however, represent several different
points on the continuum of urban-to-rural migrants. Perhaps most important,
however, are the similarities—not the differences—among the families profiled
here.

The present wave of migration to rural areas varies greatly in at least
two respects from most of the great migration movements. It is voluntary and not primarily economic (Ploch, 1978). Most of the migrant families have moved to rural areas out of choice rather than by force. They
are convinced that in a rural area they can obtain those quality-of-life attributes that are lacking in urban society. The seeking of quality-of-life satisfactions becomes more important than economic success or stability. Large
numbers of them take reductions in income or forgo opportunities for
economic or career advancement (Ploch, 1976). As can be noted in the
profiles that follow, even though the material lifestyles of the families differ greatly, they tend to share an acceptance of traditional rural values and
norms.

The Middys[2]

Bob and Mary are in their 30s. Their son Robert is 11, and Paul is 9. Both
Bob and Mary were raised near Portland, Maine. They attended high school
in Portland; for Bob it was not an enjoyable experience. He was most happy
when he could be out in the woods—fishing, hunting, trapping. After marriage, college, and short teaching stints, Bob and Mary moved to Alaska. Bob
states: "Alaska was mostly my trip. Childhood dream." But teaching school
in Fairbanks did not fulfill the dream. Occasional trips into the wilderness
helped, but the high cost of available land prevented the stay from being
permanent.

The answer became rural Maine. Bob says, "I wanted more flexibility.
Wanted to get into farming. Wanted kids to grow up in the outdoors." In
1971 they built a log cabin at the end of an abandoned road in Bradford,
a once-prosperous agricultural town. The house had no water, no electricity.
It did afford isolation. For many weeks of the year it was impossible to
drive from the hard maintained road to the cabin. When Mary worked the

late shift as a waitress in Bangor some 20 miles distant, Bob would trudge down the road to meet her at 2:00 in the morning. They took turns working so that each could share in the ruralness of their existence and still have some income for life needs.

When it was Bob's turn to stay home, he spent his time mainly in the woods, hunting, fishing, trapping, and foraging. Venison was not an unknown item on their table. The winter trapline provided some cash, but often Bob could not get to his traps because his unreliable car failed him again. In his absence, someone else would help himself to the bounty of Bob's traps.

When it came time for the boys to go to school, Bob and Mary ruled out the conventional schools in Bradford. Instead they opted for Skitikuk, an alternative "free" school some 20 miles away in Orono. When the car was not running or when Mary was using it, Bob solved the transportation problem by putting Robert on his shoulders, walking to the hard road, and hitch-hiking. Paying for the school was taken care of for a while when Bob began to teach at Skitikuk for $35.00 a week—"all they could pay."

After several years of privation in Bradford, Bob and Mary, largely through their own labor, were able to build a comfortable house of their own design. It is located in Greenbush some 15 miles from Orono and 25 miles from Bangor. The quite large, two-story prefabricated log house has running water, a bathroom, and electricity. And although it is just off a well-maintained paved road, it is somewhat isolated. Except for the entrance road, the house is enclosed by trees. There is only one nearby neighbor, a young couple without children with whom Bob and Mary are very friendly.

Both Bob and Mary work now, he as a house building supervisor in a CETA (Comprehensive Employment Training Act)–funded program; she as an outreach worker for the elderly for the local Community Action Program. Both like their work and especially enjoy having the opportunity to be of help to others in need.

Although Bob and Mary are not extreme social isolates, as are some of the back-to-the-landers, they focus most of their nonworking hours on their family. They see their semiisolated rural lifestyle as a means of maintaining their family interrelatedness. Mary says, "Even driving together puts us closer." Being out in the country forces them to drive to sources of entertainment. "Like going to the university (18 miles) on weekends. Take the kids in there to go bowling, play the machines (pinball). We go to the Bear's Den and maybe have a pitcher of beer. I don't know how much time we would spend together if we lived near my parents." The inference was that she would be spending more time away from Bob and the children.

Bob, too, recognizes the way in which their physical and social isolation enriches their family life. Although Bob is primarily outdoors oriented, he does feel that commercial entertainment and outings are important. He notes, "It's important for us to go to the Governors (a fast-food restaurant 15 miles from home). We go for the food and the kids." And both Bob and Mary appreciate the diverse experiences their children receive at the Skitikuk School.

But it is the interrelatedness associated with their rural residence that seems most important to Bob and Mary. "We have no TV, so we spend a lot of time together. We depend on each other. Bob tells the kids stories; he is very good at it. His dad used to do it for his seven kids." Even household chores have taken on a special meaning for the Middys. Mary says, "Cooking becomes important when you live like we do. Bob cooks and the kids cook. The kids even have a secret recipe."

The outdoors is also a major factor in tying the family together. Bob puts it this way, "Both of us value family closeness. Fact is, out here there is a lot of work to do together, especially the garden. We may even be mad at each other, but when we are out there working together we end up spending a lot of time together." The boys also help regularly with gardening. "This year Robert is going to plant all of our beans. We'll pay him. He has a green thumb." Bob speaks these words affectionately, warmly.

Wood is the fuel source for all heating and much of the cooking for the Middys. Getting in the wood is a task assigned to the boys and Bob. "On weekends we cut wood. That's one thing I won't give up. The kids go out with me. I cut it and drag it to the road and the kids load it. They work hard. They stacked all this wood," he says, gesturing to the kitchen woodpile.

Their family activities consume most of the Middys' discretionary physical and psychic energies. Except for close contact with one family, they visit neighbors very little. They see their friends from Bradford and other parts of Greenbush only occasionally. So far they have not become active in the community. Bob admits having attended one meeting of the local planning board. Mary hopes to get the kids, and perhaps herself, more involved in the Greenbush vacation recreation program this summer.

In general, the Middys are a family who are using their move to a rural area to live their lives as they want. This includes being relatively unencumbered by relationships outside their immediate family. Mary puts it, "I opted more for privacy than convenience." Bob says, "We came here (from the situation of more isolation and lack of household conveniences in the Bradford cabin) to upgrade our plane of living." They are doing it slowly, unobtrusively. They live their lives in a way consistent with traditional rural values—close family life, with each person assuming meaningful, productive roles for the ultimate good of all.

The McDonahs

John and Marjorie McDonah represent a type of rural inmigrant family somewhat similar to the Middys, but with its own unique aspects. They are college-educated people with advanced degrees who are combining their professions with part-time farming. In the Maine migration study (Ploch, 1978) just 10 percent of the household heads said they lived on a farm, and only 1 percent reported that their major source of income was from farming. Although their involvement with farming may be atypical of the larger group of inmigrants, they are representative of the myth surrounding much of the rural return migration movement—getting back at least to a semi-independent way of life.

John is in his late 30s or early 40s with a doctorate in English. He is a published author, is working on a book, and is an associate professor of English. Three days a week he journeys to Orono, 40 miles distant, to teach at the University of Maine. Marjorie has an M.A. in English and teaches on Tuesdays and Thursdays at the university. This schedule gives each of them ample time at home and provides for someone to be on the farm each day.

Combining farming with teaching permits John to get back to his first love. He was raised on a small farm in an area that is now part of suburban Boston. Although he appreciates the cultural advantages of metropolitan areas, John relates, "I couldn't survive in the city. I hate it with a passion. Coming out of Boston I literally breathe easier after the last traffic light." Marjorie agrees that a rural area is a much better place in which to live and to raise a family. "I grew up in the city (Brooklyn, New York) and had a wonderful family life, but I wouldn't be happy in a city."

John and Marjorie are very family oriented. Their five children (ages 13, 10, 9, 6, and 2-½) are all integrated into both family and farm activities. Even the youngest child, a girl, is learning by guidance and example. "She goes right into the barn and even tries to milk the goat—and she did get a squirt." The four older children, all boys, are expected to spend about a half-hour in barn work before they catch the school bus at about 7:30 A.M. John says, "Each child works each day; they have no choice. They do work out their own schedule. I insist they do things, grumble or not. I refuse to admit the existence of pain for them; it's good for them. The only work that is really hard is haying."

Because they heat and cook mainly with wood, bringing in the fuel supply is an important and time-consuming task. "I don't let them fell any of the trees; it's too dangerous. They do help load the wood." John and Marjorie both express love and concern for their children, but they believe in old-fashioned discipline. "I do spank the kids, that's the way I was brought up," John says.

Both home chores (dishes, bed making, floor sweeping) and farm work are supplemented with a variety of more pleasant family-centered activities. The four older children are being given music lessons on the instrument of their choice. Although neither John nor Marjorie presently plays (although John did take piano lessons) they hope that eventually they can have a family music group.

The McDonah children also participate in a number of outdoor activities. They play group sports among themselves and with a few neighbors. They are also encouraged to participate in school and extracurricular activities. Part of the incentive comes from John, who admits to "loving sports." During the season the entire family gets in the car and goes to watch the two older boys play basketball in a community league.

One of the reasons the McDonahs, with their relatively large family, prefer country living is that they do not have as many entertainment costs ("bowling, roller-skating, McDonalds") as they see associated with urban living. One recreational advantage John's land resources have given him is the opportunity to build a tennis court, which is in the early stages of construction. He enjoys tennis very much and hopes that some of the children become expert players.

Both the McDonahs, and particularly Marjorie, are concerned that small and part-time farming has not prospered in Troy as they believed that it would. Marjorie relates, "When we first came here there was a real community of inmigrants. Many raised goats like we do. They would drop by to buy a goat, have one bred, or just to talk. Now hardly anyone has goats. Mainly because the families found they wanted more money to buy things. They had to go to work so they gave up the goats. And before, we had a real live people's co-op."

There is still an area co-op, but it no longer functions as fully as it did. Oddly enough, Marjorie assigns a cause beyond anyone's direct control for the difficulties in maintaining a viable, interactive, co-op: inflation. "You can't have a co-op if people work out." She believes that the high rate of inflation has caused people to seek jobs and to work longer and harder. They are unable to remain active neighborhood and community participants.

The McDonahs' major linkage to the larger community is through the school. Troy is one of the ten towns that form SAD 3, the largest in area of all of Maine's School Administrative Districts. A current major concern for the McDonahs over SAD 3 is that it does not have a program for gifted children. Marjorie, who is considering running for school committee office in the future, states, "Our kids are brighter than many others, and that causes a problem." One of the boys is particularly able. On his behalf, as well as for a number of other children in the district, Marjorie recently appeared before the SAD 3 school committee and pleaded for the institution of a special program or services for intellectually gifted children. There were some sympathetic school board members, but her appeals were not heeded.

Although Marjorie would like to see a school program for gifted children, she does recognize that even tracking (special course content level for children of varying degrees of ability) presents problems for her children. "Tracking creates some separation; it separates the kids out. Our kids are expected to do better in school, to be at the top of the class." And the fact that their children tend to excel helps place them apart from the average student.

To save their children the hour or more afternoon bus ride, either Marjorie or John usually picks them up after school. This probably also sets the children apart from their schoolmates. But it does get them home earlier and gives them time both for their home and farm chores and family-related recreational activities.

The McDonahs have no specific goals in mind for their children. They do hope that in some way they will continue their formal education or informal learning after high school. John says, "It's not necessary that they go to college, but that they achieve some sense of vocation—that they work at it. I hope that by their 20s they can do what they want." Marjorie adds, "I hope they have a close family life. I know that, growing up in the city, I never did things with my brother. Now we are very close." She expects and hopes that their children will remain close to them, at least psychologically.

John is certainly planning on their remaining close. "I will keep half a beef critter and a hog for each of them." The oldest boy shows definite inclinations of being interested in farm life. John says he "is very responsive to animals."

The McDonahs, then, represent a rural inmigrant family who, like the Middys, place a high value on family life. They see the farm as a means to effect that goal. They also see the farm as a place to have fun. They, unlike many of their neighbors, recognize that music lessons and family tennis courts are not just for suburban effetes. While their active participation in the community is limited, they are concerned that the community provide certain support services for them, particularly a quality level of education. Marjorie may attempt to become part of the system to help assure that their educational goals are obtainable.

The Mills

Early retirement from upper-level management to ownership of a small retail business is one of the subpatterns of the urban-to-rural turnaround migration. People who have been successful managers for others want to try their hands at managing their own businesses. Bob Mill is one of these people. Employed in sales capacities for most of his life, Bob worked his way up to president of a major national transportation company headquartered in Chicago. By normal standards he was successful. Happily married to Florence, with three healthy, able children, he had a well-paid executive position and a home in the suburbs. But some five years ago Bob and Florence wanted more.

More involved coming back to New England. Both had been raised in rural Connecticut. After being disappointed with the efforts of a Vermont "opportunities locator," they struck out on their own. Almost by accident they found what they were looking for: Mill's Hardware in Belfast, Maine. It was a store that had been in the Belfast Mill family (no relation) for generations and had seen better days. Bob says, "The price was right, and certainly the name was right."

Although the Mills had no retail ownership experience and knew little about operating a hardware store, their new business met a family goal. They now had the opportunity for everyone to take an active part in a family enterprise. At the time their son was 27 and married, and their two daughters were 20 and 13. Each member, in his or her own way, identified strongly with their new community on the Maine coast. They also liked working together in *their* store—Mill's Hardware.

Before her marriage, Florence had training and experience in accounting. She became, and remains, the bookkeeper for the store. She has also melded one of her interests into the business. One corner of the two-room store is reserved for the display and sale of antiques—mainly small hand tools and household items.

Bob maintains overall control of the business, and, with Florence's assistance, is developing a mail-order business that specializes in the sale of high-quality hand tools, kitchen items including cutlery, and a varied assortment of household goods. Most of the catalog merchandise has been selected to appeal to persons with middle-class and upper-middle-class orientations.

Working together in the store not only gives family members important and definitive roles, it also brings them closer together than ever before. Bob says, "I used to be away about three weeks out of four. I guess we (he and Florence) have spent more time together in the last 5 years (since buying the store) than we did in the previous 20." Florence nods agreement. The store is open all day long, six days a week, and most of the time both of them are there. Bob admits to spending some Sundays there as well: "For me working is fun, not a chore."

Bob's enthusiasm for work is shared by all the family members. Florence glows when she talks about her bookkeeping duties and her antiques corner. But she doesn't let work shut her off from the family. "I have always put my husband and children first." She was active in hospital volunteer work in Illinois, but she has been only minimally active in community affairs since coming to Belfast.

The fact that all three of their children are involved in running the store is probably related to their early training. Florence says, "We always expected a lot from the children, and, frankly, we received it. All three worked in town (in Illinois); they were expected to."

Susie, the youngest, found no great problem in adjusting from suburban Hindsdale to villagelike Belfast. From the very beginning she fit into the community and the school. When she entered the two-year junior high school, "There were about 200 kids in the school and everybody knew me on the first day. I never felt any competition!" Growing up in Belfast was so satisfactory that she now says, "I wanted to make sure that I could stay so I married one (a local man)." Presently Susie and her husband live in the house that her parents bought on the Shore Road when they moved to Belfast. Susie appears to be happy about her choice; she practically bubbles over with enthusiasm when she talks about working in the store.

Bob and Florence have no definite plans for retiring. They do intend to turn the store over to their son and devote more of their own time to the catalog sales business and to developing a market for antiques. Both of these activities will permit them to travel—particularly to antique sales and trade exhibitions. They also hope to increase their visits to museums and historical sites—activities that have been important family ventures for many years.

The Mills, like the Middys and the McDonahs, are representative of turn-around migrants who have found it possible to combine the hope of rural or small-town living with a renewed emphasis on family life. While their business is in itself important to the Mills, the fact that two of their three children are part of it makes it even more important to them. Even though their chosen way of life does place great demands upon their time, the Mills feel a sense of escape from their former urban and suburban existence. In their responses to questions, in the nuances of their conversations, in their facial expressions when they speak of the business and their family, it is evident that their new lifestyle fits them well. They have been able to link an independent entrepreneurship with the development of strong intrafamily bonds.

Conclusions

Each of three profiled families, the Middys, the McDonahs, and the Mills, migrated to a rural or small-town area to fulfill longtime personal and family goals. For each of the families, escaping from an urban environment was important, and by escaping, each of them has created a family environment reminiscent of the traditional, if mythical, rural family. They have developed a family setting in which each person, regardless of age or sex, has important functional roles. The longtime success, in terms of family stability, of such families is difficult to predict. It is likely, however, that the norms of responsible sharing, of concern for each other, and of quiet intimacy that each family reflects will contribute to greater family stability than if they had not migrated to a rural area. Each of the families is quick to admit that their rural residence not only has changed their family life patterns, but also that living in a rural area has permitted them to develop intrafamily activities that they prefer.

As indicated earlier, there is a lack of data on how rural families are being affected by the new wave of urban-to-rural migration.[3] Therefore, in constructing a synthesis of the family effects of the recent wave of urban-to-rural migration, data must be relied upon that did not originate in studies of the phenomenon. The information sources do, however, provide a basis for conclusions and hypotheses that could be helpful in the study and understanding of the turnaround families and the communities of which they are a part.

The well-known family relations authority, Professor Urie Brofenbrenner (Byrne, 1977, p. 43), has concluded, "The family is falling apart. There is a lot of evidence to substantiate this." Although some would dispute the absoluteness of Professor Brofenbrenner's conclusions, there is no doubt that many American families are experiencing severe and disruptive problems. It may be that the threat of family collapse is one of the motivating forces drawing families to rural areas. There is evidence in each of the three family profiles presented here that family cohesion, and particularly integration of children into family functioning, was important in the decision to locate in a rural area.

In this study of interstate migration to Maine, one of the comments most often made by respondents on the mailed questionnaire is typified by the statement, "We wanted to raise our children in a clean, wholesome environment." The degree to which this goal is attainable in many rural communities is debatable. Yet the existence of this type of motivation may in itself be a factor in strengthening the rural family as a cohesive unit. And if the presumed relationship of strong families being related to strong communities is tenable, rural communities should benefit from the increase of migration.

If there is a difference between the structure and functioning of urban and rural families, then role patterns should change in the families moving from urban to rural areas. To date there is little evidence to support this conclusion. One set of circumstances, however, might be a factor in the development of role compatibility among members of inmigrant families. Noneconomic voluntary searches for improved quality-of-life conditions frequently appear as motivation of the turnaround migration (Ploch, 1978). Consequently, one might assume that family members will develop a cooperative spirit. My observational studies in Maine tend to validate this conclusion. Father, mother, children are interested in the part-time gardening and farming enterprises. Husband and wife cooperate in managing newly acquired small businesses, including weekly newspapers, hardware and general stores, boutiques, and craft enterprises. It is also common to find married or unmarried partners involved in some form of craftsmanship as well. When questioned, these people often agree that their new income-earning activity was selected not for its inherently superior economic potential but because it was personally rewarding as well as family and rurally oriented.

In addition, some of these newly acquired enterprises appear to serve as surrogate farms. To a degree, in running its business the family can re-create the interdependency of roles that exemplified the traditional family farm. Each member has a set of responsibilities that contributes to the welfare and comfort of all. In fulfilling their assigned or assumed roles, family members can bring to reality the myths that drew them to the rural environment.

Another family-reinforcing effect may occur through the cooperative work efforts of parents and their children. Young persons' perceptions of their parents as important role models and referents may be strengthened. Smith (1970, cited in Aldous, 1977, p. 109) indicates that where adolescents had positive feelings for parents there was a "willingness to turn to parents for guidance (their referent power), acceptance of parents' right to exercise control (their legitimate power), and belief in the parents' knowledge about the particular area in question (their expert power)." If this type of effect gains strength in inmigrant families, it could also begin to spread to other families in the community.

Notes

1. For details of the ways in which rural life is being affected by the reversal of rural-to-urban migration patterns, see Harry K. Schwarzweller, "Migration and the Changing Rural Scene," *Rural Sociology,* 1979, 44:7–23.

2. The surnames of the three families are fictitious. Other personal names and the names of all places are authentic.

3. One source of empirical data related to turnaround migration families will be the forthcoming analysis of the Northeast Regional Project (NE-119) titled "Impact of In and Out Migration and Population Redistribution in the Northeast." The study was conducted by state agricultural experiment stations in the Northeast. Preliminary analysis of the Maine data indicates that

migrating families, as compared with nonmigrating families: (1) tend to place more emphasis on family participation in decision making, (2) exhibit an increase in the number of family members who do things together, (3) increase the total number of shared family activities, and (4) recognize an increased sense of family togetherness.

References

Aldous, J. "Family Interaction Patterns." *Annual Review of Sociology,* 1977, 105–135.

Burchinal, L. G. and W. W. Bauder. "Adjustments to the New Institutional Environment." In Center for Agricultural and Economic Development, *Family Mobility in Our Dynamic Society.* Ames, Iowa: Iowa State University Press, 1965, 197–222.

Byrne, S. "Nobody Home: The Erosion of the American Family. A Conversation with Urie Brofenbrenner." *Psychology Today,* November 1977, 43–46.

Colfer, D. and M. Colfer. "Inside Bushler Bay: Lifeways in Counterpoint." *Rural Sociology,* 1978, 43, 204–220.

England, J. L., W. E. Gibbons, and B. Johnson. "The Impact of Rural Environment on Values." *Rural Sociology,* 1979, 44, 118–136.

Giordano, J. and I. M. Levine. "Carter's Family Policy: The Pluralist's Challenge." *Journal of Current Social Issues,* 1977, 44, 48–52.

Hennigh, L. "The Good Life and the Taxpayers' Revolt." *Rural Sociology,* 1978, 43, 178–190.

Ploch, L. A. "Maine's New Pattern of Inmigration: Some Significance and Consequences." Mimeographed. Orono, Maine: Department of Agricultural and Resource Economics, 1976.

____. "The Reversal of Migration Patterns: Some Rural Development Consequences." *Rural Sociology,* 1978, 43, 293–303.

Smith, F. E. "Foundations of Parental Influence: An Application of Social Power Theory." *American Sociology Review,* 1970, 35, 860–873.

Tweeten, L. Statement before the Select Committee on Population, U.S. House of Representatives, 1978.

PART 2

PATTERNS AND FORMS
OF RURAL FAMILIES

4
KINSHIP SYSTEMS
AND EXTENDED FAMILY TIES

Gary R. Lee and Margaret L. Cassidy

In recent years social researchers have paid little attention to kinship relations among rural populations. This is somewhat surprising in light of the great investment of research and theory in the study of urban kinship. This imbalance is probably attributable to the debate regarding the "isolated nuclear family" in the contemporary United States, which served to focus attention on urban kin relations.

The concept of the "isolated nuclear family" is generally identified with Parsons (1943, 1951), who suggested the phrase as an appropriate descriptive label for the American family system. The idea, however, predates Parsons's work (Ogburn, 1922; Ogburn and Tibbitts, 1934) and has its distal roots in the writings of early theorists such as Durkheim, Weber, Simmel, and Mannheim (see Sussman, 1965). In highly simplified form, the central message of this theory was that family bonds are weakened in modern society, so that the family becomes less prominent in the lives of its members. This process includes an attenuation of bonds between extended kin.

Wirth (1938), more explicit than most, identified the apparently declining social significance of the family with urbanization. He contended that the density of interacting individuals in the city makes the contact of entire personalities (that is, primary relationships) rare and difficult. A host of secondary relations replace small numbers of primary ties, including specifically kin ties, in the social networks of individuals. He suggested that this leads to alienation among urbanites (see Fischer, 1973, for a test of portions of this theory). Parsons's isolated nuclear family, then, was assumed to be particularly prevalent in the city and progressively more characteristic of American society as urbanization proceeded.

At this point in the development of the theory, the logical course of research would seem to have involved urban-rural comparisons of kin relations, to ascertain whether urbanization had had the hypothesized effect. But instead, the dozens of studies conducted in the 1950s and 1960s (see Sussman, 1965, and Adams, 1968, 1970, for citations) concentrated almost exclusively on urban kinship. The rationale for this strategy seemed to be that if Parsons's characterization of the nuclear family as "isolated" could not be empirically sustained among urban families, then it could not be sustained anywhere.

The problem with this approach is, of course, that the question of isolation is not answerable in absolute terms. No consensual definition of isolation exists (see Gibson, 1972; Lee, 1980), and even if all scholars agreed on a definition, it would be arbitrary nonetheless. Parsons (1965) ultimately stipulated that he intended the concept of isolation to be employed in a comparative context, but this stipulation should have been unnecessary: it is meaningless *except* in a comparative context. Unfortunately, this has not been widely recognized.

As an example, in the entirety of Sussman's (1965) review of this subject, in which he concluded that urbanization has not produced nuclear family isolation, there is only one reference to a study in which urban and rural kinship patterns are compared, and the comparison itself is not discussed. We simply cannot infer correlations between residence and kinship based on urban data alone (Winch and Blumberg, 1968; Straus, 1969; Winch, 1974), nor can we settle the debate over the isolated nuclear family simply by demonstrating that kinship relations exist in cities. One consequence of the heavy research emphasis on urban kinship is, paradoxically, that we really know very little about the effects of urbanization on kinship. A second consequence is that rural kinship patterns have not been extensively researched, allowing us to persist in an undocumented presumption that the "classical family of Western nostalgia" (Goode, 1963, p. 6) is alive and well and living on the farm.

This review will concentrate on studies that have compared urban and rural kinship patterns. By taking this approach, we certainly do not intend to imply that kinship behavior is homogeneous within either of these categories; this is demonstrably untrue. A multitude of other variables affects kinship behavior (Adams, 1970; Lee, 1979a, 1980), and many of these variables may interact with residence. For example, several studies (Klatzky, 1972; Heller and Quesada, 1977) have found that, among rural respondents, kinship interaction is less frequent and orientations to kin less strong for residents of the western United States than for others. Heller and Quesada (1977, p. 225) conclude that, while "familism is strong in each rural region," southeasterners show stronger and more pervasive ties to extended kin than do westerners, who are more oriented toward the immediate family.[1] These differences may well be attributable to the more recent migration of westerners and the greater distances between kin in the West. In Klatzky's sample, regional differences in kinship interaction disappeared when distance was controlled (Klatzky, 1972). Both migratory status and residential proximity to kin are critical factors affecting kinship interaction; we shall refer to these variables many times in the discussion that follows.

Rural-Urban Differences in Interaction with Kin

The theory reviewed thus far clearly implies that interaction with kin is more frequent and probably more meaningful among rural residents than among their urban counterparts. In fact, the very clarity of this implication may have contributed to the dearth of research on this issue: we do not need research to document something we all know to be true. Unfortunately for common sense and sociological theory, the research that has been done is quite equivocal. This is not to say that research consistently finds no relationship between residence and interaction with kin; most studies have in fact found differences. But, taken collectively, these studies do not consistently report the *same* differences.

One of the earliest and best empirical studies of the relationship between residence and interaction with kin was conducted by William Key (1961). He analyzed a probability sample drawn from five midwestern communities and measured interaction with both the immediate and extended family. His measure of the latter involved frequency of visiting and exchange of favors. A primary advantage of this study is that Key retained the five-category distribution on the residence variable, rather than dichotomizing his sample into urban and rural respondents. This refined scale allowed him to detect a curvilinear relationship between urbanization and interaction with kin: the highest scores were obtained by rural women (from unincorporated areas) and metropolitan men (cities over 100,000), with the lowest interaction occurring in villages (population less than 2,500) and small cities (2,500 to 25,000). The differences were, however, small and not statistically significant.

Key nonetheless attempted a hypothetical explanation of the pattern shown in these data. He speculated that the relatively high interaction with kin evidenced by rural residents may be attributable to spatial isolation and the lack of available alternatives; urbanites, on the other hand, may turn to kin as a source of intimate primary relations, which may be more difficult to form with nonkin in the urban environment. Small-town residents are neither spatially nor socially isolated, and satisfying nonfamily relationships may be more easily formed and maintained. Key also suggested that some of the effects attributed to the city *per se* by earlier theorists may actually have been due to rural-to-urban migration:

> It seems likely . . . that the hypotheses of the disintegration of the extended family developed early in the history of urban sociology when attention was focused on recent immigrants to the city, and before those individuals had had an opportunity to establish families. In other words, while there might have been a noticeable lack of contact with relatives during and immediately following the period of greatest immigration to the city, this seems to have been a temporary phenomenon produced by migration rather than by the city as such. (Key, 1961, p. 56)[2]

Although Key did not find the expected negative effect of urbanization on interaction with kin, a number of studies have found such an effect. Mirande (1970) compared a small sample (N = 74) of middle-class, married residents of Hillsboro, North Carolina, with a smaller (N = 39) sample of similar residents of Lincoln, Nebraska, in terms of frequency of interaction with kin. The North Carolina (rural) sample visited with kin more frequently than the Nebraska (urban) sample, but visited with friends less frequently. Mirande surmises from this comparison that traditional norms among rural populations may demand greater fidelity to kin in terms of social relations, thus restricting social activity with nonkin.

There are, of course, several problems with Mirande's sample in addition to its limited size. One is that regional differences, which we have good reason to believe may be important, are perfectly confounded with the rural-urban distinction in this sample. Another problem is that Mirande makes no attempt at multivariate analysis. For these reasons, the difference in kinship interaction between Mirande's two samples cannot be uniquely identified as an effect of residence, nor are his results clearly generalizable to any significant population.

Another study, by Shanas et al. (1968), analyzed a probability sample of about 2,500 elderly U.S. residents (aged 65 and over) collected in 1962.[3] This sample is extremely useful in terms of size and representativeness, but of course it is representative only of the elderly population and not the population in general.

Shanas et al. compared elderly people in agricultural occupations against those with urban (blue collar and white collar) occupations, so their distinctions are not precisely comparable to those made in studies employing residence as an independent variable. Nonetheless, their findings have considerable relevance for our purposes. They found that agricultural workers tended to live slightly closer to their adult children than white collar workers, but were no different than blue collar workers in this regard (Shanas et al., 1968). They also saw their children with slightly greater frequency than either blue collar or (particularly) white collar workers did. There were no occupational differences in contact with siblings. Finally, agricultural workers gave less help to their children than the others did, but they received more aid from them. This clearly appears to be a class-linked rather than a residential difference.

These results conform with traditional theory about the effects of residence on kinship interaction, but only modestly so: differences are consistently very small. Also, in many respects urban blue collar workers were more similar to agricultural than to white collar workers. This may indicate that many of the differences between occupational categories reported by Shanas et al. are in fact occupational (or at least socioeconomic) rather than residential differences. And once again no multivariate analyses were attempted; the differences, such as they are, remain unexplained.

Two other studies that found greater kinship interaction among rural than urban populations were done in the upper Midwest during the 1960s, and should thus be comparable with Key's (1961) work in many respects. Their results, however, do not agree perfectly with Key's, at least at first glance.

Straus (1969) hypothesized that contact with kin is negatively related to both urbanization and socioeconomic status. Part of his logic for the influence of urbanization, in partial conformity with Key, was that the United States has only recently become highly urban (via migration) and that migration reduces kin contact. These hypotheses were tested on a sample of married women living in Minnesota; both were clearly supported. Straus found that interaction with kin was greater among rural than urban residents and greater among blue collar than white collar wives; however, both rural classes showed higher interaction rates than either urban class.

Straus's data would seem to support classical urban theory and thus to contradict Key's findings to some extent. There are, however, at least two difficulties in interpreting these results. First, Straus's "urban" category included respondents living in cities or towns of 2,500 or more, but *not* the Minneapolis–St. Paul metropolitan area. Thus the range of the residence variable is severely restricted at the upper end. Straus may have observed the same difference in kinship interaction between rural areas and small cities reported by Key; he did not observe higher rates of kinship interaction in large cities because no such respondents were included in his sample. In light of Key's earlier findings the generalization that kinship interaction declines with urbanization (Straus, 1969:483) should not be extrapolated to highly urbanized areas on the basis of Straus's findings alone.

Second, Straus's measure of interaction with kin was a bit unusual, and as such, it is not directly comparable with the measures employed in other studies. He indexed kinship interaction by asking his respondents to name their eight most frequent social contacts; he then asked how many of these eight contacts were relatives. This method, of course, assumes that each respondent has eight at least occasional social contacts, but this assumption is not the problem here. The problem is that the measure does not index frequency of interaction with kin in either an absolute or a relative sense, but rather relative reliance on kin for social interaction. We cannot conclude from Straus's study that rural women interact more with kin than do urban (small-city) women; we can only conclude that kin constitute a greater proportion of the social contacts of rural than of urban women. This is a valuable observation in its own right, but it is not necessarily comparable to or cumulative with the findings of other studies.

A study of a statewide probability sample of Wisconsin by Winch and Greer (1968; see also Winch, 1977) also found kin to be somewhat more salient in the lives of rural than urban residents. They found small but significant negative relationships between urban residence and both interaction with kin and "functionality" of kin (exchange of services). Here again, however, two qualifications are necessary. First, Winch and Greer, like Straus, measured interaction with kin in a rather nontraditional way, thus limiting comparability with other studies: "Interaction has to do with the number of categories of households of kin with which some member of the respondent's household interacts at least monthly" (Winch and Greer, 1968, pp. 41–42). Possible categories included parents, siblings, and other relatives of the respondent and his or her spouse; scores could thus vary from zero to six. This variable does not really indicate frequency of interaction, but rather the diversity of the available kin network.

Second, Winch and Greer found that their results were significantly affected by controlling for migratory status. A respondent was defined as a migrant if he or she had moved to the community of current residence after the age of 18. Among nonmigrants, there was no association between residence and any measure of extended familism; where one or both spouses were migrants, interaction with and functionality of kin were lower in urban areas. Urbanites were more likely to be migrants than rural dwellers. Winch and Greer (1968, p. 45) summarize these results by noting that: "nonmigrant urban couples are as familistic, on the average, as non-migrant rural couples, but migrant urban couples are less familistic than migrant rural couples. . . . Non-migration is associated with the maintenance of extended kin networks, and part of the greater familism of rural areas is due to the greater stability of the population. But part of it is associated with the greater familism of migrants in rural areas."

Perhaps the most important feature of these results is the lack of difference, on any dimension of extended familism, between residentially stable urban and rural residents. Nevertheless, it is clear that the effects of migration must be examined in terms of both its relationship to residential destination and its implications for kinship interaction. An ingenious study by Hendrix (1976) focuses primarily on migration but also examines the effects of residential destination. Hendrix sampled the graduates of a high school in a small town in the Ozarks and the nongraduate siblings of those who had graduated. He classified his respondents into three categories: those who currently lived in the home community, those who had moved to another small town or rural area (population less than 50,000), and those who had moved to an urban area. Interaction with kin was measured by the percentage of respondents interacting with two or more households of kin at least weekly.

Hendrix found that those who had remained in their home town interacted with kin most frequently, whereas those who had moved to urban areas showed the lowest rates of interaction. Small-town migrants were intermediate. The relationship was then examined for only those respondents who had two or more households of kin residing in their community; the overall pattern remained unchanged. However, percentage differences were somewhat altered, such that the major difference in interaction with kin among those with two or more households present in the community was between small-town and urban migrants, rather than between migrants and non-migrants. Hendrix (1976, p. 100) concludes: "One might speculate from these findings that migration affects local kin interaction predominantly by reducing opportunities for such interaction, while urbanism further restricts kin interaction by reducing motivation when opportunity is present."

Hendrix notes, however, another possible explanation for differences in kin interaction between small-town and urban migrants. Questions about number of kin in the community were asked in the same way of all respondents, leaving the definition of "community" up to the respondent. Individuals residing in rural areas, towns, or cities of less than 50,000 population may define their communities more narrowly than those residing in metropolitan areas. Thus distance from kin, in all probability, is substantially greater for urban migrants than for those living in small towns. To the extent that distance affects interaction with kin (and that's a pretty considerable extent), it may explain differences between small-town and urban migrants. We cannot attribute this difference to motivation alone, particularly without a measure of motivation. On the other hand, we also cannot eliminate differential motivation as a possible cause. This study does show that rural emigrants who move to urban areas interact less frequently with kin than those who move to rural areas or smaller cities. It does not demonstrate conclusively *why* this is true.

Examination of a study by Klatzky (1972) sheds further light on the effects of residential proximity. She analyzed a national probability sample of married males according to frequency of interaction with fathers. An initial hypothesis was that interaction with fathers is inversely related to occupational status. Occupations were classified into four "urban" categories (upper white collar to lower blue collar) and farmers. The only significant difference Klatzky found was between farmers and all other categories, with farmers showing higher rates of interaction. This difference was greatly reduced, although not entirely eliminated, by a control for residential distance.

Klatzky also conducted two more analyses relevant to our interests here. First, she attempted to ascertain the effects of city size on interaction with fathers, independent of occupation. This analysis, unfortunately, excludes the farm sample. She found that respondents living in counties with no towns larger than 10,000 population interacted with their fathers significantly more often than did respondents in the three larger residential categories, but again most of this difference was attributable to differential distance from fathers (Klatzky, 1972).

Second, Klatzky checked for differences in interaction with fathers between urbanites with farm backgrounds and urbanites with urban backgrounds, under the assumption that differences between these two categories might reflect stronger traditions of familism among migrants from rural areas. She found no such differences, and therefore concluded that differences between farmers and nonfarmers (urbanites) in interaction with fathers "cannot be ascribed to tradition. Rather, they derive from the fact that farmers remain closer in physical distance to their parents, a situation which may mean that they cultivate land owned by or obtained from their parents, or more generally, that farming is one of the few remaining occupations where residing near the family of orientation promotes one's occupational interests." (Klatzky, 1972, p. 39.)

To summarize, Klatzky did find differences in interaction with fathers between farmers and nonfarmers and between small-town and large-city residents that favored farm and rural respondents. However, she argues that these differences are attributable primarily, if not entirely, to the fact that rural respondents tend to live closer to their parents than do urbanites. This conclusion is in agreement with the arguments of early theorists that geographic mobility, caused by industrialization and urbanization, causes a "breakdown" in extended family relations (see Straus, 1969),[4] and with findings of other researchers such as Winch and Greer (1968; see above) to the effect that residential stability is greater among rural than urban residents. It also supports Hendrix's (1976) suggestion that his differences between migrants to rural and urban locations may be due to differential distance from kin in the destination areas. However, other recent studies disagree with Klatzky on both the effects of traditional familism among rural emigrants and the ostensibly greater proximity of rural residents to their kinship networks.

Berardo (1966) studied kinship interaction among a sample of middle-class migrants to a community in Florida. Kinship interaction was measured by frequency of contact with a number of specific categories of relatives; these frequencies were summed across categories of kin and trichotomized. Since all respondents currently lived in the same community, current residence is a constant in this study. However, interesting relationships emerge when kinship interaction is analyzed according to migrants' previous residence.

First, Berardo found the highest rates of kinship interaction among migrants from the southern United States; this agrees with the findings of Heller and Quesada (1977) on greater familism among rural southerners, but it might also be explained by greater proximity, since Berardo's study was conducted in a southern state. The lowest rates of kinship interaction were found among migrants from the Northeast; midwestern and western migrants were intermediate. In this respect, Berardo's findings disagree with both Heller and Quesada (1977) and Klatzky (1972).

Of more direct relevance for our purposes, Berardo (1966) also examined the relationship between kinship interaction and size of community of origin. He discovered a negative relationship here, which was particularly apparent at the extremes of the residence continuum. People who had migrated from farms had a much higher rate of interaction with kin than people who had migrated from cities of 100,000 or more. Three intermediate residential categories were also intermediate in terms of interaction with kin, but did not differ on that dimension from one another.

Berardo's findings appear to contradict Klatzky's in terms of both empirical fact and implications. In Berardo's data, the clear differences between migrants from farm backgrounds and those from large cities may well indicate the retention of stronger traditional familism among the former. Unfortunately, Berardo did not control for distance or other possible confounding factors in his analysis. It may be that those with farm backgrounds were also more likely to have migrated from southern states, so that the apparent effect of previous residence is actually attributable to a combination of region and proximity to kin. In this connection, it is important to reiterate the fact that Berardo did not find significant differences between migrants from small towns (less than 5,000 population) and migrants from medium-sized cities (25,000 to 100,000). The appropriate empirical generalization is that farm emigrants are higher than average on kinship interaction and emigrants from large cities are lower than average.

A study by Bultena (1969) investigated variation in contact with children among the elderly by residence. The study was conducted in Wisconsin, and thus should be comparable to the Winch and Greer (1968) study discussed above, both geographically and chronologically. The results of Bultena's study, however, are markedly different.

Bultena analyzed variation in total amount of contact with all children for his sample of older people. Bivariate analysis showed no association between residence and interaction with children. This was somewhat surprising, not only in light of classical urban theory, but also because rural respondents had, on the average, more children than did urban respondents (2.9 versus 2.3). This means that, with a control for number of children, differences in interaction should favor urban elderly; this is in fact what Bultena found. He also found, as did Klatzky (1972), that a primary cause of differential interaction was distance from children, but in this case the *urban* respondents were more proximate to their children. For the members of the sample with children in the same community, slightly more rural than urban parents saw each child at least once a week. But Bultena points out that this is probably due to the (definitionally) greater size of urban communities, and the consequently larger intracommunity distances. When residence in the same county was used as the index of proximity, there were no urban-rural differences in interaction.

Bultena's data show, predictably, that differential proximity to kin influences interaction and produces residential differences in frequency of interaction. The surprising aspect of his study is that residential differences in proximity favor urban respondents. He argues that the United States is now a mature urban society; rates of rural-to-urban migration are no longer as high as they once were. The children of urban residents are now able to find education and employment, in most cases, in their native cities. Rural children must more often leave their home areas in pursuit of economic and occupational success. Since many families have now been established in urban areas for one or more generations, it makes sense to expect increasing numbers of urban adults to live closer to their parents than do rural adults: the majority of today's "grandparent" generation is now urban. In Bultena's study, greater proximity to kin among urban respondents produced slightly higher rates of interaction between aging parents and their adult children when the effects of number of children were controlled. Controlling for proximity explained this difference and eliminated it as a factor.

Finally, a study by Youmans (1963) of over 1,200 elderly residents of a rural and an urban area in Kentucky produced somewhat surprising results. Unlike Bultena, but in conformity with most other studies, Youmans found that rural residents lived a bit closer to both children and siblings than did urban residents. But, with distance controlled, the urban elderly visited with their children more frequently than did the rural elderly; the same was true for visits with siblings, although the frequency of such visits was much less than was the case for children. This casts further doubt on Hendrix's (1976) assertion that urban residence reduces the motivation for kinship contact under constant conditions of opportunity. However, Youmans argues that the relevant factors here are the limited finances and transportation facilities available to the rural elderly. He shows that older rural people depend upon their children much more than urban elderly do, but he points out that they may be constrained from interacting by the financial and physical difficulties of making such visits. They may not be the whole story, however, since urban respondents maintained higher rates of contact with children and siblings even within the most proximate residential category (nine miles or less).

Youmans's findings are superficially in agreement with Bultena's, but in one way they are a bit more extreme. Bultena found that the greater inter-action of urban elderly with their children was attributable to greater prox-imity. Youmans found that the greater interaction of urban elderly with their children occurred in spite of lesser proximity. In other words, urbanites seem to take greater advantage of the proximity that does exist. This may simply mean that urban residents are better equipped to overcome the barrier of distance because of their greater resources (Youmans, 1963). On the other hand, it could possibly mean that their affective ties to children are stronger; such a possibility cannot be conclusively eliminated.

It is important to note that the rural-urban differences reported by You-mans are, in most cases, fairly small. However, it is equally important to re-call that these data were collected in the southeastern part of the United States, where, according to Heller and Quesada (1977), *rural* kinship ties are stronger than in other regions.

Conclusions

In the course of this chapter, we have reviewed ten studies of the rela-tionship between residence and kinship interaction. Seven of these studies report that, at least on the bivariate level, kinship interaction is greater among rural than urban populations (Berardo, 1966; Shanas et al., 1968; Winch and Greer, 1968; Straus, 1969; Mirande, 1970; Klatzky, 1972; Hendrix, 1976). Two studies (Youmans, 1963; Bultena, 1969) report opposite find-ings: urban residents interact more frequently with kin than do rural residents. One study (Key, 1961) reports a small and generally nonsignificant curvi-linear relationship. Which results should be believe?

It is tempting to go with the majority of these studies and argue that kinship interaction is reduced by urban life. But such a conclusion would be much too simplistic. Even studies that agree with this conclusion dis-agree as to *why* it is true. Klatzky (1972) argues that differences in kinship interaction are attributable almost entirely to differences in proximity to kin, which favors rural dwellers. But Youmans (1963) found that urban respondents interacted more with kin in spite of disadvantages in terms of proximity, and Bultena (1969) found that his urban respondents had an *advantage* in proximity. Klatzky concluded that a rural background, perhaps indicative of stronger traditional familistic ties, is irrelevant to kinship inter-action among urbanites, but Berardo (1966) found otherwise. Winch and Greer (1968) and Hendrix (1976) found that immigrants to rural areas are more familistic in terms of interaction patterns than immigrants to urban areas, but both studies allow that this may be simply a function of greater intracommunity distances in cities; this stipulation is also pertinent to Klatzky's (1972) results. Finally, we must note once again that literally all findings of rural-urban differences in kinship interaction are susceptible to multiple interpretations. Factors such as regional variation in subcultural kinship norms, migration and differential proximity to kin, and socioeconomic status are often correlated with residence in these studies. Because these and other variables are frequently uncontrolled, we cannot attribute any rural-urban differences in kinship interaction to residence alone per se, particularly in light of the fact that controls on these variables so frequently produce differing results.

One conclusion of which we can be fairly certain is that kinship interaction is diminished by migration and consequent spatial separation from kin. However, we cannot be certain of how migration and distance are related either to residential origin or residential destination. In the late nineteenth and early twentieth centuries, when the United States was rapidly urbanizing, there was (by definition) a great deal of rural-to-urban migration. This probably meant that people who remained in the rural areas were more proximate to their kin and thus interacted with them more frequently than did those who moved away to the city. But this phenomenon may have been quite temporary. Soon people were able to move to urban areas to join kin who were already there. And now, with compounding of generations in urban areas and the greater employment opportunities for young adults in the cities, urban residents are not predominantly immigrants; they may live as close or closer to their kin than do rural residents. At least one study (Bultena, 1969) has already found this to be true. In any case, future studies of residence and kinship interaction will be of little value unless the effects of differential migration and proximity to kin are measured and thoroughly examined.

Perhaps the most useful and defensible conclusion we can reach from this review is, in some ways, a negative one. Empirical studies to date do not justify, either singly or collectively, the conclusion that urban residence destroys or seriously decreases the viability of kinship networks. The reverse side of this coin is, of course, that rural residents are not particularly "advantaged" in this regard. Reported rural-urban differences in kinship interaction are quite inconsistent, almost uniformly small, and often attributable to factors other than residence. Contrary to the assertions of earlier scholars in this area, we cannot agree that kinship relations are "weak" in the city. Our evaluation shows that they are no weaker, or not much weaker, than they are in nonurban areas. There are simply no absolute criteria of the "strength" of kin ties, so we must of necessity rely on comparative generalizations. The appropriate generalization in this case appears to be that there is not much difference in frequency of interaction with kin between rural and urban residents. Theories which imply that such differences do exist, at least in the contemporary United States, need careful scrutiny and qualification in light of the empirical evidence reviewed here.

Further research in this area is needed, of course. But this research, if it is to be theoretically and pragmatically useful, must do more than inquire into the possible existence of rural-urban differences in kinship interaction. It must concentrate on explaining whatever differences do exist. This means that additional variables must be incorporated into the analyses; some, but not all, possibly relevant variables have been discussed in this chapter. In addition, it is important to investigate the consequences of kinship interaction for both rural and urban populations. Straus (1969), for example, has done this with respect to measures of psychosocial modernization, finding that extremely high rates of kinship interaction are associated with low levels of modernization. Several other studies noted above (Mirande, 1970; Heller and Quesada, 1977) have found that kinship interaction is negatively associated with interaction with friends and/or participation in community affairs. A number of studies (Arling, 1976; Wood and Robertson, 1978; Lee, 1979b; Lee and Ihinger-Tallman, 1980) have discovered that interaction with children, grandchildren, and siblings is, surprisingly, unrelated to the morale of the elderly. We need to pay more systematic attention to these and other possible consequences of kinship interaction, as well as to the possibility that such consequences may vary according to residence.

Finally, it is clear from this review that we are not entitled to assume, on any empirical basis, that urbanization destroys kinship relations, or that kin networks are necessarily strong and viable in rural areas. Both assumptions are much too facile and simplistic to be of any scientific or practical utility.

Notes

1. The conclusion that "familism is . . . strong in each rural region" cannot, of course, be supported by these data, since Heller and Quesada analyzed only rural samples. There are no objective criteria of the strength of kin ties.

2. Migration, of course, may be influenced by the presence of kin in destination communities (Hendrix, 1975, 1979). We have evidence from other societies to the effect that rural-to-urban migration may produce temporary increases in the occurrence of extended-family households; as kin follow one another to the city, scarce housing and low wages often lead to the sharing of homes by related families. See Anderson (1973) for mid-nineteenth-century England, Handwerker (1973) for Liberia, and Stinner (1977, 1979) for the Philippines. (For a review of the implications of these findings for theories of family structure, see Lee, 1977.)

3. This study was actually cross-national in scope, encompassing Britain and Denmark as well as the United States. Only the U.S. data are discussed here, however, since they are most directly related to our purposes. Results in the other two nations were roughly comparable.

4. We should note that Litwak (1960a, 1960b) and many others have

demonstrated that kin ties can be effectively maintained in spite of both geographic and social mobility; this is the foundation of Litwak's concept of the "modified extended family." However, no one (including Litwak) has argued that distance from kin does not affect interaction frequency. Litwak's point is that viable kin relationships can be maintained in spite of the infrequent interaction resulting from residential separation.

References

Adams, B. N. *Kinship in an Urban Setting.* Chicago: Markham, 1968.

____. "Isolation, Function, and Beyond: American Kinship in the 1960s." *Journal of Marriage and the Family,* 1970, 32, 575–597.

Anderson, M. "Family, Household, and the Industrial Revolution." In M. Gordon (ed.), *The American Family in Social-Historical Perspective.* New York: St. Martin's Press, 1973.

Arling, G. "The Elderly Widow and Her Family, Neighbors, and Friends." *Journal of Marriage and the Family,* 1976, 38, 757–768.

Berardo, F. M. "Kinship Interaction and Migrant Adaptation in an Aerospace-related Community." *Journal of Marriage and the Family,* 1966, 28, 296–304.

Bultena, G. L. "Rural-Urban Differences in the Familial Interaction of the Aged." *Rural Sociology,* 1969, 34, 5–15.

Fischer, C. S. "On Urban Alienations and Anomie: Powerlessness and Social Isolation." *American Sociological Review,* 1973, 38, 311–326.

Gibson, G. "Kin Family Network: Overheralded Structure in Past Conceptualizations of Family Functioning." *Journal of Marriage and the Family,* 1972, 34, 13–23.

Goode, W. J. *World Revolution and Family Patterns.* New York: Free Press, 1963.

Handwerker, W. P. "Technology and Household Configuration in Urban Africa: The Bassa of Monrovia." *American Sociological Review,* 1973, 38, 182–197.

Heller, P. L., and G. M. Quesada. "Rural Familism: An Interregional Analysis." *Rural Sociology,* 1977, 42, 220–240.

Hendrix, L. "Kinship and Economic-rational Migration: A Comparison of Micro- and Macro-level Analyses." *Sociological Quarterly,* 1975, 16, 534–543.

____. "Kinship, Social Networks, and Integration among Ozark Residents and Out-migrants." *Journal of Marriage and the Family,* 1976, 38, 97–104.

____. "Kinship, Social Class, and Migration. *Journal of Marriage and the Family,* 1979, 41, 399–407.

Key, W. H. "Rural-Urban Differences and the Family." *Sociological Quarterly,* 1961, 2, 49–56.

Klatzky, S. R. *Patterns of Contact with Relatives.* Washington, D.C.: American Sociological Association, 1972.

Lee, G. R. *Family Structure and Interaction: A Comparative Analysis.* Philadelphia: J. B. Lippincott, 1977.

____. "The Effects of Social Networks on the Family." In W. R. Burr, R. Hill, F. I. Nye and I. L. Reiss (eds.), *Contemporary Theories About the Family,* Vol. 1. New York: Free Press, 1979 (a).

____. "Children and the Elderly: Interaction and Morale." *Research on Aging,* 1979, 1, 335–360 (b).

____. "Kinship in the Seventies: A Decade Review of Research and Theory." *Journal of Marriage and the Family,* 1980, 42.

Lee, G. R., and M. Ihinger-Tallman. "Sibling Interaction and Morale: The Effects of Family Relations on Older People." *Research on Aging,* 1980, 2.

Litwak, E. "Occupational Mobility and Extended Family Cohesion." *American Sociological Review,* 1960, 25, 9–21 (a).

____. "Geographic Mobility and Extended Family Cohesion." *American Sociological Review,* 1960, 25, 385–394 (b).

Mirande, A. M. "Extended Kinship Ties, Friendship Relations, and Community Size: An Exploratory Analysis." *Rural Sociology,* 1970, 35, 261–266.

Ogburn, W. F. *Social Change.* New York: Viking Press, 1922.

Ogburn, W. F. and C. Tibbitts. "The Family and Its Functions." In report of the President's Research Committee on Social Trends, *Recent Social Trends in the United States.* New York: McGraw-Hill, 1934.

Parsons, T. "The Kinship System of the Contemporary United States." *American Anthropologist,* 1943, 45, 22–38.

____. *The Social System.* New York: Macmillan, 1951.

____. "The Normal American Family." In S. Farber, P. Mustacchi, and R. H. Wilson (eds.), *Man and Civilization: The Family's Search for Survival.* New York: McGraw-Hill, 1965.

Shanas, E., P. Townsend, D. Wedderburn, H. Friis, P. Milhog, and J. Stehouwer. *Old People in Three Industrial Societies.* New York: Atherton Press, 1968.

Stinner, W. F. "Urbanization and Household Structure in the Philippines." *Journal of Marriage and the Family,* 1977, 39, 377–385.

____. "Modernization and Household Extension in the Philippines: A Social Demographic Analysis." *Journal of Marriage and the Family,* 1979, 41, 161–168.

Straus, M. A. "Social Class and Farm-City Differences in Interaction with Kin in Relation to Societal Modernization." *Rural Sociology,* 1969, 34, 476–495.

Sussman, M. B. "Relations of Adult Children with Their Parents." In E. Shanas and G. F. Streib (eds.), *Social Structure and the Family: Generational Relations.* Englewood Cliffs, New Jersey: Prentice-Hall, 1965.

Winch, R. F. "Some Observations on Extended Familism in the United States." In R. F. Winch and G. B. Spanier (eds.), *Selected Studies in Marriage and the Family* (fourth edition). New York: Holt, Rinehart and Winston, 1974.

____. *Familial Organization.* New York: Free Press, 1977.

Winch, R. F. and R. L. Blumberg. "Societal Complexity and Familial Organization." In R. F. Winch and L. W. Goodman (eds.), *Selected Studies in Marriage and the Family* (third edition). New York: Holt, Rinehart and Winston, 1968.

Winch, R. F. and S. A. Greer. "Urbanism, Ethnicity, and Extended Familism." *Journal of Marriage and the Family,* 1968, 30, 40–45.

Wirth, L. "Urbanism as a Way of Life." *American Journal of Sociology,* 1938, 44, 3–24.

Wood, V., and J. F. Robertson. "Friendship and Kinship Interaction: Differential Effect on the Morale of the Elderly." *Journal of Marriage and the Family,* 1978, 40, 367–375.

Youmans, E. G. *Aging Patterns in a Rural and an Urban Area of Kentucky.* Lexington, Kentucky: Agricultural Experiment Station Bulletin No. 681, University of Kentucky, 1963.

5
RURAL FAMILISM:
INTERREGIONAL ANALYSIS[1]

*Peter L. Heller, Gustavo M. Quesada,
David L. Harvey, and Lyle G. Warner*

The goal of this chapter is to present a reconceptualization of the construct "familism." This reconceptualization is based upon the belief that rural familism may be treated fruitfully as a structural phenomenon rather than as a set of activities interpreted solely within a family-as-a-group context. Unlike past and present treatments of familism that have assumed family life to center around a set of group activities and interactions located within the confines of the household, we argue for an approach to rural familism as expressing at least two forms of kinship principles.

A review of the anthropological and sociological research literature on kinship led us to the hypothesis that the conceptual homogeneity of the construct "familism" has dissolved. Specifically, we assert that at least two types of familism exist within rural America, and we support our assertion with a summary of research findings (Heller et al., 1981). The chapter concludes with a brief discussion of the need for future research and the relevance of our structural conceptualization for change agents working within diverse rural settings.

Kinship and Familism[2]

Past and present treatments of familism have assumed that family life could be treated as a set of group activities and interactions located within the confines of the household. Familism was defined as a unique form of interaction and household organization. Behaviors, perceptions, and actions toward others when defined as familistic were seen as having their origins, by and large, within the household itself. Rather than being treated as kin first, relatives were handled as members of other households who were also kin. The consequences of familism were used to explain how familism affected interaction with other households.

The household and its members' relations with other households are crucial elements in explaining familism. However, looking only at those elements offers a limited, one-sided perspective. The family group approach to the study of familism can be augmented by the view that household activity and family life can be seen as an expression of at least two forms of kinship principles. Fortes (1958) demonstrated the analytic efficacy of such an approach to the study of domestic groups.

According to the Fortes model, kinship, rather than the family group, is given priority. That is, the family and the activities of the household are conceptually seen as drawing their form and function from two sources of kinship. This perspective does not deny the concrete reality of household behavior. On the contrary, for Fortes, any theory of household behavior seen from a "kinship perspective" would have to take into account both "domestic" and "jural" domains of kinship.

The domestic domain of kinship incorporates the many sets of relations established in the economic and ecological spheres necessary for day-to-day survival. Farber (1971, p. 98) noted that "Loyalties, duties and rights emerge on an informal basis through the process of living together and having to get along." It includes concrete relations associated with adaptation to the physical and social environment of the domestic group. These adaptive relations, however, do not exhaust all of family life. Family life is also the concern of society and hence is accountable to authority outside the family. This authority outside the immediate family is called the jural domain of kinship. It refers to obligatory and/or legal relations.

From a jural perspective, the family is one mechanism through which society replaces itself. Hence, society has a large stake in the "product" of family life. The jural domain of kinship (and family life) is located in those aspects of kinship that have their origin in the larger society: the political-jural relations of larger groups. These larger social principles are expressed in the domain of family life as the shaping and proscriptive rules of descent and affiliation. Both the jural and the domestic domains permeate family life: every action in the family has consequences for both domains. From the "jural" perspective families in their day-to-day living activities can be viewed as behavioral expressions of enduring, historically defined, structural relations among kinship segments. Kinship obligations are perceived to be mandatory. Family life is, in short, jural exclusiveness centered around familial relationships; a division of the social environment into "we" (certain specified kin members)[3] and "they" (nonmembers).

Thus the domestic and jural domains of kinship can be seen as referring to two independent sources of family activity. It would thus follow that familism, as a distinct form of kinship organization, could have its roots in both domains. Familism, then, could be freely and fully conceptualized within a kinship perspective.

Most studies on American familism have either ignored or dealt in an unsystematic way with familism as a kinship phenomenon. One reason for this neglect can be traced to the theory of kinship that many sociologists have assumed in their "group-oriented" studies. Implicit in most studies of family life has been the assumption that kinship is largely a contingent affair. In opposition to the Fortes position presented above, kinship systems have been conceptualized from a family-centered orientation (including Parsons, 1943,

1959, 1965; Parsons et al., 1955). From this family group perspective, kinship structure and the behavioral activities related to it have been seen as variants, extensions, "upward and outward"; as little more than arithmetic aggregates of families. In short, kinship has been viewed as a set of "nuclear family building blocks" linked by a set of relations that find their source and justification in essentially family-based processes (Murdock, 1949). This reductionist view of kinship systems and the relationship between kinship and family, if anything, has allowed sociologists to legitimately ignore kinship and to restrict family research (familistic studies included) to the domain of nuclear household relations or to augmented sets of nuclear household relations.

To be sure, the ecological and adaptive aspects of family and household life help form the domestic aspects of kin relations. However, through their mediating norms of descent and affiliation kinship systems can also have an independent impact on family behavior, as well as on extrafamilial relations. Further it can be speculated that where kinship is based on principles of "jural exclusiveness," familism will be a "more visible" principle for ordering family life. Nevertheless, it should be remembered that the histories of families everywhere, as well as their ecological settings, introduce a wide variety of concrete household activities that tend to obscure the nature and operations of "ideal structures."[4]

The relevance of this alternative conceptualization is that the prior homogeneity of the construct known as "familism" is dissolved. If "familism" is the expression of these two corporate kinship principles, then there should be at least *two types of familism,* depending upon the relative amount of domestic or jural emphasis. In a similar manner, given any one of the structural arrangements alluded to above, variations in familistic activity could be expected to occur as a function of the demands made by different extrahousehold environments. Finally, the interactions of different kinship structures and environments might produce a phenomenon much akin to "phenotypes." That is, "familism" as stereotypically defined in the American setting might be exhibited in different populations, but might, in the last analysis, have different causal determinants. Familism is thus no longer singular. If this reasoning is correct, we should expect to encounter a plurality of familisms.

The possibility of such structurally rooted, familistic variations in America has been implicitly suggested by Farber (1968). Based on a study of state marriage laws that define incestuous alliances, Farber was able to argue the existence of two distinct kinship systems in the United States. He has referred to them as the "Biblical Kinship System" and the "Western American Kinship System." Farber notes that these two kinship systems have a general geographical distribution. The Biblical System is located in the American East, while, as the name implies, the occurrence of the Western American Kinship System is trans-Mississippian in origin. Farber, however, merely noted this geographical distribution and did not continue his analysis in the work cited. The structural emphasis of his work did not provide a basis for speculation on the historical or ecological contingencies of this distribution.

In this chapter we assume that such differences are manifested in the composition of kinship and household structures. The following familism typology is the result of an integration and extension of the Fortes and Farber conceptualizations. The typology presented here focuses explicitly upon familism as a collective response to historical and environmental exigencies in terms of jural and domestic domains of kinship. Of central importance is the notion that a given form of familism is the result of collective adaptive responses that emerge out of the family's adjustments to historical and sociological conditions and the problems these conditions pose for family functioning.

We postulate that two distinct forms of rural familism exist within the United States.[5] One form, *extended-kin-oriented* familism, is based upon the principle of jural exclusiveness and is expected to be found among rural populations living within the American Southeast—a section of America where a relatively long period of historical development has allowed a crystallization of lineages and extended-kin groupings. In extended-kin-oriented familism, nuclear and extended family identities become fused. Extended kin relationships form the basis of emotional and physical support. The nuclear family's identity and sense of worth is defined by the extended kinship system. The outside community is only secondarily considered as a positive reference group. Indeed, the outside community may be considered hostile to extended family cohesion.

Rural populations living within the American West are expected to possess a *primary-kin-oriented* form of familism, in which involvements with secondary relatives (where they occur at all) will be based upon voluntary, rather than obligatory principles. Primary-kin-oriented familism has evolved informally out of domestic activities involving daily adaptation to economic and ecological exigencies of living. In this primary-kin form of familism, an individual's identity is grounded within the nuclear family, with children's identities coming solely from their parents. The larger community serves as a positive reference group for nuclear family members, because family identity is informally achieved through family involvement in community activities.

These diverse forms of familism are perceived to be a function of differing historical and socioecological conditions. Rural areas within the western United States are sparsely populated in comparison with eastern areas, and Anglo settlement of the West has been comparatively recent. For these reasons, rural western status systems have had less time to crystallize, and migrants cannot fall back upon extended family members "left behind" for daily emotional and occupational support. Western rural living conditions reward an emphasis upon the nuclear family for daily economic survival and status attainment within the community. The rural Southeast, conversely, has a larger population density, and large numbers of kin reside within a given area. Existence of lineages over a long period of time leads to an emphasis

upon extended family systems in status allocation, and the mandatory right
to reliance upon fellow extended kin members in day-to-day living.

Extended-Kin-Oriented versus Primary-Kin-Oriented
Familism: A Typology

The following typology is based upon an integration and expansion of the
prior discussion of kinship and familism. At least two types of familism are
predicted to exist within the United States. Eastern rural family systems are
likely to be organized around extended-kin-oriented familism and are predicted to manifest a number of behavioral and attitudinal characteristics.
First, individuals will tend to view geographic mobility for better occupational opportunities as something to be undertaken only under extreme
circumstances because mobility involves leaving the security of the extended
kinship system. Secondly, individuals should possess strong emotional attachments to secondary kin involving attitudes of closeness. Thirdly, individuals
will manifest attitudes and behaviors in line with the familistic notion that
mutual aid and other forms of interaction with extended kin are obligatory
role commitments. These commitments include helping other members in
times of need and emotional and identity support through informal day-to-
day associations. Fourthly, extensive secondary kin interaction should lead
to marriages among extended kin for reasons cited by Farber (1968), but also
because the cohesiveness of extended kin ties would probably lead to romantic attachments among cousins and in-laws. Finally, since extended kin form
the boundaries of an exclusive *we* group, community and social activities
with nonkin members will be perceived as potentially threatening to kin
group solidarity. Kin members will not tend to participate in these outside
kin unit activities either individually, or as part of a nuclear family unit.
(See Figure 5.1 for a summary of the differences hypothesized between the
two types of familism.)

Western families organized in terms of primary-kin-oriented familism are
expected to manifest a quite different set of behavioral and attitudinal
characteristics. Each new marital alliance forms the beginning of a new family
system. Geographic mobility for better occupational opportunities will thus
be perceived as enhancing the status of the mobile nuclear family itself, plus
maintaining or increasing the community standing of each spouse's parents.
Geographic mobility of adult children in primary-kin-oriented familism would
not be expected to weaken bonds between adult siblings or between married
children and their parents. On the contrary, geographic mobility for occupational betterment enhances the status of multiple nuclear family groups.
Secondly, strong emotional attachments should exist among siblings and
siblings-in-law, but not necessarily among extended kin. Closeness to extended
kin members (if it occurs) is based upon achieved criteria. For example, the
kin members' personality attributes may lead to feelings of commonality and
closeness. Thirdly, the obligatory nature of role commitments associated

Figure 5.1: Behavioral and Attitudinal Characteristics Hypothesized to Occur in Family Systems Organized around Extended-Kin-Oriented versus Nuclear-Kin-Oriented Familism.

Extended-Kin-Oriented Familism	Primary-Kin-Oriented Familism
1. Individuals will be immersed within a web of secondary relatives who live within close geographic proximity.	1. Individuals will be cut off geographically from secondary relatives.
2. Individuals will emphasize remaining within their geographic area in order to remain close to secondary kin even though mobility may be perceived to result in better economic conditions.	2. Individuals will not be inhibited from moving away from their geographic area if mobility is perceived as leading to better economic conditions.
3. Sentimental ties and attitudes of closeness should remain strong for both primary and secondary relatives.	3. Sentimental ties and attitudes of closeness should be strong for nuclear family members, but should weaken extensively for secondary relatives.
4. Sentimental ties and attitudes of closeness should lead to a high incidence of marriages among secondary kin.	4. Lack of sentimental ties and feelings of closeness should lead to a seeking of mates outside the secondary kinship group.
5. Individuals should manifest attitudes and behaviors in line with ascriptive criteria, emphasizing the obligatory nature of familism regarding secondary relatives.	5. Individuals should manifest attitudes and behaviors in line with achievement criteria, emphasizing the voluntary nature of relationship between both secondary kin and non relatives.
6. Nuclear family members will not participate in social and community activities as a nuclear family unit, because nuclear family and family member identities are maintained through extended-kin support.	6. Nuclear family members will participate in community and social affairs as a nuclear family unit because nuclear family and individual family member identities are maintained through community support.

with familism will only be found among primary kinship members. Commitments and associations with extended family members will be based upon the same achievement criteria used in entering into relationships with nonfamily members. Thus, helping in times of need and giving emotional support through day-to-day associations will be no more likely to be obligatory for extended family members than it is for nonmembers. Fourthly, since the nuclear family's reference group lies mainly outside the extended kinship system, mates are more likely to be chosen from among nonrelatives. Implied here is the notion that parents must expose their children to other children whose nuclear families hold symbolic worth as a part of the parents' reference groups. Finally, nuclear families will participate in community and social affairs *as a family unit* in order to maintain symbolic worth within the community and to ensure that children will interact with other children from families belonging to the same reference group.

Summary of Previous Research Results

In two other papers (Heller and Quesada, 1977; Heller et al., 1981), we have attempted to factor out as clearly as possible the effects of two different kinship systems on the behavioral and attitudinal domains of familism by choosing samples from populations that could be said to "ideally" manifest the two forms of kinship structures summarized above. Samples were selected from married couples living in the Virginia Blue Ridge Mountain hollows lying between Luray and Shenandoah, Virginia; married ranching couples living in Elko County, Nevada; and married couples living in Akron, Ohio.[6]

The six characteristics of extended-kin-oriented versus primary-kin-oriented familism summarized in Figure 5.1 have been tested with fourteen familism measures (Heller and Quesada, 1977; Heller et al., 1981) and results from these tests are summarized in Tables 5.1 and 5.2. A cursory glance at Table 5.1 shows the extremely strong extended-kin orientation possessed by rural Virginia respondents, and similarity of familistic behaviors and attitudes between the rural Nevada and urban Akron samples. In community participation, the Nevada sample shows the extreme strength of its nuclear family unit—a phenomenon hypothesized to exist because of the isolation inherent in Nevada ranch life.

The predicted existence of disparate environments and homogeneity of familism forms within each specific environmental setting was tested by a discriminant analysis performed on the fourteen familism variables listed in Table 5.1. Relevant results of the discriminant analysis are summarized in Table 5.2. The data presented in Table 5.2, Part A, indicate that a very large relative percentage variance in familism as measured by the fourteen familism measures is explained by the two discriminant functions.

Table 5.2, Part B, shows results that more directly shed light on our attempt to ascertain the extent to which our rural and urban samples form modal types. The data indicate that all three groups can be clearly distin-

Characteristic Measured in Figure 1	Measure[b]	Va.-Nev.	Va.-Akron	Nev.-Akron	Total
1	DISTSIB	.73	.73	.04*	.39
1	DISTUNC	.85	.76	.09*	.50
1	DISTCOUS	.92	.81	-.21*	
2	GEOMO	.76	.79	.12*	.41
3	CLOSIB	.83	.88	.17*	.44
3	CLOUNC	.36	.58	.25	.39
3	CLOCOUS	.48	.67	.20*	.40
4	RELSPOUS	.91	.88	-.16*	.69
4	RELREL	.75	.86	.30	.66
5	SCALESCORE[a]	.31 (eta²)	.35 (eta²)	.04 (eta²)	.27 (eta²)
5	VISITREL 1	.81	.91	.08*	.57
5	VISITREL 2	.84	.87	.18*	.56
5	FAVORS	.57	.46	.14*	-.03*
6	COMPAR	-.86	-.31	-.63	-.53

Table 5.1: Gamma[a] Values Between Various Familism Measures and Respondent's Region of Residence.

DISTSIB: geographic distance from siblings
DISTUNC: geographic distance from uncles and aunts
DISTCOUS: geographic distance from first cousins
GEOMO: geographic mobility during respondent's life
CLOSIB: closeness felt towards siblings
CLOUNC: closeness felt towards uncles and aunts
CLOCOUS: closeness felt towards first cousins
RELSPOUS: husband and wife already related before marriage
RELREL: respondent's relative(s) married relative(s)
SCALESCORE: familism scale scores (Heller, 1970; 1976)
VISITREL 1: respondent and spouse visit couples related to them vs. couples not related to them
VISITREL 2: respondent visits relatives vs. nonrelatives during leisure time
FAVORS: respondent goes to relatives vs. nonrelatives for from none to five types of help
COMPAR: respondent's family participates in community affairs as a nuclear family unit

*Not significant at or below the .05 probability level. All other results are statistically significant.

[a]SCALESCORE was measured for degree of association by eta squared. All other findings in this table are gamma values.

[b]See Heller and Quesada (1977) for exact wording of questions to respondents and percentages of people within each ordinal category.

Table 5.2: Summary of Discriminant Analysis Results Performed on 14 Familism Variables Presented in Table 5.1.

Part A: Discriminating Power of Discriminant Functions for Three Samples of Respondents

Discriminant Function	Eigenvalue	Relative Percentage	Canonical Correlation	Functions Derived	Wilk's Lambda	Chi-square	DF	P
1	.794	78.5	.55	0	.458	253.58	28	0.00
2	.217	21.5	.42	1	.821	63.83	13	0.00

Part B: Centroids of Groups in Reduced Space

	Function 1	Function 2
Virginia	-1.522	.355
Nevada	-0.172	-0.797
Akron	0.399	0.189

Part C: Prediction Results

Actual Group	No. of Cases	Predicted Percentage of Group Membership		
		Virginia	Nevada	Akron
Virginia	48	92	4	4
Nevada	72	11	61	28
Akron	214	10	16	73

Percent of "Grouped" cases correctly classified = 73.35

guished from one another. Finally, the best test of sample homogeneity comes from the statistic, "percent of known groups correctly classified" (Table 5.2, Part C). All three groups in Table 5.2, Part C, are clearly separated when familism is measured by the linear combination of the fourteen familism variables. This classification routine was able to correctly identify 92 percent of the Virginia cases, 61 percent of the Nevada cases, and 73 percent of the Akron cases. Over all, 73 percent of the cases in the three regional samples were correctly classified as members of the groups to which they actually belong.

Summary

We have argued that familism, an historically important concept in rural sociology, has suffered from a one-sided approach that treats family activities solely within a family-as-a-group context. Following leads presented by Fortes and Farber, we have attempted to supplement this traditional approach to familism with an exploration of the relative effects that domestic and jural kinship factors have upon concrete expressions of familism. We argued that eastern rural familism had its behavioral roots in a structural base of jural exclusiveness centered around familial relationships. We hypothesized that such a kinship system, when enacted at the household level of behavior, would shape the family (including the surrounding kin group) as a closed system. Hence, the closed nature of family life (that is, familism) would be rooted in kinship proper.

We then turned to a far western sample of ranchers and showed that a superficially similar expression of "closed system" familism at the primary group level could not be rooted in jural exclusiveness but could be explained by domestic kin activities consisting of a complex set of relations established in the economic and ecological spheres necessary for daily survival in the rural, isolated environmental setting to which ranching households must adapt. Finally, results from an urban sample were included to demonstrate that, like western rural familism, urban familism is better explained in terms of domestic kin activities that have developed out of the economic and ecological environment of the city. In this way, we hoped to evaluate the relative effects the domestic and jural domains of kinship have on familistic organizations, behaviors, and attitudes.

We have sought first to demonstrate the existence of at least two familistic forms in rural America that reflect the behavioral and attitudinal characteristics summarized in Figure 5.1. Specifically we found that our Virginia respondents (1) are immersed within a web of extended kin, (2) are not prone to move away from their place of birth, (3) are steeped in emotional involvements with extended kin members and have a propensity to marry within the kinship system, (4) are engaged in everyday interaction and helping activities almost exclusively with extended kin, (5) manifest attitudes in line with the obligatory nature of familism, and (6) do not appear to stress the exclusivity of the nuclear family or to engage in community activities falling outside extended kin group involvement.

Nevada respondents, on the other hand, tend to (1) be cut off geographically from secondary relatives, (2) be mobile if mobility is connected with economic pursuits, (3) maintain strong attitudes of closeness for nuclear family members (and to a slightly lesser extent, parents' siblings), (4) marry outside the kin group, (5) interact and engage in helping activities with members outside the kin group on a daily basis, (6) be less likely to possess attitudes in line with the obligatory nature of familism, and (7) participate in many community and social activities as a nuclear family unit.

Second, we have tried to show that isolation of ranch families in northeastern Nevada has led to a marked degree of nuclear family orientation, even in comparison with Akron respondents. The *gamma* value of −.63 between Nevada and Akron samples (Table 5.1) in the amount of nuclear family participation in community affairs demonstrates the closeness of ties among members within the nuclear family unit and the strength of the relationship between the Nevada nuclear family unit and the larger community. For rural Nevadans, to an even greater extent than for Akron respondents, identity comes largely from within the nuclear family, but only insofar as family identity is established by involvement in relationships outside the kin group.

Third, we have attempted to view family life as a preeminently kinship phenomenon and have tried to isolate the relative impact of historical and socioecological forces on shaping domestic and jural domains of kinship. This has enabled us to construct a logically consistent set of theoretical and operational definitions of familism that are highly effective in discriminating types of familistic involvements within two diverse rural populations and among an urban sample. Table 5.2, Part C, shows that 92, 61, and 73 percent of the Virginia, Nevada, and Akron respondents respectively were correctly classified by discriminant function analysis.

Fourth, although the present conceptualizations have been based and tested on U.S. samples, their validities may be transcultural to a certain extent. At the present time Quesada, Heller, and Gustavo Grahl are using this kinship model in Brazil to study the use of governmentally sponsored credit and other forms of help by *latifundia* (extended-kin-oriented) and *minifundia* (primary-kin-oriented) rural family estates. It would also be intriguing to use this type of analysis (perhaps in modified form) in various European societies, and in Asian societies undergoing rapid industrialization.

Similar research is also needed for rural populations living under less extreme conditions than those existing in our Virginia and Nevada samples. The extreme differences in geographic environments were chosen purposely in order to ascertain the extent to which we could isolate the existence of "pure" types in terms of characteristics predicted in Figure 5.1. With the Virginia and Nevada samples as comparison units, it should now be possible to study populations of rural families living in randomly selected regions throughout the United States. Similar findings along regional lines would give much needed generalizable support for the ideas presented throughout this chapter.

Finally, we feel that our familism typology has relevance for applied researchers and change agents working in rural medicine and development. Extension agents and rural mental and medical health workers could develop their facilities and programs directly around family or community support systems already existing in client populations. In areas where emphasis is placed on extended-kin involvements, programs may have a better chance of success if the kin-group is approached as a whole. The more traditional nuclear family orientation, conversely, may work better in areas where strong nuclear family identity is emphasized.

Notes

1. We wish to thank the National Science Foundation for their Research Grant No. GS-29322. The interregional nature of this study made foundation support imperative. We would also like to thank Carl Backman, Doris and Gerald Ginsburg, and John Malone for their help, which was freely given throughout the project. Extensive criticisms made by two anonymous reviewers of an earlier paper and by James Copp enabled us to make meaningful modifications in our present analyses. Our intent was to write a position paper on rural familism; in no way should this chapter be considered an attempt to exhaustively summarize the literature on familism in rural America. It should be noted that although this chapter deals with rural familism, the authors feel that direct rural-urban comparisons are necessary for assessing the fate of rural familism in contemporary rural life.

2. A more detailed and research oriented version of this conceptualization appears in Heller et al., 1981.

3. Jural exclusiveness can take any number of familism forms. An almost infinite number of relatives could conceivably be included or excluded from the jurally defined kin group.

4. For a discussion of the problems involved in using structural models to interpret empirical data see Leach (1958) and Needham (1962).

5. These two forms are considered analytically distinct. Empirically, although predicted differences are expected to be great, overlapping is expected.

6. Like rural populations living within the American West, contemporary urban populations are subjected to economic and social forces that militate against a strong emphasis upon jural factors in the development of extended kin relationships. In Heller et al. (1981), it is suggested that familism in contemporary urban society is similar to that found in rural western America, with one exception. The isolated nature of western rural living may lead to a much more cohesive nuclear family group than that which is found in the city. In both rural-western and urban settings, however, familism is based upon domestic needs associated with getting along in the everyday economic and socioecological milieu associated with day-to-day life. Of course interaction with kin will exist, but the powerful "jural exclusiveness" of the eastern rural family will be missing. Like the western rural family, urbanites

will emphasize nuclear family identity, but extended kin relationships will drop off sharply and will be based upon voluntary, rather than obligatory principles. Data comparing the rural Virginia and Nevada respondents with their urban Akron, Ohio, counterparts are included here for comparison. For a more complete discussion of these findings, see Heller et al., 1981.

References

Farber, B. *Comparative Kinship Systems: A Method of Analysis.* New York: John Wiley and Sons, Inc., 1968.

____. *Kinship and Class: A Midwestern Study.* New York: Basic Books, 1971.

Fortes, M. "Introduction." In J. Goody (ed.), *The Developmental Cycle in Domestic Groups.* Cambridge, England: Cambridge University Press, 1958.

Heller, P. L. and G. M. Quesada. "Rural Familism: An Interregional Analysis." *Rural Sociology,* 1977, 42, 220–240.

Heller, P. L., G. M. Quesada, D. L. Harvey, and L. G. Warner. "Familism in Rural and Urban America: A Critique and Reconceptualization of a Construct." *Rural Sociology,* 1981.

Leach, E. R. "Concerning Trobriand Clans and the Kinship Category Tabu." In J. Goody (ed.), *The Developmental Cycle in Domestic Groups.* Cambridge, England: Cambridge University Press, 1958, 120–145.

Murdock, G. P. *Social Structure.* New York: Macmillan, 1949.

Needham, R. *Structure and Sentiment: A Test Case in Social Anthropology.* Chicago, Illinois: University of Chicago Press, 1962.

Parsons, T. "The Kinship System of the Contemporary United States." *American Anthropologist,* 1943, 45, 22–38.

____. "The Social Structure of the Family." In R. Ansken (ed.), *The Family: Its Function and Destiny.* New York: Harper, Row and Brothers, 1959, 241–274.

____. "The Normal American Family." In S. M. Farber, P. Mustacchi, and R.H.L. Wilson (eds.), *The Family's Search for Survival.* New York: McGraw-Hill, 1965, 31–50.

Parsons, T., M. Zelditch, J. Olds, and P. Slater. *Family Socialization and Interaction Process.* Glencoe, Illinois: The Free Press, 1955.

6
FAMILIES IN CULTURAL ISLANDS

Glenn R. Hawkes, Nancy G. Kutner,
Miriam J. Wells, Victor A. Christopherson,
and Edwin B. Almirol

This chapter presents a brief overview of several major ethnic and racial groups that reside in rural America. We are very much aware that whole volumes could address the differences and similarities between racial and ethnic pockets in various regions of the United States. The Germans in Wisconsin, the Dutch in Michigan, and the Scandinavians in the Dakotas in many ways present stories with similar themes. The old country is abandoned by a like-minded group. Their like-mindedness generally comes from a religious, political, or economic break with the dominant themes existing in the mother country. They make their way to the promised land. Their agrarian orientation and, in many cases, their only opportunities, push them to rural America. Here their identity is weakened through their entrance into the local power structure, and their efforts are rewarded, in part because they are absorbed into and reflect the value and cultural structure of the mainstream area they have entered. For others entrance is less easy. Their racial identification is so strong or their ethnic patterns so diverse that they defy modification in the short span of time America has existed.

The four groups we have selected display fascinating contrasts. They represent two of the most populous racial/ethnic groups and two of the smaller. They are not representative of the European stock that composed the early settlements in the East, South, and the heartland of the United States. Our selection was deliberate, and it helped us illustrate the dangers of generalizing about all facets of rural family life as though each family sprang from the same source with the same cultural heritage.

In the evolvement of agricultural rural areas, people came together for some significant reason that served as a bond of commonality. Often this bond was ethnicity, religious affiliation, or political persuasion. As the agricultural areas matured, settlements and service areas were tailored to the needs and wants of the groups served. The vendors of goods and services often brought even greater diversity because of their orientation, and the base of commonality began to erode.

In other episodes, ethnicity and race, as well as economic status, acted as a barrier to the development of isolated pockets of entrepreneurship because of class and service differentials. In these cases, groups worked side by side but failed to integrate and amalgamate because of servant/master or patron/worker status. Orientals and Blacks were denied the opportunity to own property in vast areas of this country. And interestingly, as we will discuss later, many people in decision-making positions had difficulty deciding into which slot the Filipino should be placed. These judicial and economic factors inhibited the evolution of rural integration and human rights development. Our choices of rural family groups will, we believe, illustrate these diverse patterns of family living in rural America.

The essays that follow are based on extensive literature review and author observation. Research on the rural family with an ethnic or racial approach has not been a high priority of the social and behavioral sciences. The available material clearly illustrates this lack. Care has been taken to exhaust the literature and to select that which most clearly represents the status of families in cultural islands in the United States.

With the exception of certain Mexican-American and Navajo families, the rural family systems discussed here began their American experience with farm labor. The Blacks were brought in on a slave basis, and the bulk of the Mexican and Filipino families came to assist in the extension and expansion of American agriculture by providing cheap hand labor to a then labor-intensive production system.

Families were generally welcome *if* they provided additional hands and kept the worker satisfied. Otherwise, families presented problems with no readily available solution: housing, child care, and the need to provide health and social support systems. The problems of assimilation through inter-marriage and contact on other than a work-place level were dealt with through patterns developed to provide separate resources and gathering places and strict systems of taboos. In the Filipino situation, the judiciary went to great lengths to ensure the maintenance of distance between the Filipino and his host country.

The Hispanics of California and New Mexico and the Navajos of the Southwest illustrate another dimension of the rural ethnic or racial family. Most of these families were in place in their rural environments before what was to become the dominant culture arrived, and through a series of conquests the imposing groups assumed domination.

A blending of cultures has evolved in certain areas of rural family life; they are noted below in the essay on Mexican Americans. In other areas of family life, differences still exist and conflict is apparent. Often individuals and families are beset by cultural conflicts that are disruptive to set family styles. The result can be disastrous to the individual and to the family—as detailed in the presentation on the Navajo families.

We have chosen not to present census data enumerating the racial and ethnic families in rural America. Such an aggregation of data changes too rapidly to be meaningful, and the 1980 census was not organized to provide the figures we sought. It is clear, however, that Black and Hispanic families are increasing in both rural and urban areas faster than the general population. They are the largest of the minority groups. The Navajo and Filipino families are small in numbers and are increasing less rapidly.

With the recent influx of immigrants from Asia and Cuba the diversity of family life in rural America seems not to be waning. This richness of rural American family life is not duplicated in other parts of the world. Past immigration has involved large numbers of differing racial and ethnic groups. Because of the recentness of the American past, diverse elements are still in place, and a polyglot culture remains in which the parts are greater than the sum.

THE RURAL BLACK FAMILY

Nancy G. Kutner

Although almost one-fourth of Black families in the United States reside outside a metropolitan area, research on the Black family in this country has been conducted for the most part in urban areas. Moreover, studies of the Black family have tended to emphasize family dissolution and other "culturally deviant" family characteristics (Allen, 1978). Because different values tend to characterize the industrial, urban environment as opposed to the rural or small-town environment, it need not be assumed that a stereotype drawn from studies in urban areas is also applicable to the almost one-out-of-four Black families who live outside metropolitan areas.

The majority of nonmetropolitan Black families are located in the South (Donnenwerth, Guy, and Norvell, 1978). Nonwhites compose almost one-fourth of the total population living outside southern metropolitan areas. The Black population is spread throughout the nonmetropolitan sector in the South, and most Black persons do not live in predominantly Black counties (Brown, 1978). The few available in-depth studies of rural Black families, therefore, have been conducted within the context of small, primarily Black communities in southern or border states, for example, Young (1970), Dietrich (1973), French (1977), and Martin and Martin (1978). Dietrich and Greiser (1975) and Kutner (1975) have compared data collected from Black families living in a nonmetropolitan area of east Texas with similar data collected from Black families living in downtown Houston, Texas. Finally, a small amount of information on the rural Black family can be obtained from survey research focusing on discrete aspects of family life within a stratum of the Black population or comparing Black and white populations, for example, Maxwell (1968), Chevan and Korson (1972), Donnenwerth et al. (1978), and Ryan and Warland (1978).

In existing research on the rural black family, a limited number of themes tend to consistently emerge:

* Greater prevalence of two-parent than of one-parent families;
* Variable rates of wives' employment outside the home, dependent on employment opportunities available in the immediate area;
* Prevalence of egalitarian power structures with respect to decision making by husbands and wives;
* Belief in discipline of children and acceptance of responsibility by children, within a context of acceptance and security; and
* Cultural significance of the extended family, with aged family members playing important roles within this structure.

Although anthropologists and sociologists have employed different perspectives in studying the rural Black family, their conclusions about these five family dimensions tend to be reinforcing.

Young (1970) conducted an intensive anthropological investigation of Black family life in "Georgiatown," a county seat in Georgia whose population of less than 10,000 was approximately 20 to 25 percent Black. The field study, in which the investigator observed and recorded in detail the behavior of parents and children in their own homes and yards, focused on forty-one lower-class and five middle-class households with young children. All households were located in three Black sections of town and in a rural hamlet adjoining the town. Many residents were the first generation to have left the countryside, and rural family traditions prevailed.

Dietrich (1973, p. 6) described nonmetropolitan Black families residing in a town of 4,900 and two nearby rural villages located in a predominantly rural county of east Texas. According to Dietrich, the area is "distinguished by a way of life and thinking more akin to the traditional culture of the 'Deep South' than any other region of Texas. In culture, industry, and topography, east Texas closely resembles the bordering state, Louisiana." Black families in the east Texas town and villages were residentially segregated from the white population and were of low-income status. Blacks composed 30 percent of the town population. As in Georgiatown, the research focus was on families having at least one dependent child in the household. An additional study requirement was the presence of a female homemaker who was less than 65 years old; information about family patterns was obtained through interviews with the homemaker. A total of 259 families were studied (approximately one-half of the Black families in the area). Almost all villagers and more than a third of the town residents had lived over half of their lives in rural areas.

Research on Black residents of small mountain communities is almost nonexistent. French (1977) has reported on twenty-eight family interviews held with Black residents of two small communities, Tannery Flats and The

Hill Community, which are adjacent to Sylva, the county seat of Jackson County, North Carolina, in Appalachia. Located across the river and railroad tracks from Sylva proper, they face the back street of Sylva and consist mainly of unpainted single-dwelling shacks. French estimated that 260 blacks lived in these two communities, accounting for about 70 percent of the county's black population. He described the area (p. 362) as being "for the most part a cultural anachronism, an area where physical and cultural isolation seem to be strongly correlated." Almost 70 percent of the families surveyed had lived their whole lives in the two communities. Although young people often left the area in search of employment, a spouse, or just excitement, many became disillusioned and eventually returned to the community. The influence of religion was strong in the area, and local Blacks almost never were arrested or involved in any type of crime, although there was heavy alcohol consumption among adult males.

The study by Martin and Martin (1978) of thirty Black families living in a small-town area of central Missouri and a small-town area of northern Florida provides intriguing insights into the Black extended family institution. Unstructured interviews, group discussions, and personal observation over an 8-year period, 1969–1977, were the major sources of information for their study. Family histories were gathered from family documents such as Bibles, and the investigators constructed a genealogy for each family they studied. Interviews were conducted with individuals regarded by each family as key members of the extended unit. As in Georgiatown, east Texas, and Appalachia, stability and continuity characterized the communities studied by the Martins; family activities revolved around one family-based household, which was always considered "home" by family members.

In contrast to the prevalent stereotype of the Black family as broken rather than intact, Black families in rural areas are more likely to be husband-wife units than female-headed units. Estimates of the prevalence of two-parent families were 54 percent in the Appalachian community studied by French (1977) and 64 percent in the two east Texas villages and 69 percent in the east Texas small town studied by Dietrich (1973). A comparison of nonmetropolitan east Texas families with families living in metropolitan Houston indicated a significantly higher frequency of husband-wife units among the former (44 percent versus 22 percent among poverty-level families, 81 percent versus 70 percent among nonpoverty-level families). Thus, even at the poverty level, almost half of the Black families living in the nonmetropolitan area were husband-wife units (Kutner, 1975).

Although multiple sequential marriages and frequent dissolution of marriages were observed in Georgiatown, these phenomena were viewed by Young (1970, p. 273) as "necessary concomitants of the emotional underpinning of the system." Free response to emotions and continuing compatibility between man and woman were important values in the community; these values were reflected in males' movement between households. Illegitimate births were common before a woman's first marriage, but most women seemed to have established a relatively stable marriage by the time they were in their mid-20s. When marriages dissolved, remarriage was common, and most middle-aged persons in the community were married.

Ryan and Warland (1978) reported that Black male agricultural laborers (rural farm workers) had higher earnings if they were married and if they had children, contradicting the thesis that the low-income Black male fails to function as economic provider for his family. Estimates of the frequency of working wives among rural Black families range from 45 percent in Thomas County, Georgia (Maxwell, 1968) and 50 percent in two east Texas villages, to 66 percent in an east Texas small town (Dietrich, 1973). The higher employment rate among wives in the latter community was a function of the variety of occupations available there—manufacturing of wood and food products as well as small businesses (grocery stores, beauty shops, barbecue stands) located in the town's Black ghetto. Employment of women who did not have a spouse present in the home was also higher in the east Texas small town than in the east Texas villages. Women in nonmetropolitan east Texas were more likely to be employed than were women living in metropolitan Houston—45 percent versus 42 percent among poverty-level families, 74 percent versus 55 percent among nonpoverty-level families (Kutner, 1975).

Maxwell (1968) utilized questionnaire responses from 190 eleventh- and twelfth-grade lower-class Black students from rural areas in Thomas County, Georgia, to compare fathers' family participation in families having working wives and families having nonworking (outside the home) wives. He concluded that the lower-class Black father is "a prominent participant in family activities," regardless of wife's employment status, but that the wife's employment appears to increase the amount of the father's participation, especially with regard to household tasks, child-care tasks, and economic functions such as shopping. Interestingly, nonmetropolitan Black families in east Texas, which were characterized by higher female employment than in their metropolitan counterparts in Houston, also showed greater participation and authority on the part of the father than did the Houston families (Dietrich and Greiser, 1975).

Wives' employment also has implications for conjugal power structure. In the study by Maxwell (1968) husbands of working wives were significantly less likely than husbands of nonworking wives to act alone in paying monthly bills and in buying clothes or shoes for the family. Wives' employment apparently gave them a greater share in disposition of the family income. In families in which wives were employed outside the home, husband and wife were regarded by 48 percent of the youths surveyed by Maxwell as sharing the responsibility of providing for the family.

Unlike the prevalent stereotype of the Black family as matriarchal, existing evidence points to an egalitarian power structure among Black families in rural areas. Dietrich (1975) found that egalitarian power structures more often characterized nonmetropolitan Black families. Martin and Martin (1978) reported that the ideal pattern in extended families is for dominance to be shared by husband and wife; only if the husband dies first does the wife assume the role of dominant family figure.

Decision making was shared by most husbands and wives in the east Texas town and villages, although wives often had the responsibility of translating decisions into actions. Maxwell's (1968) research suggests that husbands' action taking, especially with regard to household and child-care tasks, is increased when the wife is employed outside the home. These data suggest that the particular measures employed may give somewhat different pictures of conjugal power structure (Dietrich, 1975; Kutner, 1971).

Despite wives' frequent employment, in almost all families in the east Texas study in which a husband was present, the husband was the family's main income source (Dietrich, 1973). Similarly, Young (1970) found that the wages earned by men in Georgiatown far exceeded their wives' earnings. Additional evidence against the concept of matriarchy in Georgiatown was the observed social importance of family ties through men and of men's emotional attachments to their kin, despite the importance of mother-daughter ties. Men were accorded deference in the community, and many persons remembered their fathers as strict authoritarian figures.

Respect for parents' and grandparents' authority and the appropriateness of strict discipline were stressed by parents in east Texas (Dietrich, 1973) and in the Missouri and Florida communities studied by Martin and Martin (1978). Nonmetropolitan Black homemakers in east Texas were more likely than metropolitan Black homemakers in Houston to agree that respect for parents is the most important thing kids should learn, that most kids should be toilet trained early, that most kids should be spanked more often, that a child should be weaned as soon as possible, and that a parent's main goal is to see that the kids stay out of trouble (Kutner, 1975).

Young (1970) reported that older children were expected to assume responsibility toward their younger brothers and sisters. Martin and Martin (1978) found that occasionally a young woman would assume a subdominant or even a dominant role in the family, putting the family's well-being above her own desire for marriage or additional children of her own. Both Young and the Martins stressed the caring, supportive environment surrounding children of both "legitimate" and "illegitimate" status.

The Martins (1978) reported that children within extended families were encouraged by aged family members to get a "good" education. Similarly, east Texas homemakers held high educational and occupational aspirations for their children, desiring college educations and professional occupations for their sons and daughters (Dietrich, 1973).

Probably the most distinctive characteristic of the rural Black family is the significance that extended family ties have for family members. Dietrich and Greiser (1975) reported greater emphasis on extended family ties among nonmetropolitan Black families in east Texas than among metropolitan Black families in Houston. Strong ties across as many as three or four generations were observed in Georgiatown (Young, 1970). Although *households* were not necessarily organized on a multigenerational basis, the grandparent tie on either the mother's or the father's side was "easily and often invoked in a variety of arrangements." French (1977) reported that it was not unusual "to have a three-generation extended family sharing one dwelling" in the Appalachian Black community. In east Texas, one-third or more of the families in both the villages and the small town were extended units (Dietrich, 1973). One-parent and two-parent families were almost equally likely to be extended in both types of communities. The large majority of homemakers in east Texas expressed an extended family orientation[1] and reported that they gave and received help more from kin than from nonkin, discussed problems more with kin than with nonkin, and spent more time with kin than with nonkin (Dietrich, 1973). The central role of kinship among Blacks in the South has also been recognized by Shimkin and Lowe (1971), Doughtery (1974), Moerman (1974), and Jones (1976).

French (1977, p. 368) pointed to the dual economic and psychological functions of the Black extended family: "The families can pool their financial resources while at the same time provide a strong sense of family cohesion." These are themes emphasized by the Martins in their portrayal of the structure and dynamics of Black extended family households and networks. The following definition of a Black extended family grew out of the Martins' study:

> a multigenerational, interdependent kinship system which is welded together by a sense of obligation to relatives; is organized around a "family base" household; is generally guided by a "dominant family figure"; extends across geographical boundaries to connect family units to an extended family network; and has a built-in mutual aid system for the welfare of its members and the maintenance of the family as a whole (Martin and Martin, 1978, p. 1).

Thus, major functions of the extended family are (1) leadership—providing family members with a sense of security, a sense of family, and a sense of group direction and identity; and (2) promoting the welfare of dependent family members—dealing with crisis situations, providing family members with the basic necessities of life, and giving family members a feeling of economic security.

Informal adoption of children was a characteristic of extended families frequently observed by the Martins (1978). It occurred primarily because of economic necessity when parents could not provide for a child, but informal adoption also occurred when a child was born out of wedlock and the mother continued to live with her own family, when parents physically or emotionally could not care for a child, when relatives believed the child was being abused or neglected, or when a family member who was living alone wanted the satisfaction of raising a child. A person taking a relative's child gained status within the family. Some family members felt an obligation to adopt relatives' children because they themselves had been cared for by relatives during their childhood.

In almost all of the extended families studied by the Martins (1978), the dominant family figure was elderly—often the oldest member of the family network. Aged dominant figures enjoyed a sense of fulfillment because of being needed and respected by the family. Chevan and Korson (1972), who examined social and demographic factors related to the phenomenon of living alone among widowed persons, found a high probability that widowed Black females living in rural areas would reside with "others," usually kin. They noted (p. 48) that the Black widow "frequently serves as a focal person in a household which may include children, relatives, and nonrelatives in various combinations." Even when they are not the dominant family figure, there is evidence that elderly Blacks living in rural areas remain more integral family members than do elderly Blacks living in urban areas. Donnenwerth et al. (1978), who interviewed over 2,000 older persons (age 60 or more) living in a predominantly urban and a predominantly rural county in western Tennessee, found a higher frequency of social contacts among rural Blacks than among urban Blacks, when "social contacts" was defined as frequency of seeing friends and relatives.

Rural Black families represent a "cultural island" in the sense of being geographically isolated to a large extent from the dominant metropolitan influences of American society, especially in areas such as Appalachia. In addition, the rural Black family is essentially a southern phenomenon, located in a region that is distinctive in a number of ways from other regions of the country (Hill, 1977). For example, emphasis on kinship ties appears to be a regional value characterizing not only Black families but also many white families and other ethnic groups in the South (French, 1977; Hill, 1977).

Gillin (1955) argued that the family life patterns of southern Blacks are a product of their greater spatial and cultural isolation from white, middle-class norms. It appears, however, that rural Black families in the South may actually approach ideal white middle-class family norms more closely than do urban Blacks of similar socioeconomic status. At the same time, it has been suggested that because rural Black families on the average tend to include more children and dependent family members than do metropolitan Black families and that because rural Black parents are less permissive in their child-rearing practices, "nonmetropolitan poor blacks might be more handicapped than metropolitan poor blacks with respect to potential socioeconomic mobility" (Dietrich and Greiser, 1975, p. 70). In addition, Black community studies in rural areas have emphasized the stability of these communities, implying resistance to change within a society that has change as a central characteristic.

The rural Black family *can* be viewed as a "cultural island," set in a region of the United States that is itself a cultural island in some ways. At the same time, the rural Black family is an institution that reflects a number of characteristics attributed to "cultural mainstream" families and contradicts in a number of ways the prevalent stereotype of the (urban) Black family. Recognition of the strengths of the Black family in the rural setting is no doubt an important reason for the disillusionment that rural Black migrants to cities reportedly experience, encouraging them to return "back home" to their people.

THE RURAL MEXICAN-AMERICAN FAMILY

Miriam J. Wells

Mexican Americans are the second largest minority in the United States and one traditionally associated with the rural Southwest. Residential concentration in the states of Texas, Arizona, New Mexico, Colorado, and California still characterizes the group: in 1970 approximately 90 percent of the national Mexican-American population lived in the Southwest, about three-fourths of them in California and Texas (U.S. Bureau of the Census, 1973). Most Mexican Americans who live outside the Southwest reside in the midwestern states of Illinois, Michigan, Minnesota, Wisconsin, Indiana, Kansas, and Ohio. Mexican Americans are no longer the agriculturalists of popular image, however, as only 19 percent of the Mexican-origin population lived in rural areas in 1978, and less than 7 percent of them worked in farm-related occupations (U.S. Bureau of the Census, 1978). Their urban concentration varies somewhat by region: they are about 90 percent urban in California and the Midwest, while only 65 percent urban in New Mexico (U.S. Bureau of the Census, 1973). The pace of urbanization has been especially rapid for Chicanos[2] since World War II, with the progressive contraction of the agricultural labor market and the absence of farm-ownership possibilities to keep them in rural areas (Moore, 1976). Increasing opportunities for nonagricultural employment have also fostered the movement to the city.

Mexican Americans, then, are a group that has participated heavily in the rural-to-urban migration of recent decades and has suffered considerably from the economic decline of rural areas. While rural and nonmetropolitan Chicanos are a minority of the contemporary population, their patterns of family life are of interest not only because they can offer some insight into sources of social adaptation in marginal and rapidly changing environments, but also because they can cast some light on the causes and dimensions of Mexican-American family patterns in general.

The central characteristic of the traditional Mexican-American family, according to most observers, is familism: the primacy of kin ties as close social relationships (Alvirez and Bean, 1976; Mirande, 1977; Montiel, 1970).

While researchers vary in the emphasis they accord to different aspects of Chicano familism, a composite picture includes the following dimensions: (1) the extended family household as a residential unit, (2) the extended family as a nonresidential support network, (3) the normative belief that the needs of the family should supersede those of the individual, (4) the tendency to extend family status to significant friends through the institution of *compadrazgo* (coparenthood), and (5) the tendency for members of the family group to constitute each others' primary source of emotional support and identification.

Because of long-standing assumptions regarding the nature of urbanism, this traditional family structure has been expected to decline in urban areas and to be enhanced and sustained by the isolation and relatively small size of rural settings. Review of the urban empirical evidence has not supported this expectation, however (Miller, 1978). While some facets of traditional familism, such as the trigenerational household, are not evident among urban Chicanos, others, such as the primacy of the extended family as a source of emotional and emergency material support, have been maintained or transformed. This irregular urban record suggests comparable caution in assuming that rurality has a single and unidirectional impact on family relations.

The following discussion aims to describe and suggest explanations for patterns of rural Mexican-American familism. In order to clarify the causes of differences in the nature and extent of familism between rural and urban dwellers, as well as among different rural regions, I begin with an inquiry into the place of rurality in explanations of Chicano family life. I then go on to clarify the traditional image of Chicano familism and its variable relationship to cultural norms and environmental constraints. Finally, I examine rural Chicano familism in four geographical regions.

The shape and determinants of rural Mexican-American familism are poorly understood. In part this is a consequence of the unevenness of empirical documentation. One early scholar (Jones, 1948, pp. 450–452), after reviewing over 3,000 works relating to Mexicans in the United States, concluded: "Little of this material represents really basic or prolonged research. . . . A tremendous amount of duplication exists. References to family life are scattered and seldom documented." The contemporary record is not greatly improved. There have been few studies of Mexican Americans in which the family is the primary focus, and information about family life must often be gleaned indirectly through studies of folk culture, health practices, employment conditions, and delinquency. Thorough studies of the settled non-metropolitan Chicano population have been almost entirely restricted to the Texas-Mexico border region and to the long-standing Hispanic villages of New Mexico and Colorado. These areas have been subject to severe economic dislocations in the decades following their study, yet contemporary examinations of family life in these regions are few. In addition, the only large-scale survey to provide data of interregional comparability on family life concentrates on the metropolitan centers of Los Angeles and San Antonio (Grebler,

Moore, and Guzman, 1970). Despite its considerable contribution to the study of Mexican family patterns, this study provides no information on non-metropolitan Chicanos in the Southwest, nor on Chicanos outside the Southwest.

In addition to the substantive limitations of existing research, description and explanation of rural Chicano familism have been hindered by a stereotype of the traditional family that derives from historical studies of Mexican values. According to this image, traditional Mexican and Mexican-American households contain not only parents and children, but also grandparents, aunts and uncles, and often the families of married sons. Outside the residential extended family is a wide bilateral network of relatives who interact frequently, try to live near one another, and are mutually dependent for emotional and many sorts of material support. For the individual, the family is the primary focus of identification and fulfillment and is sharply distinguished from the supposedly hostile and threatening outside world. The happiness and welfare of Mexican-American family members are largely subordinated to that of the group, sometimes to the detriment of individual advancement. Friends tend to be chosen from the extended family circle, and nonrelatives are often brought symbolically into the family through the institution of *compadrazgo*. This custom makes important friends "coparents" of a child, thus initiating a lifelong relationship of reciprocal obligation between parent and godparent, and between godparent and child.

While long-standing in the literature and strongly associated with the agrarian past and present of Mexicans and Mexican Americans, the empirical status of this image of traditional familism is nonetheless problematic. First, the accuracy of the image depends upon the validity of direct inferences from rural Mexican family life of the 1940s (Lewis, 1960) to the values of nonmetropolitan Mexican Americans of the 1980s. Not only have the accounts of Mexican values drawn heavily on psychoanalytical paradigms of questionable merit (Montiel, 1970), but these accounts imply a single Mexican value orientation and ignore variation by region, class, ethnicity, and time of immigration.

In addition to underrepresenting potential variation in the values brought from Mexico, the traditional image also neglects important sources of internal differentiation among Mexican populations in the United States. This is primarily a consequence of an overemphasis on cultural norms as determinants of family life and an underestimation of the impact of environmental constraints. Repeatedly, the literature on Mexican-American familism confuses these two levels of analysis, assuming that studies of stated values suffice as descriptions of actual family life. As Schneider and Smith (1943) point out in their study of American kinship, the values and the actual social organization of families are quite different phenomena. While cultural norms constitute the "oughts" of family interaction, actual family patterns may diverge considerably from these ideals because of the constraints of their daily environments.

It is in this connection that the significance of rural residence for Mexican-

American familism must be examined. To clarify the role of rurality for variations in familism, one must go beyond statements about traditional values and characterize the settings in which family life is carried out. The task, of course, can only be begun here given the limitations of space and the shortcomings of existing literature.

Mexican-origin settlement in the United States may be divided into four broad regions: Texas-Arizona, New Mexico–Colorado, California, and the Midwest. These regions exhibit much historical and contemporary diversity in their socioeconomic and physical environments. Such variables as the longevity and stability of residence, the proximity of settlements to one another and to Mexico, the extent of social and cultural isolation, and the economic status and opportunities of the Chicano population in the region all shape the extent to which familistic norms are reinforced or undermined, and to which familistic activity is advantageous or disadvantageous.

Nonmetropolitan Chicanos are clustered in the southern counties of Texas and Arizona, most of them in the small towns and on the large ranches of the Lower Rio Grande Valley, the rest in an east-west line of Arizona mining and farming towns. Huge influxes of farm laborers from Mexico in the late 1800s initiated heavy Mexican settlement of the region and inundated previous Hispanic colonists. Ethnic stratification is the most extreme in this region, the manual laboring character of the Chicano population most pronounced, and its ties to Mexico and Mexican culture most vital (Uhlenberg, 1972). While the region has the largest proportion of recent immigrants and temporary sojourners, it also has a sizeable proportion of permanent residents, many of them descendants of original settlers. Shrinking local and migratory farm labor opportunities have impelled a slow shift to urban employment here, although Chicanos still remain in high-turnover, low-paying, underprotected positions in the secondary labor market (Briggs, Fogel, and Schmidt, 1977).

The bilateral extended family appears to be the most significant facet of life for both residentially stable and migratory Chicanos in this region. While the large family is pictured as the focus of emotional identification and as a refuge from hostile Anglos and potentially envious Mexican neighbors (Madsen, 1964; Rubel, 1966; Ulibarri, 1966), in some cases the necessity of economic and political cooperation has motivated the symbolic expansion of the family grouping to include all barrio members (Foley, Mota, Post, and Lozano, 1977; Baca Zinn, 1975). A large number and variety of *compadres* (coparents), chosen primarily from respected friends of equal status, are also drawn into the family, although recent studies report a decline in *compadrazgo* obligations (Foley et al., 1977; Moore, 1976). While preconquest Hispanic ranchers apparently lived in trigenerational households, today coresidence is neither valued nor practiced in any but emergency situations, although nuclear families commonly settle next to one another (Foley et al., 1977; Madsen, 1964; Miller, 1970; Rubel, 1966). Extended families commonly offer the support that formal social services provide elsewhere (Moore, 1976) and serve as a buffer against economic uncertainty by dispersing members into a variety of local and migratory economic niches and by sharing the small and unpredictable returns from their labors. Substantial monetary support of relatives outside the nuclear family is rare for impoverished southwestern migrants, however, suggesting that the ideal of familism is not upheld to the detriment of individual survival (Miller, 1970; Ulibarri, 1966). Chicanos in this area are much more likely than Anglos to rely on family connections to find a job (Briggs, 1977). Old people, women, and children may work for little or no pay in the small family stores that are the barrios' main places of business. In a pattern characteristic of migrants from all regions, farm workers often travel in family groups, leave children at home with relatives, and obtain temporary lodging, job information, loans, and legal protection from kin along the migrant trail. Familism thus facilitates the recruitment of migrants to regions of economic opportunity, although it is local employment conditions and institutional barriers that determine their ultimate economic mobility (Tienda, 1979).

The Spanish-American villages of northern New Mexico and southern Colorado are the oldest and historically most stable and isolated rural Mexican settlements. They evolved over a period of several centuries from the mixed Spanish and Mexican values of their founders in almost total isolation from Anglo-Americans and from Mexico. Small, noncontiguous, self-sufficient villages composed of interrelated extended families dotted the mountain valleys and engaged in subsistence farming, herding, and trade with the Indians. Today the rural areas remain predominantly Spanish-speaking and have the highest proportion of native-born Mexicans of native parentage. They also have a narrower class range, greater degree of Anglo control and discrimination, and lower rate of Spanish-American social mobility than is characteristic of the region as a whole (Alvarez, 1973; Leonard and Hannon, 1977; Luebben, 1970; Moore, 1976). In the 1900s the economic basis of village life has been severely eroded, out-migration is substantial, and poverty in some rural counties is so severe that over half the population is on welfare (Knowlton, 1961, 1969; Leonard and Hannon, 1977; Moore, 1976).

The bilateral extended Spanish-American family, although shaken in its internal role structure, continues to be the primary focus of identification and social support in the rural areas. Villages are still composed of interrelated families with few social contacts outside the kindred; the salience of kinship is indicated by a recent survey of northern New Mexico (Leonard and Hannon, 1977, p. 390), in which 94 percent of the Spanish Americans reported that "my greatest happiness in life comes from my family." Those who leave the villages have tended to settle in nearby urban centers where residence near urban relatives, along with visits, letters, and even continued landholding in the home village maintain family ties (Kluckhohn and Strodtbeck, 1961; Knowlton, 1959; Luebben, 1970). Some studies have found the hostility toward nonkin associated with traditional familism, although this may be a consequence of the dominance of Anglos in the region (Knowlton, 1969). *Compadrazgo* is still vital in the villages studied, although it is no longer used to strengthen rights and obligations throughout the village but is confined to the extended family unit (Knowlton, 1969; Luebben, 1970). There appears to have been some intervillage variation in residential patterns in the past, probably evolved in their centuries of mutual isolation (Knowlton, 1961). Uxorilocal residence is reported in some areas, although virilocal residence seems to have been more common. While in the past the families of offspring in some villages moved into the parental residence, today the nuclear family household is the norm and reality (Gonzalez, 1967; Leonard and Hannon, 1977). This seems to be related to the fact that subsistence activities no longer require close familial cooperation and are frequently unable to support even the nuclear household. There is also some indication that the advent of values and economic opportunities outside the traditional family eroded its normative hold on members and hastened the economic decline of the villages (Atencio, 1964). Today social services have replaced many of the welfare functions of the traditional family. Even cooperation in running a business is not an option for most families, since Anglos tend to own the stores in rural areas. The extended family does, however, improve access to the job market. The men from some villages, for example, seek work with the same firm, help each other in getting jobs, fill in for each other, and drive to work together. Migrant workers travel with a trustworthy group of relatives and those who plan a move to the city can draw on a network of extended kin for temporary lodging and job information (Kluckhohn, 1961; Knowlton, 1969). The norm of income sharing among closely related families, which provided a critical buffer against starvation for many villagers during the depression and was still found in the 1950s, appears to have disappeared, although kinsmen still rely on each other in the frequent small emergencies of daily life (Bodine, 1967; Gonzalez, 1967; Kluckhohn and Strodtbeck, 1961).

There have been several major sorts of rural settlement in California in this century, the present state of which is only sketchily known through the literature. Aside from the preconquest rancher and mestizo settlements, some of which continued their traditional customs well into the twentieth century (Tuck, 1946), Mexican rural settlements evolved from the pattern of their mass employment in mining, on the railroads, and in agriculture. Small, impoverished, homogeneous Mexican communities grew up in proximity to these sources of employment. Lacking most municipal services and geographically separate from Anglo communities, interethnic social relations were so stratified as to be termed "castelike" (Goldschmidt, 1947; Lasswell, 1953; Tuck, 1946). Most of these towns grew from the agricultural immigration in the 1920s and 1930s and were situated close to farm-related employment: wineries, packing houses, truck farms, and citrus groves (McWilliams, 1968). By World War II, however, the rate of urbanization quickened, employment opportunities in defense-related industries opened, and many Mexican *colonias* (settlements) were engulfed by cities. This development marked the advent of more open, class-based social relations and more remunerative and stable employment for Mexicans on the urban periphery. The agricultural towns of the Imperial, San Joaquin, and Coachella Valleys, however, have not experienced such an expansion of opportunities and may well continue to exhibit the sharp social discrimination of the earlier period (Alvarez, 1973; Moore, 1976).

Although rural Californian Chicanos tend to live near relatives in all-Mexican-American neighborhoods, they are today more likely to work and attend school with non-Mexicans than are Chicanos elsewhere in the Southwest. Many still, however, rely almost exclusively on relatives for emotional support and, once settled, are much more likely than Anglos to remain and gather kin about them (Keefe, Padilla, and Carlos, 1977). Families here maintain intimate ties to relatives in Mexico, often returning to visit in the winter and providing housing and job leads to kinsmen who work the migrant circuit or who want to immigrate. While *compadrazgo* appears to be declining in the cities (Penalosa, 1967; Tuck, 1946), there is little information as to its status in rural areas. The extended family appears to have been a normative and actual residential unit in pre- and postconquest California, with almost half of the mestizo and Hispanic population of the isolated rural settlement of Los Angeles living in extended family households before 1850 (Griswold del Castillo, 1975). Extended residence was apparently facilitated by cooperation in cattle ranching and also provided a stable basis for the social mobility of wealthy *hacendados* (landholders) in the early urban period. Inundation of the region by a population with more individualistic values, plus the advent of economic and educational options outside the family, appear to have undermined the *hacendado* extended household. It is not clear that later Mexican immigrants even brought the value of extended residence; certainly their migratory lifestyle and marginal economic circumstances discouraged it. Studies of migrants and town dwellers show that the vast majority live in nuclear households today, although extended family involvement in terms of preference of association and support persist (Hawkes, Taylor, and Bastian, 1973; Penalosa, 1959). Here, as elsewhere, the extended family serves as a means of job recruitment and a source of emergency support. Men with jobs in cities often pass news of openings to relatives in the surrounding area. In addition, the availability of a flexible pool of family workers improves access to farm labor positions, in the absence of formal credentials and recruitment mechanisms and given the variability of seasonal labor demands (Wells, 1980). Exchanges of material aid, as well as expansion of the family circle to include those in the political movement for Chicano power, appear to be more frequent among the better-off, suggesting a potential increase in and transformation of familism with social mobility (Clark, 1959; Keefe et al., 1977).

Chicanos have been drawn to the Midwest since before World War II by jobs and higher wages in industry and seasonal agriculture. While most settled in the large cities, some have settled in the surrounding rural areas where they can tap both agricultural and industrial labor markets. Rural settlement ballooned in the 1960s as mechanization forced farm workers out of the Texas-midwestern migrant stream and the federal government accepted responsibility for relocating them (Cardenas, 1976). Rural Chicanos in the Midwest are thus more likely to be recent arrivals and to have a history of migratory farm labor and previous residence in Texas. Their average incomes and available economic opportunities are greater than those of their southwestern counterparts.

Living in small, predominantly Anglo towns, rural Chicanos in this region do not have the proximity to the border and a large circle of relatives, the indigenous regional ties to Mexican culture, or the sharp geographical and social separation from Anglos that help maintain traditional familism in the Southwest. Nevertheless, extended family ties were a central reason for many to relocate and are a continuing focus of social relations and identification (Choldin and Trout, 1969; Macklin, 1963; Sena-Rivera, 1979). Rural settlers typically come as families, settle near relatives, and, depending on the constraints of distance, write letters, visit, and exchange favors with relatives in the migrant stream or in nearby cities or elsewhere in the Midwest, in Texas, and in Mexico. Economic interdependence appears to be strongest for the most and least affluent, although most households are financially independent (Sena-Rivera, 1979). Family ties are critical to job recruitment in this area and are encouraged by industrial and agricultural employers who value the guarantee of performance that such connections provide. Chicano employment and advancement, however, are ultimately dependent not on the strength of family recommendations, but on local labor-market conditions (Wells, 1979). Friendship and intermarriage appear to increase with longevity of residence, but this contact does not disrupt familism, since Anglo spouses are usually incorporated into the family (Choldin and Trout, 1969; Sena-Rivera, 1979). Although rural households tend to be larger than urban households, the nuclear household is desired and most common in this region. Members regard periods of coresidence forced by temporary hardship as necessary but stressful obligations (Sena-Rivera, 1979). Lacking the resources and personnel of a large ethnic community, the force of *compadrazgo* is minimal.

Existing evidence suggests that rurality does not have a single, unidirectional impact on Chicano familism. Rather, familism is shaped by a series of variables that may differentially characterize urban as well as rural milieus. Familism is seen to have both pragmatic and normative benefits; it improves the ability of individuals and groups to cope with certain situations and, insofar as they observe a custom of internalized worth, it enhances their sense of emotional security and well-being. Both of these dimensions appear to be operant in the continued vitality and transformation of rural familism. In general, extended family size and cohesion appear to be greatest in rural Texas, New Mexico, and in the interior valleys of California. While family bonds seem to be less strongly obligatory and more voluntary than they were in the past, in all regions they continue as the primary focus of reciprocal concern, identification, and support. In no region does familism appear to require foregoing individual advancement in a way inconsistent with the amount of sharing common among Anglo families. The character of kinship obligations appears to be geared to the circumstances of the family or individual in question, so that, for example, lower status families are less likely to expect or engage in substantial monetary exchanges.

Longevity, stability, and proximity of residence, the amount of interchange with the core culture area, the degree of ethnic stratification, and the economic status and environment of the population in the region all seem to affect the extent and shape of rural familism. While more research is needed to definitely determine the impacts of these variables, some preliminary conclusions can be drawn. The extent to which individuals are able to actualize familistic norms, and thus the primacy, number, and variety of family contacts, seems to be enhanced by stability and geographical concentration of residence, although familism may continue to serve important functions under contrary circumstances of ethnic and kin dispersal and migrancy. Sharp geographic, social, and economic separation from non-Mexicans in a region decreases the possibility of forming satisfying relations outside the group and appears to increase the potency of intragroup bonds. The extent to which these ties are confined to the family unit or elaborated throughout the ethnic community seems to depend less on cultural values than on political and economic circumstances encouraging extrafamilial cooperation. The strength of traditional familism is enhanced by the exchange of personnel with the region of origin, while extreme and prolonged isolation from outside influences causes differentiation of familistic norms.

It is doubtful that the trigenerational household has ever been a universal cultural norm, either in Mexico or in the United States. The value of extended residence appeared mainly among Spanish and mestizo upper-class families during the Mexican colonial period, while for peasants coresidence has been primarily an emergency expedient (Sena, 1973). In colonial Texas, New Mexico, and Los Angeles, where coresidence seems to have been normative and practiced to some extent, it was associated with Hispanic culture and with subsistence economies in which the family cooperated closely in productive activities and in which the level of living afforded was adequate. Erosion of the economic base of the producing family unit brought a corresponding reduction in coresidence and in the ascriptive strength of familistic values. The current prevalence of nuclear households in these regions could be a consequence both of this development and of the current dominance in Texas and California of immigrants who lack the normative history of extended residence.

The material circumstances of rural Chicanos have also fostered familism. While there are distinct variations within and among regions, rural Chicanos tend to be poorer, less differentiated in class structure, and more likely to be confined to the secondary labor market than are urban dwellers. The jobs they obtain are low-paying, high-turnover, and sporadic or seasonal in duration. They generally lack formal credentials, recruitment mechanisms, and guarantees of subsistence security. In such circumstances, the resource-sharing and economic-niche diversification of familism provides a hedge against economic uncertainty. Family networks also serve as informal job-recruitment mechanisms, providing family members with information about job openings and likely success and offering employers a guarantee of performance and defrayal of recruitment expenses. They do not, however, ensure economic mobility.

A final lesson from this review is that rural Chicano familism should not be viewed solely within the paradigm of tradition. In fact, the current adoption of the family metaphor by the Chicano political movement suggests that innovation and change will be the hallmarks of future family patterns among both urban and rural Mexican Americans.

THE RURAL NAVAJO FAMILY

Victor A. Christopherson

The "People" is the translation of "Nadene" or "Dene," and it is the word Navajos use for themselves. The Navajos constitute the largest Native American group in the United States today, numbering some 130,000 people. They are the most rapidly growing group of Native Americans, and they occupy the largest contiguous reservation land area. The Navajo reservation is approximately 24,000 square miles plus 3,500,000 acres of Navajo-owned land near the reservation (Gilbreath, 1973). The Navajos, along with the Apaches, are members of a linguistic group known as Athapascans. The difference between the language spoken by contemporary Navajos and Apaches is largely a matter of dialect (Dobyns and Euler, 1972).

The Navajos are primarily camp dwellers rather than nomads. Their livestock herding seldom transcends a radius of 10 miles, whereas, in the past, herding areas might have averaged 30 or 40 miles in radius. The change has come about because of several factors: the livestock reduction program in the late 1930s and early 1940s, the expanding population, and the land-use system. Grazing permits were issued—to Navajo women only—up to the 1930s. These permits define customary use areas that are passed on to someone in the family, usually the oldest daughter, but the land has become increasingly inadequate to support the expanding population base.

The degree of acculturation observable among the Navajos varies significantly in different parts of the reservation, and the variation is proportional, in large measure, to the proximity of Anglo centers of various kinds. The insulation and isolation of the families in the interior of the reservation—for example, in the former Joint Use area, a 1.8 million-acre tract that was divided equally between the Navajos and Hopis in 1977—is such that life goes on much as it did many years ago, but in areas closer to urban centers, some change seems apparent. Overall, however, there seems to be a good bit of validity to the French expression, *Plus ça change, plus c'est la même chose!*—The more things change, the more they remain the same.

The young people or teens on the reservation are caught between two cultures. They are neither what their parents were nor what they themselves might one day become. Teenagers are in a kind of "transitional marginality," and they appear to be reacting in a way suggestive of the term "youth culture." In short, adolescence, in the cultural sense, has arrived on the reservation. Alcohol, glue and gasoline sniffing, venereal disease, and a variety of delinquent behaviors are much in evidence. Parents are upset, and they lament the loss of control over children. Bureau of Indian Affairs (BIA) personnel are frustrated over the apparent lack of success of the boarding school programs ostensibly designed to enable the students to become independent and productive both on and off the reservation (Collier, 1972).

Sex roles within the context of Navajo adolescence have definite dimorphic qualities. The females are more traditional in the sense that they prefer to marry and settle down at an early age, many in their teens. The males, on the other hand, do not reflect qualities of sociological adulthood until their very late 20s or early 30s. Until then, males typically defer marriage, maintain their peer-group orientations, and have very little job stability (Office of Indian Education, 1978).

This state of affairs appears to be in rather sharp contrast with the characterization given by Leighton and Kluckhohn (1947). Of course, their observations were made some thirty-three years ago, which allows sufficient time for significant cultural change to have taken place. According to their account, both male and female are usually ready for marriage at physical maturity. Now, however, the teen years through the 20s are spent in preparing for poorly understood and complex work roles or in temporary and itinerant employment and for the Navajo male constitute a type of psychological moratorium. Maturity and an inclination to take on family responsibilities often do not emerge until the early 30s.

A number of elements in the Navajo family combine to perpetuate the unique culture, which, in earlier times, was highly adaptive in the reservation setting. It has become less so with the departure from the traditional way, as Navajos grow somewhat closer to the institutions of the larger society. The semiacculturated status that is characteristic at present seems adaptive for neither setting. In many respects, Navajo children still experience much of the traditional impact of the family in their socialization. Coming out of this setting into the more peer- and Anglo-oriented situations, particularly the BIA boarding schools, results in a cultural dislocation. That the Navajo family exerts an enduring and massive influence upon its young is attested to by the difficulty Navajo youth have in living comfortably in or with the non-Navajo world. A closer look at the Navajo family, particularly its organization, may provide some clues as to the sources of difficulty in bridging the two cultures.

Shepardson and Hammond (1970) suggest three critical aspects of Navajo family organization and function: they are kinship, coresidence, and cooperation. Every society utilizes some system of relating an individual to his biological and affinal kin. Even fictive relationships may be accounted for in some of their ceremonial and functional aspects. Much of the basis of the Navajo kinship system depends upon the concept of clans. There are estimated to be from fifty to seventy-five clans in the Navajo tribe.

Clans are based on common ancestors and constitute a consanguineal-type group, although often the consanguinity is fictive in nature. Clans are exogamous, and, next to the tribe, are the suprastructural element in the Navajo society. The clan effectively regulates marriage between all cousins, both cross and parallel, as well as between members of the same clan. In practice, marriage can and sometimes does take place within the father's clan.

Kinship enjoys a more prominant position in the social organization of the Navajo than in Anglo society. Kinship terms are used both as a form of address and as a system of reference. The distinctions implied in terms of address are generalized and do not always imply categories similar to those utilized in Anglo kinship designations. For example, one's father's sisters' children are called cousins by the individual. Father's brothers' children are called sister or brother. One's aunts are often referred to as "little mother." An uncle on the mother's side is called "uncle," but an uncle of the father's side may be referred to as "little father." "My mother" is a term of respect that may be used to address any older woman, and "my grandfather" is a designation of respect that may be applied to any older man. The term "relative" is commonly used to include members of the extended family or even those belonging to the same clan. These terms represent but a few of the many designations for relationships and reference in the Navajo kinship system. (For detailed accounts of Navajo kinship, see Schuske, 1965; Witherspoon, 1975; Shepardson and Hammond, 1970; and Edmonson, 1970).

The Navajo residence pattern is essentially one of family camps. The camps are often situated in customary use areas and may vary in size from one or two nuclear households (hogans) to ten or more. Some extended family household units may be separated by 20 or 30 miles. While the general pattern is matrilocal, neolocality and patrilocality are not uncommon. The male who moves near the home of his wife's mother also thinks of where his own mother lives as home. The maintenance of two residence orientations on the part of the male—those involving the families of orientation and procreation—constitute one of the chronic sources of irritation and difficulty between Navajo couples.

Kluckhohn and Leighton (1962) suggest that there is an extension of the family to those who regularly cooperate for certain purposes. The term for such a group is "outfit." The outfit probably could be considered synonymous with a far-flung, loose-knit or linked clan. The outfit, however, may not be a functional unit at the present time. BIA officials in Chinle, Arizona, which is close to the isolated former Joint Use area, were familiar with the term, but they could not recall any evidence of its current designation or function. Usually cooperation—primarily economic—can be obtained from relatives or other clan members.

Structurally, the typical family is nuclear, with descent being reckoned matrilineally. There are, however, often one or more collateral relatives living with the nuclear or conjugal group. When possible such relatives as older widows, aged parents, or sisters live in their own hogans and have some sort of assistance arrangement with the nuclear unit. In terms of classification, the Navajos are polygynous; that is, in a society where polygyny is a sanctioned pattern, even though a minority pattern, the society is termed polygynous. The sanction, however, is wearing thin due to the negative feedback from missionaries, the BIA, and other agents of acculturation. The sanction, in fact, is implicit rather than explicit or formal. When polygyny does occur, it usually involves a marriage between a man and two or more sisters. Kluckhohn and Leighton (1962) estimated a 7 percent incidence in the 1940s. No reliable figures are available for the current time, but officials in the BIA believe the 7 percent figure has not diminished appreciably in the intervening years. Isolation, propinquity within the isolated or remote areas, and the philosophical and traditional acceptance of plural marriage all combine to give polygyny a tenacity that, while somewhat attenuated, has successfully resisted the onslaughts by non-Navajo agents determined to eradicate the practice. In short, polygyny is still alive, if not entirely well.

Very likely mutual help patterns and forms of sharing in subsistence economies constitute a kind of adaptive behavior that is evolutionary in origin. Sharing one's resources with relatives in need is the "natural" thing to do, and it is not considered generous or altruistic. On the other hand, not sharing is the basis for severe negative sanctions. Dimorphism in this regard, however, is not only evident but may also be increasing as a result of certain kinds of contact with the outside world. For example, Navajo women tend to own and control those resources associated with the operation of the home, often including the sheep. Sharing most resources with other relatives, including the husband, is common and expected. Men, on the other hand, who acquire other kinds of wealth, principally money, cattle, and horses, will share with other males but are often reluctant to share with their wives or to use their money for household or family expenses. Navajo women are learning that such behavior is neither inevitable nor immutable, and they are beginning to seek redress in the courts with increasing frequency.

While the normative patterns of sharing include those who are considered family and relatives, few nonrelatives would be denied such help in time of need. The matter, unfortunately, is not that simple. Complex attitudes, both traditional and acquired from acculturation, combine to create ambivalence about wealth accumulation and distribution. Jealousy, fear, resentment, and hostility result from unequal success in accumulation of wealth and from demands made upon personal wealth by others. Navajos frequently carry a burden of tension and frustration that is controlled to a point by a veneer of apparent imperturbability. This veneer is rather thin, however, and under a number of kinds of provocation dramatic swings in mood, often resulting in violence, are not uncommon (personal communication, Mr. Steve Allman, BIA official, Chinle, Arizona, 1979).

Almost all Navajo families own sheep and often a few cattle and horses. The holdings are considerably more modest now than in former times as a result of the livestock reduction program of the late 1930s and early 1940s. The legal limit for herd size at present is seventy-four sheep (Downs, 1972). Women tend to own the sheep while the men own the other livestock. Children also own sheep, and often children increase their holdings over time through natural reproductive increase and by gifts from relatives. Children, however, are also expected to take their turns in contributing an occasional animal for family meals or for a ceremony. At the present time ownership and inheritance patterns are much more varied than in former times, when both owner-ship and property transfer through inheritance were maternal prerogatives. The practices now range from strict observance of maternal dominance in such matters to the adoption of white ownership and inheritance customs, including the making of wills. Kluckhohn and Leighton (1962, p. 106) point out that "Attempts of some Navajo to emulate white practices with respect to wood and water rights are among the most bitterly resisted of all innova-tions."

Among the Navajos, marriage has a strong cultural deterministic impetus. Leighton and Kluckhohn (1947) speak of it as being virtually inevitable. The basis for mate selection may be considered to vary with the degree of accul-turation. Even today in the more isolated areas and among the grandparental generation romantic love is of little consequence. In prior generations marriages were arranged by the parents, usually the boy's parents, but today individual choice is the norm. A gift from the parents of the boy to the girl's family is often still proffered, but the custom is no longer mandatory, and it is much less common than in former times (personal communication, Peter Todechini, Native American, Chinle, Arizona, 1978). As Leighton and Kluckhohn (1947) point out, this is not the equivalent of the "bride price" but merely a cus-tomary gift.

Divorce among the Navajo has a tradition of being much more casual than in the Anglo culture. Often it amounts to little more than one of the partners in the marriage leaving the common residence place and going back to the maternal home. Sometimes when the female's relatives suspect neglect or abuse on the part of the husband, he is encouraged to leave.

Divorce figures are very difficult to obtain, and, even with numbers in hand, the figures need interpretation. Separation is probably more common than formal divorce. If domestic tranquility does not prevail, other partners may enter the scene with little or no formal sanction having taken place of either the separation or the new living arrangement. In the formal sense, divorce incidence is estimated to be low (BIA, Chinle, Arizona, 1979). In the functional sense, so is marital stability.

In school, nowadays, where the sexes are so much together, yet separated, romantic-type relationships are inevitable. Romantic attraction is the principal mode of mate selection among the great majority of youth today. This pat-tern, however, is not necessarily adaptive in a context where practical subsis-tence matters are of the essence. Romantic attraction, translated as sexual attraction, is an ephemeral and protean quality and frequently leads to mar-riages that do not have the traditional Navajo family support structure.

The Navajo family is in a vulnerable position economically. The usable land base and the limited water supply effectively impose agricultural con-straints. The jobs on the reservation come largely from the following sources: The Navajo tribe, the Bureau of Indian Affairs, and the Public Health Service. These sources provide approximately 70 percent of all reservation jobs. In addition, the other job sources are the Office of Economic Opportunity, the public schools, occasional contract jobs, sheep herding, the Peabody Coal

Company, the Navajo Forest Products Industry, miscellaneous service jobs and the Navajo Tribe Utility Authority. Of those who seek employment in off-reservation settings, approximately 30 percent remain more than five years, and the others return to the reservation to seek employment there (Office of Indian Education, 1979). A number of these remain chronically unemployed. In short, both the self-determination and the termination concept, or the virtual withdrawal of federal subsidy, have left the problem of adequate employment unsolved. There seems to be little in the reservation framework to attract large investors, with the exception of the government, and even here disenchantment has appeared.

Johnson (1972) has suggested that the federal government has the capacity to provide the necessary number of jobs. She estimates that material poverty could be ameliorated with the provision of about 40,000 jobs for rural Native Americans. Considering the fact that civilian employment increased at a rate of about one million jobs a year in the last decade and also considering the economic capacity of our nation, it would appear that poverty among Native Americans is more a source of annoyance and embarrassment that a potentially serious drain on the national economy. The per capita income for the Navajos has consistently been below the poverty level. For example, in 1970 it was estimated to be $831 as compared with $3,331 for the state of Arizona (Gilbreath, 1973). This suggests that both skills and opportunities are in short supply.

The Navajo family is hard pressed both economically and culturally. Culturally there is a failure to fit within the encroaching off-reservation society as the elements of white control increasingly circumscribe the traditional Navajo Way. The young generation has one foot in each world and stability in neither. Kluckhohn and Leighton (1962, p. 30) write: "Instead of a patterned mosaic, Navajo culture is becoming an ugly patchwork of meaningless and totally unrelated pieces. Personal and social chaos are the byproducts." Economically neither the old ways nor the new ways are providing for a dignified or adequate lifestyle. Poverty abounds.

There has been a greater role decrement for the male Navajo than for the female. The female still has meaningful functions in the family—childbearing, child rearing, ownership of property and wealth transfer, imputed lineage status, and other general functions associated with homemaking. Also, Navajo women have experienced expanding occupational opportunities. All of these activities involve role assumptions that are laden with significance and meaning. The male, while sharing some of these roles with the female, has lost a role that once served as an important basis of peer and self-esteem—that of the warrior. The limitation on the legal size of livestock herds also prevents a man from enjoying the prestige that he might otherwise acquire by amassing large holdings. The male, moreover, is highly visible in his own perception and that of others with respect to his less than dramatic success in the labor market, both on and off the reservation.

An almost universal interest in and emphasis on the rodeo by the male Navajo may indicate an unconscious attempt to regain some of the elements of prestige once supplied by the warrior role. The rodeo is not only a one- or two-time-a-year event. Males of all ages practice rodeo skills almost unceasingly, and many a male head is turned in admiration toward one who is known for his expertise in rodeo events. Women tend, on the other hand, to view the rodeo as little more than a game. Navajo parents designated the rodeo as one of the causes of "bad behavior"—that is, nontraditional or disrespectful behavior—along with other reservation activities, such as dances, and the lack of guidance at schools (Christopherson and Dingle, 1979). At any rate, the rodeo appears to meet a complex need among the male subculture that has to do with entertainment, participation, and status acquisition. In this sense, the rodeo carries a cultural burden not entirely evident to the casual observer.

Having some grasp of the structure of the Navajo family provides insight toward understanding the Navajo people. Underlying and, in a sense, energizing the family and its functions, is the unique Navajo culture, or the "Navajo Way." For the Anglo-European-Western mind to grasp the essentials of a culture that rests and operates on a different set of assumptions as to cause and effect, history, human nature, and, indeed, the nature of reality, is probably too much to expect. There is a real question as to whether one not reared as a Navajo could ever manage to grasp their world view. For the most part we settle for compartmentalized concepts, in effect, bits and pieces. Kluckhohn and Leighton's books (1947 and 1962, revised edition) are among the most informative and insightful accounts by way of orientation. It is important to keep in mind, however, that there are significant regional variations in culture and the Kluckhohn and Leighton accounts deal primarily with the New Mexico Navajo.

To date the social engineering efforts with the Navajo people leave much to be desired. Paternalism has not succeeded nor has self-determinism. Surely there is a way to shore up the resources of the vast Navajo reservation, to help the "People" develop skills with which they can provide for a satisfying lifestyle, and to preserve at the same time, the Navajo Way—perhaps the quality at greatest hazard. The ultimate solution will not be easy. It will be a compromise, but it must take into account the basic concerns of the Navajo people. Otherwise there is more to be lost than gained.

THE RURAL FILIPINO FAMILY

Edwin B. Almirol

Most American families are held together by a network of rights and obligations. In the Filipino-American family, these rights and obligations go much further. Not only are there more rights and obligations, but they attach to a far wider circle of family and kin. This extended concept of family kinship provides the mechanism by which the Filipino ethnic community maintains its sense of identity and also serves to sustain its members in times of economic adversity and in the face of outside social discrimination. A study of the Filipino family is therefore an important ingredient in the study of the status and position of the Filipino in the United States.

This study examines the structure of the Filipino-American family, particularly how it manages a system of rights and obligations among its members. The extended kinship boundaries of the Filipino-American family provide a wide base for family interdependence and ethnic mutual support. Economic adaptation is related to family organization and function.

Although Filipinos appeared in California in the early 1920s, there were no Filipino settlements comparable to the German settlements in the Midwest or the Italian settlements in Canada. The early Filipinos were predominately male; the sex ratio was fourteen men to one woman. They were young, with 85 percent under 25 years old, and single. The few who were married invariably came alone, leaving their families behind. The American labor recruiters sought only able-bodied men, assiduously inspecting the hands of those who wanted to come to the United States. Rough hands meant the men were hardworking and assured them a ticket to the States (Almirol, 1977). Many early Filipino immigrants report that they would rub their palms on rocks on the road in order to pass the "rough hands" inspection. Only men obtained this free passage from labor contractors and other would-be employers. The women had to pay their own fare, and in the steerage to which Filipinos were confined there were no facilities for women passengers. The Hawaii Sugar Planters' Association expressed concern over the unbalanced sex ratio among Filipino farm laborers but their official explanation (Clifford, 1954) was that Filipino women feared that there were no organized Catholic churches in the new land!

The first Filipinos to arrive in the United States ended up in either domestic labor or farm work. Those who found domestic work were employed as houseboys, waiters, busboys, cooks, elevator boys, and dishwashers (cf. Block, 1930). Those in farm labor followed the crop cycle; in the spring and autumn they worked in the lettuce and asparagus farms in Salinas and Stockton; in the winter, they were found in the cantaloupe and vegetable farms in Imperial Valley; in the summer, they worked in the salmon canneries in Alaska and farms in Washington state. Due to their mobility, a stable Filipino community was not to be established until after World War II.

Census data show that Filipinos are not in the U.S. economic mainstream. They have a high unemployment rate and earn less than the Anglos, Mexicans, Japanese, and Chinese, despite education comparable if not better than that of other ethnic groups. The Filipinos have great difficulty acquiring jobs corresponding to their education, training, and experience. In 1960, Filipinos in California, where more than one-half of the total Filipino population in the United States resides, had the lowest median annual income (compared with Blacks, Chinese, Japanese, whites, and persons of Spanish surnames). In 1970, the Filipinos still had the highest unemployment rate (compared with the same groups). In the United States as a whole almost 40 percent of all Filipino men work in relatively low-skilled, low-income jobs such as domestic service occupations, farm work, and unskilled labor. This is more than twice the proportion for the United States as a whole (U.S. Department of Health, Education and Welfare, 1974, p. 93). On the other hand, only 3 percent of all Filipino men in the United States are managers or administrators; far below the U.S. average of 11 percent. This suggests that there are barriers against Filipino entrepreneurial and managerial efforts.

In California, 42 percent of all Filipino women are employed in clerical and sales jobs. This is the U.S. average for women, but since a larger number of these Filipinos have professional backgrounds, their being in lower-skilled white collar jobs represents underemployment (U.S. Department of Health, Education and Welfare, 1974, p. 97). Education and income levels among Filipinos in the United States are not correlated. The median level of educational attainment among Filipinos in the United States and in California is 12.2 years, or slightly better than the median for the United States as a whole. Yet 40 percent of Filipino men work as laborers, farm workers, and domestic servants. Although 27 percent of Filipino women in the United States have college degrees, 56 percent make less than $4,000 a year (U.S. Bureau of the Census, 1970).

In 1960, over one-fourth of the Filipinos in the United States lived in rural areas, and 23 percent of all Filipino men worked in farm-related occupations. By 1970, however, with the arrival of large numbers of new, urban-oriented Filipino immigrants to the cities, only 14 percent of the entire Filipino population still lived in rural areas. The percentage of Filipino men working on farms is down by nearly half (12 percent) from the previous decade. However, this percentage is 1.5 times higher than for the total U.S. population (U.S. Department of Health, Education and Welfare, 1974, p. 20).

For the Filipino, the most important ties start from the family and kin group. The kin group relationship is embedded in a complex and complicated system of reciprocal rights and obligations; loyalty and unity are prescribed for family and kin members, while nonkin are often regarded with suspicion and jealousy, and subjected to gossip. Thus the ties that they establish with kin for support, loyalty, and status also tend to cut them off from other people. The family and kin group occupy a significant place in the social and personal lives of Filipinos. The incentives (and constraints) to participation in community affairs, in clubs and associations, in church-related and other social activities, are all closely tied to the family and wider kinship network.

The Filipino family is bilateral, that is, kinship descent is traced through both maternal and paternal sides of the family, although the family name is carried patrilineally. Filipinos are expected to be loyal to all the persons related to them through both parents and through marriage. To the Filipino, the family means not only spouse, children, parents, and siblings, but also grandparents, uncles, aunts, and cousins; in short, all blood and affinal relatives. The individual household then is really just a subunit of the extended kin group and not the basic family unit, as it is for most white Americans.

However, the nuclear family is still the basic socioeconomic unit. It provides the individual with a basic moral code; it dictates what kinds of loyalties one can and cannot, should and should not, contract and maintain; it assures protection and assistance. And among the loyalties thus implanted, the one by which a Filipino is basically judged is that to his extended family. His social status is most closely linked to his capacity to maintain or improve his family's economic position, maintain its harmony and cohesion, and safeguard the honor of his women kin. Safeguarding one's collective family honor includes being vigilant against gossip adverse to it and against scandals, even while participating in them if they do not involve one's own family and kin group.

As already remarked, early Filipino immigration to California was limited to young single males. Filipino women were few, and family life, as Filipinos knew it, was practically nonexistent. Even when Filipino women began to arrive and a few families were established, it was obvious that Filipino family patterns could not be transferred to the new land. Filipino families were isolated in the sense that they were reduced to the nuclear family and deprived of the wider family-based community found in the Philippines. The preponderance of highly mobile single male population, and the scarcity of women and children, naturally inhibited the development of a secure family life. Although with obvious differences, the Filipino community bore some analogies with the classic western frontier town: the individual was the most efficient economic unit, and the family had secondary importance. Community life was, at best, mythical, and family ties were insecure.

Because chastity in its women kin is central to a Filipino family's honor, the Filipino community exacts strict rules for its women members. Traditionally, women in the Philippines are insulated from contact with men except in guarded social encounters. In the United States, Filipino women had to work beside other men in the fields to help keep the family going, and this provided grounds as well as opportunity for marital suspicion and jealousy. The ratio between Filipino men and women favored the woman immensely. The husband always feared that because there were always more men, the wife could easily replace him. In fact, it was not uncommon to find Filipino family households with a husband, a wife, perhaps a few children, and three or four male boarders, who often attempted to extend their privileges beyond the conventional bed and board.

The need to follow the crops and the long working hours of the men also greatly inhibited settlement and family life. Since the women frequently worked in the fields, it was hard for the children to become educated and socialized. In turn, because of the absence of parents and other older kin, the children were required to take on family responsibilities early. They were expected to perform household chores much younger than was normal in the Philippines, washing their own clothes and sometimes their parents' as well, taking care of younger siblings, and cleaning the house. Household responsibilities had to be placed on individual family members rather than on a kin category—for example, uncles, aunts, grandparents—as would be usual in the Philippines. Sons and daughters equally acquired household duties with only slight variations based on age differences.

To understand the forces that inhibited the development of a secure Filipino family life, one must also appreciate the attitudes of the larger American society, which insisted on viewing the Filipino population as a "menace," an extension of the dreaded "Yellow Peril" (the Chinese and the Japanese). The Filipinos were seen as economic threats. "They represent cheap and irresponsible labor of a type that cannot be assimilated, and as such they threaten American standards of wages and living conditions." (Scharrenberg, 1929, p. 52). In fact, since the Filipinos were chiefly in agriculture and domestic work, jobs that interested only but a few whites, the Filipinos posed no economic threat at all (cf. Melendy, 1972).

The Anglo concept of the "Filipino menace" was not restricted to economic matters; it extended to the very moral fiber of America. A former superintendent of the Department of Public Instruction in the Philippines, professor of political science, and later the president of the University of California wrote: "The Filipinos' natural weakness is a moral weakness. He is smart enough. For a small race he has an unusual endowment, if it can be built up and freed of chronic disorders. But morally, he is deplorable." (Letter to Casper Hodgson, June 3, 1929, Barrows Papers; quoted by Clifford, 1975, p. 9.)

In 1930, the attorney general of California announced his support for exclusionary legislation against the Filipinos to protect "the racial purity and moral integrity of the United States." (Evening Pajaronian, January 18, 1930.) The executive secretary of the California Joint Immigration Committee testified during a hearing before the Committee on Immigration and Naturalization of the House of Representatives in Washington, D.C., that "the sex problem presents a special difficulty we face in connection with Filipino immigration . . . the Filipino does not bring his women with him. You can realize his preference for white women." (Hearings, 1930, pp. 35–36.) It was not mentioned that wives were discouraged from joining their husbands by the lack of facilities for women in the labor camps and by the cost of bringing them to the United States.

There were strong and concerted efforts to exclude Filipino immigration to the United States, to repatriate those who were here, to prohibit Filipinos from leasing or buying lands, owning property, or marrying white women. There were court proceedings to determine whether Filipinos were "Mongolian" or "Malayan," what percentage of "white" blood a Spanish Filipino would have, whether a Filipino could marry a Mexican with one-sixteenth "Indian" blood (Bogardus, 1932; Foster, 1932). Although marriages between whites and Filipinos were prohibited by law, a California judge predicted "that there will be 40,000 half-breeds in the state of California before ten years have passed." He lamented that this "union of East and West will produce a group that in all measures will be a detriment to the attainment of a higher standard of man and woman-hood." (Evening Pajaronian, January 10, 1930.) Another judge nullified Filipino-Anglo marriages, and a California Legislature amendment in 1933 included the Filipinos in the state ban on interracial marriages.

After World War II, many of the Filipinos who joined the all-Filipino First and Second U.S. Regiments returned to the United States with their wives and children. In 1942, U.S. House Resolution 1844 was passed to enable Filipino residents in the United States to become naturalized citizens (Buaken, 1948). Since 1945, Filipino residents have been able to buy land in California (Feria, 1946, p. 50). The antimiscegenation law against Asians was also repealed on October 1, 1948 (McDonagh and Richards, 1953). But despite all this, and although the larger American society showed more tolerance and it became easier to bring over Filipino wives and families, the development of the Filipino family in the United States was still hampered by economic uncertainties.

As one examines the present organization and function of the Filipino family in the United States, one cannot fail to observe the existence of a complex structure of loyalty and interdependence. These are not mere vestiges of "old country" tradition but rational and effective strategies to achieve economic viability and social capability.

Family rights and obligations apply to all members of a kin group, but the rights and obligations one might expect, receive, or exercise diminish as genealogical distance increases. Thus, one feels stronger responsibility to a father's brother than to a father's sister's husband, despite their both being addressed by the same referential term. Conversely, one's father's brother can be expected to offer more assistance, support, and protection than one's father's sister's husband.

Family obligations and rights come in many and varied ways. For instance, "oldtimers" (a term used for Filipinos who arrived in the 1920s and 1930s) and postwar immigrants feel a strong sense of obligation to send money, dry foods, medicines, appliances, clothes, etc. to relatives in the Philippines. Kin members borrow money from each other and exchange food supplies with each other. In general, it is taboo to refuse any kin in need. The obligation to support a kin member who runs for an office in one of the ethnic associations is also strong. It has been shown elsewhere that voluntary associations are essentially extensions of the family; at the same time, Filipino associations are used as mechanisms for establishing political alliances and mutual dependence between families (cf. Almirol, 1978). Kin members are obliged to provide assistance in the preparations for the various rites of passage. Further examples of obligations and accompanying rights are described below. Although reciprocal aid, loyalty, and friendship may be extended to all consanguinal kin, obligatory expectations and pressures are extended as far as second cousins only. In general, mutual support and loyalty have been effectively extended to cousins on both the mother's and father's sides of the family. Loyalty and support is strongest among members of the nuclear family.

But the kinship network among Filipinos is not a closed system; recruitment into the kin group is not restricted to blood and marriage. Fictive kin ties are formed to link not only individuals but also kin groups. The most common way is through the *compadrazgo* (coparenthood) system. The *compadrazgo* system is characterized by "simulated familism, mutual concern and support, and increase in the number of persons to whom one extends the prerogatives and responsibilities of particularistic privilege" (Tumin, 1952, p. 125). Filipinos generally recruit their own countrymen, especially those who come from their own home towns, or provinces, or who speak their own Philippine language. *Compadrazgo* recruitment is also extended to fellow members of the same home town or same church. There are very few Filipinos who would recruit non-Filipinos for *compadrazgo* relationship, unless they are already related through marriage. But *compadrazgo* relationships are not usually established between social equals; they are established between people from different social ranks and statuses.

Generally, the bases for recruiting a *compadre* (coparent) are social influence, status, wealth, and access to power. For a Filipino, the child's *padrino* (godfather) or *madrina* (godmother) is someone from whom one can ask for help and can depend upon to grant favors. One can expect the *compadre* or *comadre* to come to one's aid whenever necessary, to intercede for one when there is trouble, to protect one's interests when they are threatened. As a result, community leaders, the wealthy and influential members of the community, are often asked to become *padrinos* or *madrinas*. But it would be erroneous to infer that *compadrazgo* recruitment is based solely on wealth, status, or power. In most cases, Filipinos choose those with whom they can establish *kasunduan* or *confianza* (confidence, understanding, trust).

Compadres and *comadres* play an important part in the family network of rights and obligations, through a role that has altered somewhat in the United States. As an informant reports, "it used to be that when one is a godparent, one is supposed to take care and raise the godchild if his or her parents died. When the parents are still alive, the godparents are supposed to act like complementary parents. Godparents used to be more involved than now." Indeed, godparents were (and to a certain extent still are) viewed not only as surrogate parents but as active participants in the socialization and education of the child. Today, an increasing number of people simply expect godparents to pay part of the baptismal expenses and give gifts at Christmas, birthdays, first communion, confirmation, graduation, wedding, and other rites of passage.

Godparents are supposed to be attentive, generous, and solicitous to their godchildren; those who are not risk estranged relations. Of course, since godparents belong to one's kin group, they have rights as well. The direction of attention, generosity, and sustenance is reversed when the godchild grows up, especially if the godparents become ill and cannot take care of themselves. If the godparents have no children of their own, their godchildren are expected to take care of them. An "oldtimer" who had neither children nor close family members suffered from a stroke, and while he was recuperating in a nursing home, his godchildren and *compadres* were among his regular visitors. And when a godparent needs help, not only his godchildren but also their parents are obliged to give it. Likewise, when the godchild's parents are sick and require help, the *compadres* visit, bring food, or stay and do household chores. When either parent or godparent is preparing a birthday party or baptism or any social gathering, the other comes to help. When one needs to borrow money, one can approach one's *compadre* without hesitation. *Compadres* are even called upon to mediate quarreling spouses. Clearly, the *compadrazgo* system considerably extends the Filipino family's ties of loyalty and interdependence. By this extension the Filipino community is better able to meet its collective needs and develop a sense of solidarity.

Filipino immigration patterns and early settlement conditions further explain the need to extend and elaborate the network of rights and obligations. Many Filipinos came to the United States through the help of their relatives. Immigrants not only had their passage paid; frequently relatives drew up immigration petitions to the U.S. Immigration and Naturalization Service, signed affidavits of support, provided money for living expenses upon arrival, and arranged accommodation. This kin-based assistance caused what can be termed "chain migration," defined by McDonald and McDonald (1964, p. 82) as "that movement in which prospective immigrants learn of opportunities, are provided transportation and have initial accommodations and employment arranged by means of primary social relationships with previous immigrants." Only for the Filipino, chain migration occurs not solely through "primary social relations" but through extended kin arrangements as well.

Finding the first job is one of an immigrant's most urgent problems. Solving it means acquiring information about the availability and prerequisites of jobs. This information comes primarily from relatives and secondarily from friends. The settled immigrants bring the newly arrived relative to their place of work and inquire about openings or ask their friends about other job possibilities. The members of the family and kin group not only help each other migrate and look for jobs, they also assist each other during rites of passage such as baptisms, birth, confirmations, marriages, and deaths. When a woman gives birth, the members of her and her husband's family come to do her chores and cook for the family. Her younger children are taken to their homes or looked after until she is again able to care for her own household. Grandparents, especially if they are no longer working, are usually called on to supervise and help in the house. The role of grandparents in child care is very important. When parents go to work or attend parties, the grandparents are the first to be asked to baby-sit. When a child is born to a family with no close relatives, the family may petition a relative from the Philippines to come and help in the house.

Many grandparents help to pay for the schooling of their grandchildren. A retired informant explains why he still occasionally does seasonal farm work. "I am expected to, and I want to, help my grandchildren go to school. It is essential that they become better than us." His drive to help his grandchildren is as strong as his hope that they will return his help when he needs it. He said the best investment a Filipino can make for his old age is to take care of the younger, implying that when he can support himself no longer, he expects his children and grandchildren to look after him. In some cases grandparents have taken a grandchild, usually the eldest, into their own home; again the young child is strongly expected to help and work for his grandparents when they need it. Children do not take care of elderly parents and grandparents just for money, though money is certainly not a negligible factor. Most children welcome having their elderly parents come stay with them and vie with each other for the privilege. Usually parents bring their old-age pensions with them, but no one admits to this being the main reason for taking them in.

In general, there is a pervasive feeling of obligation and *utang na loob* (literal translation: internal debt). Since Filipinos can expect help and protection from the members of this family and kin group, they also have obligations to them. If they can render service and hospitality, return support, and provide protection, they are obliged to do so. If they do not, they are likely to be regarded as *walang hiya* (shameless). *Hiya* means shame or losing face, and it must be avoided at all cost. To be *walang hiya* is to incur strong public censure and condemnation. Fear of losing face provides a strong incentive to meet one's obligations, especially family obligations. *Utang na loob* and *hiya* are concepts important to understanding family and social ties. *Utang na loob* is embedded in a moral principle that dictates that a favor received must be returned. In most cases, this triggers off an unending traffic of receiving and returning favors. It is a form of social control that assures reciprocity and social balance. When a person who can return a past favor refuses to, "ostracism is the lightest punishment that can be meted out to him." (Agoncillo and Alfonso, 1967, p. 10). *Utang na loob* is a debt of gratitude that is found not only in the family and kin group but also in all levels of Filipino contact and interaction.

For baptisms, marriages, and funerals, invitations to family and close kin are sent by word of mouth. They are expected not only to attend, but also to help with the preparation and finances. The lavishness of these occasions and the large number of guests show how successful they are. The guests include friends as well as relatives, and friends' friends; and it is commonly said that a friend is sure to bring at least six other friends along. Filipinos coming from the same Philippine home town or belonging to the same Filipino fraternities are expected to attend these various rites of passage. In order to accommodate all these guests, large reception halls, including the Filipino community hall, are rented for the occasion.

Social affairs are likewise lavish and again, the more people, the better; Filipinos compete with each other in making their celebrations as lavish and as inclusive as possible. A celebration has "class" when it is inclusive, not exclusive. Families give *bienvenida* parties for arriving relatives and *despedida* parties for departing ones. The *bienvenida* does not simply announce that a family or a kin group has a new member; it also displays additional prestige, since the bigger the family group, the wider its base of support and loyalty and thus the higher its social status. Furthermore, during a *bienvenida*, the hosts invite influential Filipinos in the community who may be instrumental in helping the new immigrant get a job.

During these rites of passage and special occasions, kin and friends talk in Ilocano, Tagalog, and Cebuano and exchange news about mutual friends and the "old country." During these parties, English is usually spoken only by American-born Filipinos and mestizos who cannot speak any Philippine language—and they will nonetheless claim to understand a "little bit." Filipino dishes are served and occasionally Filipino folk dances are performed. Some of the elder Filipinos wear their Philippine costumes; grandparents, children, and grandchildren eat, sing, drink, and dance together to the music of recorded Filipino folk songs. These rites of passage bring together and reaffirm family and kin group ties while providing an arena for observing and preserving cultural traditions, thus re-creating ethnic consciousness and a sense of belonging.

Many single Filipinos find it "good" and "practical" to live with their parents even if they are adults and can afford to live elsewhere. Even married Filipinos do not mind living with their parents if they see the arrangement as temporary. Living independently is better, but no stigma attaches to adult or married children living with their parents. A high proportion of children over 18 live with their parents, though these arrangements are ideally seen as temporary. As one married Philippine-born informant explains, "if one lives with one's family for a while, one gets a reprieve from meeting one's own problems alone. One has ready baby-sitters, household tasks are lighter, and on the whole, it is more practical." One Filipino mestizo, employed and in his late 20s, returned to live with his parents after he was divorced by his Anglo wife.

Working adults living at home are expected to share in the household expenses. In fact, every working member of the family contributes to a collective family coffer, the mother usually being the purse holder. Many Filipino families have more than one source of income. Some have a back garden that yields vegetables and fruit. There is much traffic in homegrown produce between *compadres,* kin members, friends, and neighbors, which easily saves money for the average family. Filipinos often further augment their income by taking a second job or by doing various odd jobs (Almirol, 1977). Filipinos live together, share resources, and hold their monies collectively as a way of coping economically.

The Filipinos' economic situation compels them to develop and maintain a dependable support network: the family and kin group. The individual derives mutual support, social status, honor, and protection from the family. The family protects its immigrant members from the shocks encountered in their new surroundings. The family and kin group provide a complex system of rights and obligations, of reciprocal assistance and support. The kinship ties, as well as ethnic loyalties, are regularly reaffirmed through the rites of passage. Through the *compadrazgo* system, the circle of family and kin is broadened, which makes the kin group more effective in dealing with economic problems. Family roles and social statuses are allocated and defined in ways that are mutually satisfying for the individuals and consonant with the community's needs and resources. The extensive and vast network of rights and obligations within the Filipino family is at once a response to the larger society's economic pressures and an assertion of cultural identity and group solidarity.

Notes

1. Family orientation was measured by the scale developed by Litwak (1960).

2. The terms Mexican American and Chicano are used interchangeably throughout the text to refer to Americans of Mexican descent.

References

The Rural Black Family

Allen, W. R. "Black Family Research in the United States: A Review, Assessment, and Extension." *Journal of Comparative Family Studies,* 1978, 9, 167–189.

Brown, D. L. "Racial Disparity and Urbanization, 1960 and 1970." *Rural Sociology,* 1978, 43, 403–425.

Chevan, A. and J. H. Korson. "The Widowed Who Live Alone: An Examination of Social and Demographic Factors." *Social Forces,* 1972, 51, 45–53.

Dietrich, K. T. *Black Families in a Nonmetropolitan Southern County: Social, Economic, and Psychological Attributes.* Departmental Information Report 73-10. College Station: Texas Agricultural Experiment Station, Texas A&M University, 1973.

___. "A Reexamination of the Myth of Black Matriarchy." *Journal of Marriage and the Family,* 1975, 37, 367–374.

Dietrich, K. T. and L. Greiser. *Residence Differences in Characteristics of Black, Lower-Class Families.* Departmental Information Report 74-10. College Station: Texas Agricultural Experiment Station, Texas A&M University, 1975.

Donnenwerth, G. V., R. F. Guy, and M. J. Norvell. "Life Satisfaction among Older Persons: Rural-Urban and Racial Comparisons." *Social Science Quarterly,* 1978, 59, 578–583.

Doughtery, M. "Kinship and Descent in a Rural Black Community." Paper presented at the 73rd annual meeting of the American Anthropological Association, Mexico City, 1974.

French, L. "The Isolated Appalachian Black Community." *Journal of Social and Behavioral Sciences,* 1977, 23, 361–370.

Gillin, J. "National and Regional Cultural Values in the United States." *Social Forces,* 1955, 34, 107–113.

Hill, C. E. "Anthropological Studies in the American South: Review and Directions." *Current Anthropology,* 1977, 18, 309–336.

Jones, Y. *Ethnicity and Political Process in a Southern Rural Community: An Examination of Black/White Articulation in Decision Making.* Unpublished Ph.D. dissertation, American University, Washington, D.C., 1976.

Kutner, N. G. "Who is the 'Head of the Family'? Some Evidence from Lower-

Class Negro Couples." Paper presented at the 34th annual meeting of the Southern Sociological Society, Miami, 1971.

___. *An Interethnic and Place of Residence Examination of the 'Culture of Poverty'*. Departmental Technical Report 75-3. College Station: Texas Agricultural Experiment Station, Texas A&M University, 1975.

Litwak, E. "Geographic Mobility and Extended Family Cohesion." *American Sociological Review,* 1960, 25, 385–394.

Martin, E. P. and J. M. Martin. *The Black Extended Family.* Chicago: University of Chicago Press, 1978.

Maxwell, J. W. "Rural Negro Father Participation in Family Activities." *Rural Sociology,* 1968, 33, 80–83.

Moerman, D. *Extended Family and Popular Medicine on St. Helena Island, South Carolina: Adaptation to Marginality.* Unpublished Ph.D. dissertation, University of Michigan, Ann Arbor, 1974.

Ryan, V. D. and R. H. Warland. "Race and the Effect of Family Status Among Male Agricultural Laborers." *Rural Sociology,* 1978, 43, 335–347.

Shimkin, D. and G. Lowe. *The Black Extended Family: A Basic Rural Institution and a Mechanism of Urban Adaptation.* MS. University of Illinois (Urbana) and Center for Advanced Study in the Behavioral Sciences (Stanford), 1971.

Young, V. H. "Family and Childhood in a Southern Negro Community." *American Anthropologist,* 1970, 72, 269–288.

The Rural Mexican-American Family

Alvarez, R. "The Psycho-Historical and Socioeconomic Development of the Chicano Community in the United States." *Social Science Quarterly,* 1973, 53, 920–942.

Alvirez, D. and F. D. Bean. "The Mexican American Family." In C. H. Mindel and R. W. Haberstein (eds.), *Ethnic Families in America: Patterns and Variations.* New York: Elsevier, 1976, 271–292.

Atencio, T. C. "The Human Dimensions of Land Use and Land Displacement in Northern New Mexican Villages." In C. W. Knowlton (ed.), *Indian and Spanish American Adjustments to Arid and Semi-Arid Environments.* Lubbock: Texas Tech College, 1964, 44–52.

Baca Zinn, M. "Political Familism: Toward Sex Role Equality in Chicano Families." *Aztlan,* 1975, 6, 13–26.

Bodine, J. J. "A Tri-Ethnic Trap: The Spanish Americans in Taos." In *Spanish-Speaking People in the United States: Proceedings of the 1968 Annual Spring Meeting of the American Ethnological Society.* Seattle: University of Washington Press, 1968, 145–153.

Briggs, V. M., Jr., W. Fogel, and F. Schmidt. *The Chicano Worker.* Austin: University of Texas Press, 1977.

Cardenas, G. "Los Desarraigados: Chicanos in the Midwestern Region of the United States." *Aztlan,* 1976, 7, 153–186.

Choldin, H. M. and G. D. Trout. "Mexican-Americans in Transition: Migration and Employment in Michigan Cities." Final Report to U.S. Department of Labor. East Lansing, Michigan: Department of Sociology, Rural Manpower Center and Agricultural Experiment Station, Michigan State University, 1969.

Clark, M. *Health in the Mexican American Culture*. Los Angeles: University of California Press, 1959.

Foley, D. E., C. Mota, D. Post, and I. Lozano. *From Peones to Politicos: Ethnic Relations in a South Texas Town, 1900 to 1977*. Austin, Texas: Center for Mexican American Studies, University of Texas, 1977.

Goldschmidt, W. *As You Sow*. New York: Harcourt, Brace and Co., 1947.

Gonzalez, N. *The Spanish-Americans of New Mexico*. Albuquerque, New Mexico: University of New Mexico Press, 1967.

Grebler, L., J. Moore, and R. Guzman. *The Mexican American People*. New York: The Free Press, 1970.

Griswold del Castillo, R. "La Familia Chicana: Social Changes in the Chicano Family of Los Angeles: 1850-1880." *Journal of Ethnic Studies*, 1975, 3, 41-58.

Hawkes, G., M. Taylor, and B. Bastian. *Patterns of Living in California's Migrant Labor Families*. Research Monograph No. 12. Davis, California: Department of Applied Behavioral Sciences, University of California, Davis, 1973.

Jones, R. C. "Ethnic Family Patterns: The Mexican Family in the United States." *The American Journal of Sociology*, 1948, 53, 450-452.

Keefe, S., A. Padilla, and M. Carlos. *The Mexican American Extended Family as an Emotional Support System*. Washington, D.C.: Educational Resources Information Center, 1977.

Kluckhohn, F. R. and F. L. Strodtbeck. *Variations in Value Orientations*. Westport, Connecticut: Greenwood Press, 1961.

Knowlton, C. "The Spanish Americans in New Mexico." *Sociology and Social Research*, 1961, 45, 445-448.

____. "Changing Spanish American Villages of Northern New Mexico." *Sociology and Social Research*, 1969, 53, 455-474.

Lasswell, T. E. "Status Stratification in a Selected Community." Unpublished Ph.D. dissertation, University of Southern California, 1953.

Leonard, O. E. and J. H. Hannon. "Those Left Behind: Recent Social Changes in a Heavy Emigration Area of North Central New Mexico." *Human Organization*, 1977, 36, 384-394.

Lewis, O. *Tepoztlan*. New York: Holt, Rinehart and Winston, 1960.

Luebben, R. A. "Spanish-Americans of the Upper Rio Grande Drainage." In J. Burma (ed.), *Mexican-Americans in the United States: A Reader*. Cambridge, Massachusetts: Schenkman Publishing Co., Inc., 1970, 441-457.

Macklin, B. J. *Structural Stability and Culture Change in a Mexican American Community*. Ph.D. dissertation. Philadelphia: University of Pennsylvania, 1963.

Madsen, W. *Mexican-Americans of South Texas*. New York: Holt, Rinehart and Winston, 1964.

McWilliams, C. *North From Mexico.* New York: Greenwood Press, 1968.

Miller, M. V. and R. L. Maril. *Poverty in the Lower Rio Grande Valley of Texas: Historical and Contemporary Dimensions.* College Station, Texas: The Texas Agricultural Experiment Station, Texas A&M University, 1979.

Miller, P. B. "The Role of Labor Market Institutions in the Lower Rio Grande Valley of Texas." College Station, Texas: Department of Economics, Texas A&M University, 1970.

Mirande, A. "The Chicano Family: A Reanalysis of Conflicting Views." *Journal of Marriage and the Family,* 1977, 39, 747–756.

Montiel, M. "The Social Science Myth of the Mexican American Family." *El Grito,* 1970, 3, 56–63.

Moore, J. *Mexican Americans* (2nd ed.). Englewood Cliffs, New Jersey: Prentice-Hall, 1976.

Pensalosa, F. "The Changing Mexican-American in Southern California." *Sociology and Social Research,* 1967, 51, 405–417.

Rubel, A. J. *Across the Tracks—Mexican-Americans in a Texas City.* Austin, Texas: University of Texas Press, 1966.

Schneider, D. M. and R. T. Smith. *Class Differences and Sex Roles in American Kinship and Family Structure.* Englewood Cliffs, New Jersey: Prentice-Hall, 1973.

Sena, J. R. "The Survival of the Mexican Extended Family in the United States: Evidence From a Southern California Town." Ph.D. dissertation. Los Angeles: University of California, Los Angeles, 1973.

Sena-Rivera, J. "La Familia Chicana." In *Families Today: Volume I.* Washington, D.C.: National Institute of Mental Health Science Monographs, U.S. Department of Health, Education and Welfare, 1979, 67–128.

Swadesh, F. L. "Property and Kinship in Northern New Mexico." *Rocky Mountain Social Science Journal,* 1965, 2, 209–214.

Tienda, M. "Familism and Structural Assimilation of Mexican Immigrants in the United States." Madison, Wisconsin: Center for Demography and Ecology, University of Wisconsin, Working Paper 79–11, 1979.

Tuck, R. D. *Not With the Fist: Mexican-Americans in a Southwest City.* New York: Harcourt, Brace and Co., 1946.

Uhlenberg, P. "Marital Instability Among Mexican Americans: Following the Patterns of Blacks?" *Social Problems,* 1972, 20, 49–56.

Ulibarri, H. "Social and Attitudinal Characteristics of Spanish-Speaking Migrant and Ex-Migrant Workers in the Southwest." *Sociology and Social Research,* 1966, 50, 361–370.

U.S. Bureau of the Census. "Persons of Spanish Origin in the United States; March, 1978." (Tables 4, 7). *Current Population Reports,* P-20, No. 328. U.S. Government Printing Office, 1978.

____. *U.S. Census of Population: 1970. Subject Reports. Persons of Spanish Origin.* Final Report PC(2)-1C, Table 1. Washington, D.C.: U.S. Government Printing Office, 1973.

Wells, M. J. "Brokerage, Economic Opportunity, and the Growth of Ethnic Movements." *Ethnology,* 1979, 18, 399–414.

____. "Regional Forces and Industrial Constraints: Changing Labor Market Structure in the California Strawberry Industry." Davis, California: Department of Applied Behavioral Sciences, University of California, 1980.

The Navajo Rural Family

Christopherson, V. A. and S. F. Dingle. "Rural Navajo Youth: A Challenge for Resource Development." Paper presented at the annual meetings of the Rural Sociological Society in Burlington, Vermont, August 1979.

Collier, P. "The Red Man's Burden." In H. M. Bahr, B. A. Chadwick, and R. C. Day (eds.), *Native Americans Today: Sociological Perspectives.* New York: Harper and Row, 1972.

Dobyns, H. F. and R. C. Euler. *The Navajo People.* Phoenix: Indian Tribal Series, 1972.

Edmonson, M. S. "Kinship System." In E. A. Vogt and E. M. Albert (eds.), *People of Rimrock.* New York: Atheneum, 1970.

Gilbreath, K. *Red Capitalism: An Analysis of the Navajo Economy.* Norman, Oklahoma: University of Oklahoma Press, 1973.

Johnson, H. "Rural Indians in Poverty." In H. M. Bahr, B. A. Chadwick, and R. C. Day (eds.), *Native Americans Today: Sociological Perspectives.* New York: Harper and Row, 1972, 24–30.

Kluckhohn, C. and D. Leighton. *The Navajo* (revised edition). Garden City, New York: Doubleday and Company, Inc., 1962.

Leighton, D. and C. Kluckhohn. *Children of the People: The Navajo Individual and His Development.* Cambridge: Harvard University Press, 1947.

Office of Indian Education. Personal communication with Steve Allman, Chinle, Arizona, 1978.

Schuske, E. L. *Manual for Kinship Analysis: Studies in Anthropological Method.* New York: Holt, Rinehart and Winston, 1965.

Shepardson, M. and B. Hammond. *The Navajo Mountain Community: Social Organization and Kinship Terminology.* Berkeley: University of California Press, 1970.

Witherspoon, G. *Navajo Kinship and Marriage.* Chicago: University of Chicago Press, 1975.

The Rural Filipino Family

Agoncillo, T. A. and O. Alfonso. *History of the Filipino People.* Quezon City: Malaya Books, 1965.

Almirol, E. B. "Ethnic Identity and Social Negotiation: A Study of Filipino Community in California." Unpublished Ph.D. dissertation. University of Illinois, 1977.

____. "Filipino Voluntary Associations: Balancing Social Pressures and Ethnic Images." *Ethnic Groups,* 1978, 2 (1), 65–92.

Block, L. *Facts About Filipino Immigration into California.* San Francisco: California Department of Industrial Relations, 1930.

Bogardus, E. "Filipino Immigrant Attitudes." *Sociology and Social Research,* 1929, 14 (1), 469–479.

____. "What Race are Filipinos?" *Sociology and Social Research*, 1932, 20, 67–71.

Buaken, M. *I Have Lived with the American People*. Caldwell, Idaho: Caxton Printers, 1948.

Clifford, D. "Filipino Immigration to Hawaii." Unpublished M.A. thesis, University of Hawaii, Honolulu, 1954.

____. "California's Struggle Against the Filipino Invasion: 1929–1934." Unpublished manuscript, 1975.

Evening Pajaronian. "Judge Rohrback on Filipinos." January 10 and 18, 1930, Watsonville, California.

Feria, R. T. "War and Status of Filipino Immigrants." *Sociology and Social Research*, 1946, 31, 48–53.

Foster, N. "Legal Status of Filipino Intermarriages." *Sociology and Social Research*, 1932, 16 (5), 441–454.

Hearings Before the Committee on Immigration and Naturalization. "Hearings on Exclusion of Immigration from the Philippine Islands." House of Representatives, 71st Congress, 2nd Session, Washington, D.C., 1930.

McDonagh, E. and E. Richards. *Ethnic Relations in the United States*. New York: Appleton-Century-Crofts, 1953.

McDonald, J. S. and L. D. McDonald. "Urbanization, Ethnic Groups, and Social Segmentation." *Social Research*, 1962, 29, 433–448.

Melendy, B. "California's Discrimination Against Filipinos, 1927–1935." In R. Daniels and S. C. Olin (eds.), *Racism in California*. New York: MacMillan, 1972.

Scharrenberg, P. "The Philippines Problem." *Pacific Affairs*, 1929, 2 (2), 49–54.

Tumin, M. M. *Caste in a Peasant Society*. New Jersey: Princeton University Press, 1952.

U.S. Bureau of the Census. *Census of Population, Subject Reports on Japanese, Chinese, and Filipinos in the United States*. Washington, D.C.: General Printing Office, 1970.

U.S. Department of Health, Education and Welfare. *Study of Selected Socioeconomic Characteristics of Ethnic Minorities. Based on Census 1970, Vol. II; Asian Americans*. Washington, D.C.: U.S. Government Printing Office, DHEW Publication No. (OS) 75-121, 1974.

PART 3

FAMILY DYNAMICS

7
INTERPERSONAL PROCESSES
IN RURAL FAMILIES[1]

Walter R. Schumm and Stephan R. Bollman

A decade ago a prominent family sociologist challenged the generalizability of a family sociology derived almost exclusively from the responses of wives (Safilios-Rothschild, 1969). Since then, researchers have been more careful to obtain and compare the perceptions of different family members. Today it may be more relevant to question the generalizability of what amounts to the sociology of the urban or suburban family. Although certain rural-urban differences in demographic characteristics have been well documented, the literature on rural-urban attitudinal differences remains largely speculative (Glenn and Alston, 1967), and our understanding of the interpersonal processes of rural family life has not changed substantially in spite of many laments (Burchinal, 1964; Landis, 1948; Lind, 1976; Nelson, 1948; Rosenblatt, Nevaldine, and Titus, 1978). Family researchers have been content to assume that results from relatively convenient urban samples could be readily extended to rural families, given the debate over the usefulness of the rural-urban variable (Lowe and Peek, 1974; van Es and Brown, 1974), the supposed convergence of urban and rural culture (Smith and Zopf, 1970), the apparent decline of the sociology of the family in general (Larson and Stehr, 1973), and the decline of the family as a topic within rural sociology (Sewell, 1965). Indeed, Rosenblatt et al. (1978) acknowledged the similarity between farm families, rural nonfarm families, and urban families in the culture of the United States, as contrasted with differences in other nations.

Yet, for the most part, the empirical bases for generalizations about the rural family are scanty, and it is important, therefore, to summarize and integrate precisely what is known about rural family relationships in order to consider the implications for future research and policymaking. In addition, where appropriate, we have expanded the current literature by reporting a preliminary analysis of data collected on rural and urban families in Kansas as part of a larger national study.[2] The review below focuses on the following issues: (1) family size and composition, (2) satisfaction with family relationships, (3) quality of life and family satisfactions, (4) characteristics of rural families, (5) parent-child relations, and (6) marital satisfaction.

Current Research on Interpersonal Processes in Rural Families

Family Size and Composition

In their standard text, Nye and Berardo (1973, p. 363) commented, "That families in rural areas are on the average larger than those in cities might well be stated as a sociological law." Nye and Berardo attribute the difference in family size to lesser use of birth control by rural couples, for whom additional children are not as costly a responsibility as they may be for urban couples. Rural couples generally desire more children than do urban couples (Glenn and Alston, 1967). A higher fertility rate among rural families is one of the societal factors presented by Cogswell and Sussman (1979) in their overview of the literature pertaining to family fertility. Edwards and Booth's (1976) report that frequency of intercourse is not different for rural than for urban couples tends to support the view that decreased emphasis on family planning is the cause of the rural-urban difference. Others have found that urban couples are more opposed to larger families (Lowe and Peek, 1974) and that rural mothers and daughters favor larger families (Woods, 1959). However, with average family size on the decline during the past decade, there is mixed evidence regarding the differences between urban and rural family size. Some report that significant differences continue to exist (Tarver, 1969; Wood and Bean, 1977; Defronzo, 1976) while others propose that the differences are narrowing (Burchinal, 1964; Tarver et al., 1970). At least one survey found no difference in family size between urban and rural families (Hafstrom et al., 1974), and our own survey of Kansas communities found no significant differences in family size. However, national census data indicate that rural families are slightly larger, on the average. In 1970 and 1977 respectively, the average numbers of related children under 18 years for metropolitan families were 2.32 and 2.07; for nonmetropolitan families the corresponding figures were 2.42 and 2.16 (U.S. Census, 1978, pp. 44–45). Census data indicate that the rural family continues to be larger in size than the urban family, although all families have decreased in size between 1970 and 1977.

The implications of the larger size of the rural family are that there are more dyadic relationships, especially sibling relationships, to contend with, and that parental management of the children without the help of older children might be more complicated. Parents may have to adopt different guidelines to adequately control their larger number of children, for whose behavior rural parents feel especially responsible (Glenn and Alston, 1967). Some differences in rural family interaction may be a direct result of the larger family size.

Rural families are more likely to be headed by a married couple than are urban families. Family stability is greater in rural areas, in the sense that fewer divorces occur (though until recently, divorce rates have been rising in rural as well as urban areas). If a divorce does occur, remarriage follows more quickly than in urban areas (Woodrow et al., 1978). Recent census data confirm that a smaller percentage of rural individuals are divorced than urban individuals (U.S. Census, 1978, pp. 32–33). Like family size, family stability is a traditionally accepted characteristic of rural families.

Bumpass and Sweet (1972) found that divorce was not related to rural or urban residence while growing up. Mueller and Pope (1977), looking at percentages of divorced offspring of divorced and nondivorced parents, found that rural-urban socialization had no effect on the transmission of parental marital instability to offspring's marital instability. The rate of divorce among offspring was not dependent on the area of residence as a function of parental divorce. These results suggest that the lower rates of divorce in rural areas may be a function of *current rural social norms* rather than norms internalized during socialization. Goode's finding (1956) that rural women considered divorce longer before actually filing and Lowe and Peek's (1974) finding that rural individuals are less favorable towards lenient divorce laws are consistent with this interpretation. Woods (1959) also reported data that indicate rural people are more apt to be opposed to divorce, regardless of the circumstances. Smith and Zopf (1970) have proposed familism as the means of social control that fosters family permanence in rural areas. If divorce rates in rural areas are lower because rural residents are hesitant to act contrary to local norms, then there may be more rural marriages in trouble but still intact, fitting the stable-unsatisfactory pattern discussed by Lederer and Jackson (1968).

Satisfaction with Family Relationships

Early reviews of the field have come to opposite conclusions regarding rural-urban differences in family satisfaction. Landis (1948) concluded that rural families were better adjusted on the basis of three studies (Burgess and Cottrell, 1938; Duvall and Motz, 1945; Lydgate, 1946). However, Burchinal (1964) found two studies indicating no overall differences in satisfaction (Blood and Wolfe, 1960; Burchinal, 1961) and seven studies indicating that rural families were experiencing less satisfaction with family life (Beers, 1937; Gurin et al., 1960; Landis, 1951; McVoy and Nelson, 1943; Sheeley et al., 1949; Taves, 1952; Thorpe, 1957). Burchinal also reported three studies in which parent-adolescent relationships were less happy in rural areas (Burgess, 1934; Nye, 1950; Sheeley et al., 1949).

More recent studies tend to suggest that there are only slight, if any, differences in satisfaction between rural and urban families. Hafstrom et al. (1974) found no rural-urban differences in Illinois wives' satisfaction with their husbands. In a National Opinion Research Center (NORC) national probability sample survey of the elderly (over age 60) in 1973, Hynson (1975) reported no significant differences between rural and urban areas in family satisfaction, even though the rural elderly were more happy in general. Mitchell (1976), using 1974 NORC data, found that rural-urban residence did not explain differences in social satisfactions. National sample data of Campbell et al. (1976) revealed only insignificant differences in marital and family satisfaction between those raised in or presently living in rural and urban areas.

The data collected in our Kansas study indicated no statistically significant differences in satisfaction with number of children; with family, spouse, or children; or with marriage between adult urban and rural respondents. However, the picture is quite different from the perspectives of an adolescent in each of the same families. There are trends for adolescents in rural areas to report greater satisfaction with family life (p = 0.07), with parents' relationship with each other (p = 0.06), with relationship with parents (p = 0.14), and with relationships with siblings (p = 0.05). Additionally, rural adolescents rated family life (p = 0.04), parents' relationship with each other (p = 0.08), relationship with parents (p = 0.18), and relationships with siblings (p = 0.44) as more important than did urban adolescents. An inspection of the distributions of the responses of the rural and urban adolescents suggests that the mean differences are caused by a tendency for urban adolescents to report intermediate levels of satisfaction more often than rural adolescents, whose distributions tended to be consistently skewed towards higher levels of satisfaction. Thus, our urban sample did not tap a group of very dissatisfied teenagers but rather more who were having ambivalent feelings about their family relationships.

For those who are prepared to argue that rural and urban families do not differ in family satisfaction, three explanations are often advanced. First, social and psychological factors that influence family satisfaction are probably only indirectly influenced by area of residence, inasmuch as social norms may vary from one area to another. Second, some would argue that within the United States, the impact of a common national culture and various regional subcultures may obscure the impact of the rural-urban variable, where it exists. Third, the sources of family satisfaction are varied enough that rural culture offers both advantages and disadvantages, combining to "wash out" differences between rural and urban areas.

Quality of Life and Family Satisfactions

The issue under investigation here is: Do rural family members relate their family satisfactions to their overall satisfaction with life differently than urban family members? The more important family satisfactions are in determining overall satisfaction, the more important family variables become in a comprehensive policy framework for the group under consideration. Almost no research has been directed specifically to this problem and therefore it is necessary to review first national data for both rural and urban individuals combined.

Campbell et al. (1976) reported data from a national sample of 2,100 respondents. The correlations of satisfaction with family, marriage, and standard of living with well-being were .53, .40, and .48, respectively (p. 76). Andrews and Withey (1976, p. 112) present similar results for three samples, conducted in 1972 and 1973. Table 7.1 presents the correlations of marital satisfaction and standard of living satisfaction with Andrews and Withey's best measure of well-being (p. 107). Although Andrews and Withey suggested that demographic differences did not seem to alter the relative ability of their variables to predict overall well-being (1976, p. 147), results from their Toledo sample may suggest that in urban areas marital satisfaction has a slight edge over socioeconomic well-being in predicting overall quality of life.

Table 7.1

Correlations of Satisfaction with Marriage and Standard of Living with an Index of Well-Being in Three Surveys.

Variables	Surveys		
	May[a] 1972	November[b] 1972	July[c] 1973
Marital Satisfaction	.38	.52	.60
Standard of Living Satisfaction	.47	.57	.49

[a] A national probability sample, N=1297, eta used as measure of association.

[b] A national probability sample, N=1072, eta used as measure of association.

[c] A local survey of Toledo, Ohio, N=222, Pearson r used as measure of association.

NOTE: This table was constructed from data reported in Andrews and Withey (1976).

Combining these and other variables in a variety of regression equations yielded the results that the family and standard of living variables were always among the four most substantial predictors of well-being, with the family variable being the better predictor relative to standard of living in four of five regression equations (p. 124). Therefore, in both the Campbell et al. (1976) and Andrews and Withey (1976) studies, the foremost conclusion that can be drawn is that both family and socioeconomic satisfactions play a major role in the perception or determination of overall well-being.

Data from our rural and urban Kansas samples permit an illumination of this relationship through an analysis of differences in the relative impact of family satisfaction and standard of living satisfaction upon overall quality of life, as a function of residence. Our analysis compared the relative impact of family and standard of living satisfactions upon quality of life for four groups of rural husbands, rural wives, urban husbands, and urban wives.[3] The correlations are presented in Table 7.2, which indicates few statistically significant differences. Rural and urban couples in this sample apparently perceived their quality of life as relatively equal functions of standard of living and of family satisfaction.

Characteristics of Rural Families

Much more has been said about characteristics of the rural family than has been verified through objective research. What has been investigated often fits into rather narrow aspects of overall family life. However, those interested

Table 7.2

Zero-order Correlations between Quality of Life and Selected Components of Quality of Life as Perceived by Rural and Urban Spouses; Differences between Correlations within and between Rural and Urban Groups.

Groups		Components		Differences Across Components Within Groups
		Standard of Living Satisfaction	Family Satisfaction	
Rural				
	Husbands	.55***(80)[a]	.57***(79)	-.02 ns
	Wives	.75***(80)	.63***(81)	.12 ns
Urban				
	Husbands	.46***(94)	.36***(98)	.10 ns
	Wives	.29***(96)	.47***(97)	-.17 ns
Differences Between Groups For Each Component				
	Husbands	.09 ns	.21*	
	Wives	.46***	.16 ns	

*p .05
**p .01
***p .001
a - N after missing data have been deleted

in working with rural families, who understand their processes and functions and are aware of what is speculation and what is not, will have a head start in designing effective programs.

What are the goals of rural families? How might they differ from those of urban families? Burchinal (1964, p. 188) has suggested:

Consideration of alternative norms for evaluating marital relationships leads to what appear to be the most significant differences in rural and urban family patterns. These differences concern the role of companionate or affectionate relationships in family relationships, the importance of attempting to meet interpersonal needs of family members, and the emphasis put upon developing interpersonal competence skills among family members. The present ways in which urban families are structuring their marital relationships do not represent perfect models. However, the meager data which are available suggest that greater emphasis is being given to these matters among urban families, and apparently more satisfactory results are being attained by urban than by rural families.

There are very meager data on the goals of rural families, particularly in terms of the relative importance of various interpersonal objectives. The lack of research is surprising, in view of the suggestion by Rokeach (1973) that interpersonal conflict was largely a function of individuals holding different terminal values (goals). Smith and Zopf (1970) noted that one aspect of familism in the rural family is the subordination of personal goals to those of the family. Perhaps this assumption has deterred researchers from measuring the relative importance of the goals of rural families or evaluating the impact of family consensus on goals. Some evidence does suggest that farm families do have some substantial consensus on goals (Wilkening and Bharadwaj, 1967), but the goal consensus of rural and urban families has not been compared. Social interventions designed to support families in rural society may be futile until there is a better grasp of the goals of rural families as they perceive them.

Family power, in the narrow context of decision making as measured through survey research, has been extensively studied in rural families. Rural families are often stereotyped as being patriarchal, in the sense of the husband being dominant in all decisions that are made. While some evidence suggests that there is more paternal authority in rural homes, chiefly from evaluations of one's parents' patterns (Fischer, 1975; Larson, 1974), most studies contradict the notion of male dominance, especially as perceived by spouses for their own marriage. Decision making appears to be similar to that in urban families, predominantly joint and egalitarian (Baumert and Lupri, 1963; Beck and Burchinal, 1961; Blood and Wolfe, 1960; Hafstrom et al., 1974; Jeries, 1977; Larson, 1974a; Wilkening and Bharadwaj, 1967; Wilkening and Morrison, 1963). Not surprisingly, decisions tend to be made as much in accordance with who will perform the tasks that implement a decision as by normative sex role allocations (Wilkening and Bharadwaj, 1967, 1968).

Since the merits of family-power research have been challenged very severely since 1970 by several family scholars, rather little has been done with family power of late. However, data collected in our Kansas study did explore the perceptions of husbands and wives regarding who was most likely to "give in" when a conflict arose in thirteen different aspects of family life. Although some differences were identified, our analysis did not detect any major differences due to area of residence. Of the twenty-six t-tests that were performed on perceived compromising, only two significant differences were found between rural and urban spouses.

The situation with respect to the division of labor and family roles is more controversial. Several studies have noted that family tasks are allocated along traditional sex role lines in rural families (Bayer, 1975; Blood, 1958; Larson, 1974a), with wives becoming more traditional if they have more children, have less education, or are older (Lind, 1976). Our Kansas data included several items on roles. In reference to actual and ideal roles for women, in terms of homemaking versus career orientation, we found no rural-urban differences. However, rural wives perceived fewer differences with their husbands in the areas of bringing up children and tasks and responsibilities. Rural wives also believed they had fewer intense arguments over the same issues and felt they had more satisfaction with tasks and responsibilities, as well as with their employment and finances. Therefore, our Kansas data suggest either that rural-urban differences are small in the populations studied or that rural wives may be slightly more satisfied with the performance of certain typical family roles.

Early studies indicated that rural couples were less expressive of love and affection than urban couples (Beers, 1937; Blood and Wolfe, 1960) and spent less time in private (Thorpe, 1957). Bollman et al. (1975) reported that rural families did spend a great deal of time interacting, although this does not guarantee that couples themselves have much privacy. Palisi (1977), using an Australian sample of rural and urban families, found that urban couples were more "companionate" than rural couples. Smith and Zopf (1970, p. 320) believed that there was more affectional interaction in rural families.

There has not been much research on communication between rural family members. However, an adaptation of the Barrett-Lennard Relationship Inventory was part of our Kansas survey, permitting a test of rural-urban differences in the dimensions of regard, empathy, and congruence or openness. Of thirty-six possible differences, only three statistically significant differences were found between our rural and urban samples. Hence, our data suggest that rural couples do not see themselves as less empathic or congruent in their self-disclosure than do urban couples. Given the importance of communication, at least in theory, in the success of marriage, more research is urgently needed in this area on rural families.

Another important aspect of marital interaction is sexuality. It seems that the subject has seldom been dealt with in rural family research. Landis (1951) found a sample of rural wives expressing more dissatisfaction with their sexual adjustment than did a comparison sample of urban wives. However, other than the Kinsey studies, which found few rural-urban differences (Burchinal, 1964), the authors could not find research of a rigorous nature on sexual relations in rural families.

Our Kansas data would seem to contradict Landis's findings. Rural wives reported higher levels of satisfaction with sexual relations than did urban wives in our study, although rural and urban husbands were equally satisfied. In particular, the urban wife more often saw herself as giving in to her husband's wishes in the area of sexual relations. Although more research is needed, researchers may expect to find more resistance in rural families than in urban families to discussion of the topic in interviews, if de Lissovoy's (1973) difficulties in interviewing rural couples is representative of the rural population.

Parent-Child Relations

One study did find unusually high correlations between the opinions of rural farm fathers and their college sons on the topics of Vietnam and drug usage, but not on five other issues including sexual behavior, inflation, pollution, campus unrest, and segregation (Jacobsen, Berry, and Olson, 1975). However, overall consensus between fathers and sons was not significantly different between farm and urban families. Unfortunately, Jacobsen's correlational analysis did not provide a conclusive measure of consensus, since scores with very similar means can be uncorrelated. Even though greater orientation toward parents than peers has been shown to correlate with rural youths' perceptions of parental support (Floyd and South, 1972; Larson, 1974b), at least one study has suggested that rural adolescents are no more parent oriented than urban teenagers (Brittain, 1969). Therefore, it appears that the evidence regarding the relative closeness of rural adolescents to their parents is inconclusive, given the lack of research at present. Much more work is needed in this area, especially in comparing the quality of marital relationships to the quality of parent-child relationships. Larson (1974b) has reported a moderate correlation between marital satisfaction and the rural adolescent's perception of the quality of his relationships with his parents. In our Kansas data we compared adolescents' perceptions of 128 aspects of family life regarding their interaction with their parents and their parents' marital relationships. Only seven items revealed rural-urban differences, only one more than would be expected by chance. Hence, our preliminary findings are that, other than in the areas of satisfaction, rural and urban adolescents perceive their relationships with their families similarly. In the area of sibling relationships within rural families, virtually nothing can be stated, since so little work has been done with sibling relationships in general (Cicirelli, 1977; Pfouts, 1976). Brown (1952) and Bultena (1969) have commented very briefly on sibling relationships, but they have dealt only with those siblings who have begun their own families. It is obvious that much more research is needed before we can answer questions about how brothers and sisters interact in rural families or how parents deal with conflicts between siblings.

Correlates of Marital and Family Satisfaction

So far there has been no firm indication that rural families differ from urban families in overall levels of family satisfaction. However, it is possible that the relative importance of sources of family satisfaction differs between rural and urban families. Lacking previous research on the matter, we explored the relative importance of satisfaction with children and marriage for perceptions of family satisfaction, using our rural and urban Kansas samples. Our findings are presented in Table 7.3. It appears either that rural females conceive of family satisfaction more in terms of marital satisfaction or that marital satisfaction is a more important determinant of their sense of family satisfaction. Otherwise, the correlations are notable for their similarity rather than for their differences.

Marital Satisfaction in Rural Families

A review of the literature can give us some guidance concerning marital

Table 7.3
Zero-order Correlations between Family Satisfaction and Selected Components of Family Satisfaction as Perceived by Rural and Urban Spouses; Differences between Correlations within and between Rural and Urban Groups.

Groups		Components		Differences Across Components Within Groups
		Satisfaction With Children	Satisfaction With Marriage	
Rural				
	Husbands	.51***(73)[a]	.72***(74)	-.21**
	Wives	.36***(78)	.64***(83)	-.28**
Urban				
	Husbands	.59***(88)	.62***(76)	-.03[ns]
	Wives	.57***(93)	.57***(97)	.00[ns]
Differences Between Groups For Each Component				
	Husbands	-.08[ns]	.10[ns]	
	Wives	-.21*	.07[ns]	

*p   .05
**p   .01
***p .001
a - N after missing data have been deleted

satisfaction in rural families, although the issues often have been covered very thinly. Marital satisfaction appears to decrease, on the average, as family size increases for both rural and urban families (Corrales, 1974; Larson, 1974b; Miller, 1976). Joint decision making seems to be associated with higher marital satisfaction in both rural and urban couples (Evans and Smith, 1969; Jeries, 1977). Open communication and marital satisfaction were correlated in Corrales's (1974) research comparing rural and urban couples in Minnesota. Mutual power over each other was associated with marital happiness in Bahr's (1974) rural sample. However, Thornton-Stahura (1976) and Burchinal (1961) suggest that the causes of marital satisfaction may differ from rural to urban areas. De Lissovoy (1973) also noted that standard predictors of marital success did not always operate in his study of disadvantaged young rural couples. However, our Kansas data reveal few rural-urban differences in sources of marital satisfaction (Barnes, 1980). Again, therefore, we are in the position of proposing further research.

Conclusion

Burchinal (1964) and Smith and Zopf (1970), among others, have predicted a convergence of rural and urban values. Certainly, the broad view of the scanty literature that is available and our own preliminary analysis of Kansas survey data suggest that major rural-urban differences in the dynamics of family relationships may be rare. Changes in rural family functioning have occurred, however, and we don't know if the antecedents of these familial changes are the same or different for urban and rural families (Coward and Smith, 1981).

The situation poses a difficult dilemma: rural practitioners need to know more about the rural family, but researchers are probably hesitant to continue research in an area that appears to have little promise for finding significant differences but is, in many respects, a costly source of respondents due to the distances involved. Perhaps if researchers will follow the lead of intuitive hypotheses provided by those working with rural families and use a variety of research designs complementary to survey methods, the dilemma will be lessened. Furthermore, researchers may find more advanced methods of statistical analysis useful in clarifying the direct and indirect effects of rurality while controlling for confounding demographic and socioeconomic factors (Schumm, Southerly, and Figley, 1980).

Several issues seem important for further research. First, premarital relationship development among noncollege rural populations has scarcely been studied, especially in terms of the current major theoretical frameworks. Second, the impact of the larger size of the rural family has seldom been controlled for in rural-urban studies. Since increasing family size does appear to complicate family relations, lack of control for this variable could easily distort the interpretation of how rural and urban families differ. Since children may have different meaning for rural families (Burchinal, 1964), it is also important to assess the rural families' perception of larger family size.

Another area of particular interest is the divorce differential between rural and urban families. Is the cause of the differential related to rural pressures against divorce? Lewis and Spanier (1979) have listed a variety of factors that measure the threshold level beyond which couples with low-quality marriages choose to divorce. The factors include marital expectations, commitment, tolerance, religious doctrine and faith, external pressures and social stigma, divorce law and legal aid available, as well as real and perceived alternatives to the current family situation. What happens as a rural area becomes urbanized? How does the threshold change as a result of factors related to urbanization? Is there a sharp increment in divorces, as dissatisfied couples decide to no longer accept their situation? There may be a greater perceived need for community education programs designed to improve the quality of marriage, as some couples seek to raise the quality of their marriage rather than opt for separation or divorce. However, programs based on urban values may run the risk of changing threshold levels without changing the level of marital quality, since the former may be more easily changed than the latter. In such cases, programs might appear to "backfire," actually increasing the divorce rate. Program design, therefore, should consider both threshold factors and the direct antecedents of marital quality. Does urbanization of a rural area foster a sharp increment in divorces with rapid exposure to urban norms, perhaps changing people's comparison levels for evaluating the value of continuing less than satisfying commitments? How substantial and what are the needs of the group of spouses who in an urban setting would file for divorce but stick out an unhappy situation because of community pressures? The implications for rural practioners are evident, especially in terms of "rocking the boat" with programs based on more urban values.

Our investigations of family satisfactions between rural and urban families yielded few rural-urban differences. However, our sample of rural adolescents did appear to evaluate family life more positively than did urban adolescents. Since they did not differ significantly on variables thought to be causally related to family satisfaction (for example, family violence and communication patterns), it may be that rural adolescents are more tolerant of their families' problems. Another difference more evident in our Kansas sample was a trend for rural wives to differ from urban wives in their evaluations of family life. Rural spouses in our sample appeared to evaluate their marital satisfaction as more critical to their family satisfaction, but also to perceive quality of life more in terms of both family and nonfamily satisfactions than urban spouses. More research is needed to determine whether these effects represent causal relationships or reflect different ways of defining the quality of life and family satisfaction. The data also posed some interesting questions, inasmuch as there were some indications that rural wives were more satisfied with their sexual relations and with the division of labor (tasks and responsibilities) than were urban wives.

Policy and Program Implications

Policymakers and human service professionals responsible for the delivery of rural family programs do not have the benefit of adequate research findings. However, it remains to be demonstrated that primary family relationships differ in any consistent, substantial manner from rural to urban areas. Regional policy should probably allocate funding on the basis of local needs, as reported by family specialists, rather than on any rural-urban formula per se.

In terms of program design, the key word is flexibility, allowing practitioners freedom to match programs with localized needs. Further research should permit generalization beyond existing state-level studies that may reflect regional differences as much as rural-urban differences.

The family specialist who is in close contact with the community being served must remain a major source of input in statewide program planning and regional policy analysis. Current research is presently most useful for stimulating the professional intuition of the family specialist rather than conclusively providing policy guidelines. As more carefully designed studies are performed and analyzed with methods realistically geared to the complexities of family life, research can become more useful in the creation and implementation of policies pertaining to rural families.

Notes

1. This research was supported through funds from the Kansas Agricultural Experiment Station, under Organized Research Project No. 0935, Contribution No. 80-58-B, Department of Family and Child Development, College of Home Economics, Kansas State University.

2. The "Kansas data" referred to in this chapter consists of the responses of eighty-three rural and ninety-eight urban families to a survey conducted by the authors and Dr. Anthony P. Jurich in the fall of 1977 and spring of 1978 as Kansas's contribution to the NC-128 Technical Committee of the research grant OR No. 0935, "Quality of Life and Area of Residence," USDA Cooperative Research. The rural sample was collected in Neodesha, Kansas (population 4,500), and the urban sample in Wichita, Kansas (population 260,000). Further information on regional and state publications from the project data are available upon request from the second author.

The research project NC-128, "Quality of Life as Influenced by Area of Residence," is sponsored by the Agricultural Experiment Stations of Arizona, California, Colorado, Illinois, Indiana, Iowa, Kansas, Michigan, Minnesota, Missouri, Nebraska, Nevada, Ohio, and Texas in cooperation with the Science and Education Administration, Cooperative Research, and the U.S. Department of Agriculture.

3. Formulas from Cohen and Cohen (1975) for comparing correlation coefficients from within the same and across different samples were used for this analysis. The SES measure was computed from the sum of three questions that assessed perceived adequacy of income, satisfaction with income, and satisfaction with standard of living. Single items were used to assess perceived family satisfaction and quality of life.

References

Andrews, F. M., and S. B. Withey. *Social Indicators of Well-Being: Americans' Perceptions of Life Quality.* New York: Plenum, 1976.

Bahr, S. J. "Conjugal Power and Marital Satisfaction." *Family Perspective,* 1974, 9 (1), 19–29.

Barnes, H. L. "The Impact of Empathy, Congruence and Regard on Satisfaction with Family Relationships: A Cross Generational Study." Unpublished thesis, Kansas State University, 1980.

Baumert, G. and E. Lupri. "New Aspects of Rural-Urban Differentials in Family Values and Family Structure." *Current Sociology,* 1963, 12, 46–54.

Bayer, A. E. "Sexist Students in American Colleges: A Descriptive Note." *Journal of Marriage and the Family,* 1975, 37 (2), 391–398.

Beck, E. W. and L. G. Burchinal. "Comparisons of Spousal Relations, Community Participation, and Kinship Relation Patterns Between Farm and Nonfarm Families." A paper presented at the Midwest Sociological Society meeting, Omaha, April, 1961.

Beers, H. W. "A Portrait of the Farm Family in Central New York State." *American Sociological Review*, 1937, 2, 591–600.

Blood, R. O., Jr. "The Division of Labor in City and Farm Families." *Marriage and Family Living*, 1958, 20 (2), 170–174.

Blood, R. O., Jr. and D. M. Wolfe. *Husbands and Wives*. Glencoe, Illinois: Free Press, 1960.

Bollman, S. R., V. M. Moxley, and N. C. Elliott. "Family and Community Activities of Rural Nonfarm Families with Children." *Journal of Leisure Research*, 1975, 7 (1), 53–62.

Brittain, C. V. "A Comparison of Rural and Urban Adolescents with Respect to Peer vs. Parent Compliance." *Adolescence*, 1969, 4 (13), 59–68.

Brown, J. S. "The Conjugal Family and the Extended Family Group." *American Sociological Review*, 1952, 17, 297–306.

Bultena, G. L. "Rural-Urban Differences in the Familial Interaction of the Aged. *Rural Sociology*, 1969, 34 (1), 5–15.

Bumpass, L. L. and J. A. Sweet. "Differentials in Marital Stability: 1970." *American Sociological Review*, 1972, 37, 754–766.

Burchinal, L. G. "Correlates of Marital Satisfaction for Rural Married Couples." *Rural Sociology*, 1961, 26, 282–289.

_____. "The Rural Family of the Future." In J. H. Copp (ed.), *Our Changing Rural Society: Perspectives and Trends*. Ames, Iowa: Iowa State University Press, 1964.

Burgess, E. W. (ed.) White House Conference on Child Health and Protection: "The Adolescent in the Family." Report of the Subcommittee on the Function of House Activities in the Education of the Child. New York: Appleton-Century-Croft, 1934.

Burgess, E. W. and L. S. Cottrell. *Predicting Success or Failure in Marriage*. Englewood Cliffs, N.J.: Prentice-Hall, 1938.

Campbell, A., P. E. Converse, and W. L. Rodgers. *The Quality of American Life: Perceptions, Evaluations, and Satisfactions*. New York: Russell Sage, 1976.

Cicirelli, V. G. "Family Structure and Interaction: Sibling Effects on Socialization. In M. McMillan and H. Sergio (eds.), *Child Psychiatry: Treatment and Research*. New York: Brunner/Mazel, 1977.

Cogswell, B. E. and M. B. Sussman. "Family and Fertility: The Effects of Experience." In W. R. Burr, R. Hill, R. I. Nye, and I. L. Reiss (eds.), *Contemporary Theories About the Family: Research Based Theories*, Vol. 1. New York: Free Press, 1979, 180–202.

Cohen, J., and P. Cohen. *Applied Multiple Regression/Correlation Analysis for the Behavioral Sciences*. New York: Wiley, 1975.

Corrales, R. G. "The Influence of Family Life Cycle Categories, Marital Power, Spousal Agreement, and Communication Styles upon Marital

Satisfaction in the First Six Years of Marriage." Ph.D. dissertation, University of Minnesota, 1974. *Dissertation Abstracts International,* 1974, 35, 3141A. University Microfilms No. 74-26, 179.

Coward, R. T. and W. M. Smith, Jr. "Families in Rural Society." In D. A. Dillman and D. S. Hobbs (eds.), *Rural Society: Research Issues for the 1980s.* Boulder, Colorado: Westview Press, 1981, forthcoming.

Defronzo, J. "Cross-sectional Areal Analysis of Factors Affecting Marital Fertility: Actual Versus Relative Income." *Journal of Marriage and the Family,* 1976, 38 (4), 669–676.

de Lissovoy, V. "High School Marriages: A Longitudinal Study." *Journal of Marriage and the Family,* 1973, 35 (2), 245–255.

Duvall, E. M., and A. B. Motz. "Are Country Girls So Different?" *Rural Sociology,* 1945, 10, 263–274.

Edwards, J. N. and A. Booth. "Sexual Behavior In and Out of Marriage: An Assessment of Correlates." *Journal of Marriage and the Family,* 1976, 38 (1), 873–881.

Evans, R. H. and N. R. Smith. "A Selected Paradigm of Family Behavior." *Journal of Marriage and the Family,* 1969, 31 (3), 512–517.

Fischer, C. S. "The Effect of Urban Life on Traditional Values." *Social Forces,* 1975, 53 (3), 420–432.

Floyd, H. H., Jr. and D. R. South. "Dilemma of Youth: The Choice of Parents or Peers as a Frame of Reference for Behavior." *Journal of Marriage and the Family,* 1972, 34 (4), 627–634.

Glenn, N. D. and J. P. Alston. "Rural-Urban Differences in Reported Attitudes and Behavior." *The Southwestern Social Science Quarterly,* 1967, 47, 381–400.

Goode, W. J. *After Divorce.* Glencoe, Illinois: Free Press, 1956.

Gurin, G., J. Veroff, and S. Feld. *Americans View Their Mental Health.* New York: Basic Books, 1960.

Hafstrom, J. L., M. M. Dunsing, and A. W. Gustafson. "Early Background and Later Life Style." *Illinois Research,* 1974, 16 (4), 18–19.

Hynson, L. M., Jr. "Rural-Urban Differences in Satisfaction among the Elderly." *Rural Sociology,* 1975, 40 (1), 64–66.

Jacobsen, R. B., K. J. Berry, and K. F. Olson. "An Empirical Test of the Generation Gap: A Comparative Intrafamily Study." *Journal of Marriage and the Family,* 1975, 37 (4), 841–852.

Jeries, N. "Wives' Perceptions of Marital Decision Making." *Journal of Home Economics Research,* 1977, 5 (3), 146–153.

Landis, P. H. *Rural Life in Process.* New York: McGraw-Hill, 1948.

____. "Two Generations of Rural and Urban Women Appraise Marital Happiness." Pullman, Washington: Washington Agricultural Experiment Station Bulletin No. 524, March 1951.

Larson, L. E. "System and Subsystem Perception of Family Roles." *Journal of Marriage and the Family,* 1974, 36 (1), 123–138 (a).

____. "An Examination of the Salience Hierarchy During Adolescence: The Influence of the Family." *Adolescence,* 1974, IX (35), 317–332 (b).

Larson, L. E. and N. Stehr. "The Family as an Area of Specialization in Sociology." *International Journal of Sociology of the Family,* 1973, 3, 198–206.

Lederer, W. J. and D. D. Jackson. *The Mirages of Marriage.* New York: W. W. Norton, 1968.

Lewis, R. A. and G. B. Spanier. "Theorizing about the Quality and Stability of Marriage." In W. R. Burr, R. Hill, R. E. Nye, and I. L. Reiss (eds.), *Contemporary Theories About the Family: Research-Based Theories,* Vol. I. New York: Free Press, 1979, 268–294.

Lind, R. W. "Sex Knowledge, Birth Control, and Marital Attitudes of a Rural Population." *Journal of Home Economics Research,* 1976, 5 (1), 47–53.

Lowe, G. D. and C. W. Peek. "Location and Lifestyle: The Comparative Explanatory Ability of Urbanism and Rurality." *Rural Sociology,* 1974, 39 (3), 392–420.

Lydgate, W. A. "The Chief Faults of Wives—and Husbands." *Redbook,* June 1946, 28–29, 121–122, 126.

McVoy, E. C. and L. Nelson. "Satisfaction in Living: Farm versus Village." Minneapolis, Minnesota: Minnesota Agricultural Experiment Station Bulletin 370, 1943.

Miller, B. C. "A Multivariate Developmental Model of Marital Satisfaction." *Journal of Marriage and the Family,* 1976, 38 (4), 643–657.

Mitchell, R. M. "Paths to Happiness: Residence Locality and Interpersonal Relations." Ph.D. dissertation, University of Notre Dame, 1976. *Dissertation Abstracts International,* 1976, 37, 3944A–3945A. University Microfilms, No. 76-27, 291.

Mueller, C. W. and H. Pope. "Marital Instability: A Study of Its Transmission Between Generations." *Journal of Marriage and the Family,* 1977, 39 (1), 83–93.

Nelson, L. *Rural Sociology.* New York: American Book Company, 1948.

Nye, F. I. "Adolescent-parent Adjustment—Rurality as a Variable." *Rural Sociology,* 1950, 15, 334–339.

Nye, F. I. and F. M. Berardo. *The Family: Its Structure and Interaction.* New York: MacMillan, 1973.

Palisi, B. J. "Wife's Statuses and Husband-wife Companionship in an Australian Metropolitan Area." *Journal of Marriage and the Family,* 1977, 39 (1), 185–191.

Pfouts, J. H. "The Sibling Relationship: A Forgotten Dimension." *Social Work,* 1976, 21 (3), 200–204.

Rokeach, M. *The Nature of Human Values.* New York: The Free Press, 1973.

Rosenblatt, P. C., A. Nevaldine, and S. L. Titus. "Farm Families: Relation of Significant Attributes of Farming to Family Interaction." *International Journal of Sociology of the Family,* 1978, 8, 89–99.

Safilios-Rothschild, C. "Family Sociology or Wives' Family Sociology? A Cross-cultural Examination of Decision-making." *Journal of Marriage and the Family,* 1969, 31 (2), 290–301.

Schumm, W. R., W. T. Southerly, and C. R. Figley. "Stumbling Block or

Stepping Stone: Path Analysis in Family Studies." *Journal of Marriage and the Family,* 1980, 42, 251–262.

Sewell, W. H. "Rural Sociological Research, 1936–1965." *Rural Sociology,* 1965, 30 (4), 428–451.

Sheeley, A., P. H. Landis, and V. Davies. "Marital and Family Adjustment in Rural and Urban Families of Two Generations." Pullman, Washington: Washington Agricultural Experiment Station Bulletin 506, 1949.

Smith, T. L., and P. E. Zopf, Jr. *Principles of Inductive Rural Sociology.* Philadelphia: F. A. Davis, 1970.

Tarver, J. D. "Gradients of Urban Influence on the Educational, Employment, and Fertility Patterns of Women." *Rural Sociology,* 1969, 34 (3), 356–367.

Tarver, J. D., C. Cyrus, K. Kiser, C. Lee, and R. Moran. "Urban Influence on the Fertility and Employment Patterns of Women Living in Homogenous Areas." *Journal of Marriage and the Family,* 1970, 32 (2), 237–241.

Taves, M. J. "Farm versus Village Living: A Decade of Change." *Rural Sociology,* 1952, 17, 47–55.

Thornton-Stahura, B. "Rural-Urban Differences in Marital Happiness and Family Satisfaction: Towards a General Model." Mimeographed paper, Department of Sociology and Anthropology, Purdue University, 1976.

Thorpe, A. C. "Patterns of Family Interaction in Farm and Town Homes." East Lansing, Michigan: Michigan Agricultural Experiment Station Technical Bulletin 260, 1957.

U.S. Bureau of the Census. "Special Studies: Social and Economic Characteristics of the Metropolitan and Nonmetropolitan Population, 1977 and 1970." *Current Population Reports,* Series P-23, No. 75. Washington, D.C.: U.S. Government Printing Office, 1978.

van Es, J. C. and J. E. Brown, Jr. "The Rural-Urban Variable Once More: Some Individual Level Observations." *Rural Sociology,* 1974, 39 (3), 373–391.

Wilkening, E. A. and L. K. Bharadwaj. "Aspirations and Task Involvement as Related to Decision-making among Farm Husbands and Wives." *Rural Sociology,* 1968, 33, 30–45.

____. "Dimensions of Aspirations, Work Roles, and Decision-making of Farm Husbands and Wives in Wisconsin." *Journal of Marriage and the Family,* 1967, 29 (4), 703–711.

Wilkening, E. A. and D. E. Morrison. "A Comparison of Husband and Wife Responses Concerning Who Makes Farm and Home Decisions." *Marriage and Family Living,* 1963, 25, 349–351.

Wood, C. H. and F. D. Bean. "Offspring Gender and Family Size: Implications from a Comparison of Mexican Americans and Anglo Americans." *Journal of Marriage and the Family,* 1977, 39 (1), 129–139.

Woodrow, K., D. W. Hastings, and E. J. Tu. "Rural-Urban Patterns of Marriage, Divorce, and Mortality: Tennessee, 1970." *Rural Sociology,* 1978, 43 (1), 70–86.

Woods, F. J. *The American Family System.* New York: Harper, 1959.

8

INTERACTION IN FARM FAMILIES: TENSION AND STRESS[1]

Paul C. Rosenblatt and Roxanne M. Anderson

By a farm family we mean a family that raises crops or livestock, earning the largest share of its net income from that. By family we mean a coresiding collectivity of two or more people related by blood, adoption, or marriage. Although the modern farm family is in many ways more like other families than farm families were even a generation or two ago, there are some characteristics that tend to differentiate farm families from urban and from rural nonfarm families. These characteristics affect family interaction, particularly as it is linked with tension and stress. For social scientists, attention to the characteristics that tend to differentiate farm families from other families would seem to be important in developing and probing family theory. The study of farm families will also, of course, yield better understanding of the service needs of farm families and nonfarm families with similar characteristics (particularly business-operating families).

Among the characteristics of farm families that tend to differentiate them from other families are the following: family members work together on a common enterprise; compared to other families they often experience wide seasonal variations in work requirements; they may have periods (extending into years) of no or few days off from work; they are more likely to have parents and minor or adult children working together; their income comes in irregularly and is relatively unpredictable; they have an occupation requiring a very substantial cash investment; they have a high rate of "industrial" accidents; they often have to deal with important, income-related decision making; and they are relatively isolated from other families and from entertainment and services. Each of these factors is central to the discussions in this chapter. Although we emphasize generalizations, it must be remembered that farm families are quite diverse (Salamon and O'Reilly, 1979), and their diversity must eventually be taken into account.

Working Together

In North America, members of farm families, more than members of most nonfarm families, work together (Capener and Berkowitz, 1976). Husbands and wives, parents and children, grandparents and grandchildren, and siblings work together in farm enterprises much more than in nonfarm occupations. The work may be parallel or nonparallel, there may be a distinct division of labor, parallel work at the same tasks, or a certain amount of shifting around of efforts. There may be a partial hierarchical organization, a complete one, or apparent nonhierarchy; the work may involve formal, even legal, agreements. What are the consequences of working together for family interaction?

Mutual Dependence

Mutual dependence makes it hard for people to end a relationship (Coppinger and Rosenblatt, 1968; Hagood, 1949; Sorokin and Zimmerman, 1929). By definition, each needs the work of the other. In modern farm families, one may not be able to farm without the work of one's spouse or some other family member, and any breakup of the family that would divide its assets might make it economically impossible to farm. Thus, a farm family with a high level of internal tension is less likely to break up than a nonfarm family with similar tension. In fact, divorce rates, though rising in farm families, are still lower than urban rates (Brown, 1977; Kohl, 1976). There are, no doubt, many ways of explaining the lower divorce rate; one implication is that couples with high levels of tension are more likely to stay together when they are in farming than when they are not. The situation is, however, not that simple. Divorces in farm families may actually, to some extent, result from mutual dependence. Perhaps divorce is more likely in those farm couples in which the quality of the operation, the spouse's comportment, or the couple's strife makes the farm income too small.

What do people who "cannot" split up do in order to deal with their tensions? Many families delimit their contact in order to delimit tension (Rosenblatt and Titus, 1976; Rosenblatt, Titus, Nevaldine, and Cunningham, 1979; Rosenblatt, Titus, and Cunningham, 1979). Delimited contact may be harder to achieve for families locked into a mutually dependent economic relationship, and this question needs to be explored in further research.

Some couples with tense relationships actively work at alleviating tensions— for example, finding ways to be more tolerant of one another or going through painful discussion after painful discussion in an effort to work out their problems. Others try to create distance from each other—for example, devoting inordinately large amounts of time to their work or to organizations, separating from one another when both are home with television, sleep, or reading.

Women's Work

Mutual dependence in contemporary farm couples is complicated by contemporary changes in sex roles and by resistance to such changes. Although farm women of the past worked hard and may have had covert if not overt power, changes in sex roles have put pressure on some farm couples to adopt a new division of labor and of formal responsibility (see the chapter by Wilkening in this volume). Lack of role models and lack of shared expectations and understandings certainly add to the problems experienced by a farm couple (Berkowitz and Hedlund, 1979; Hannan and Katsiaouni, 1977). A nonfarm couple must work out issues of cooking and other household chores, but farm couples have to work out the details of work on the farm enterprise as well.

Although much of this chapter is written as if people of either sex may farm and people of either sex may work interchangeably, the fact is that men are usually defined as farmers and in many farm families there is relatively clear-cut division of labor by sex. Although there were women farmers at least as far back as the nineteenth century (cf. Kohl, 1979), and although there have always been farms in which men and women worked interchangeably, the sex role revolution has been making an impact in farm communities. Women are taking on more of the management aspects, and have organized groups such as WIFE (Women Involved in Farm Economics) and American Agri-Women (see Chapter 2). The change or potential change in the status and role of a farm woman can be a real source of tension for her and her family.

In many families, tensions are minimized by routinization of activities. Once routinization is disrupted—for example, because a woman takes on new management tasks—tension can become acute without the routine to protect family members from having to deal with value differences or ineffective communication. Family members can also have mixed feelings about the change, even though all see it as helpful. The sex role revolution may be occurring more in younger farm families, and perhaps in these families new patterns of relating are being worked out. All this is not to say that the battle is fought only in the home; some battles are political or legal—for example, in Saskatchewan (Women's Division, 1977) the matrimonial property law existing in 1977 did not provide any guarantee to a married woman of a share in the assets accumulated in the enterprise during her marriage.

Work Off the Farm

In many farm families, one or more family members work part or full time off the farm. Although the reasons for outside work and its effects on family relations have not been fully researched (see Chapter 2), the choice to work off the farm in some families may be partly a response to family tension—a need to get more distance, to respond to tensions resulting from economic difficulty, or to find a sense of self-worth not being found at home. A woman's work off the farm can give her a feeling of autonomy because she is producing an income of her own that she can maintain control over. The work of a family member off the farm sometimes serves to tie family members together, but such work may also put greater work demands on other family members and thus push the family apart. Research is needed to explore the implications of the rapidly increasing phenomenon of off-farm work.

Parents and Children Working Together

Parents and minor children who work together do not have the option of divorcing each other; they cannot choose to separate as spouses or other adults can. There is potential for both stress and gain in this situation, and what is stressful may change as children come closer to being adult partners in the enterprise.

Minor Children

Parents in farm families have many opportunities to interact with their children in the sense of having a wide range of work situations in which their children may be directly involved. Particularly for fathers, there tends to be more contact with offspring old enough to do chores than there is in the typical nonfarm family. The higher level of contact means that there is more opportunity for parents to have influence, particularly in the areas of work and responsibility. Socialization for completing work, for sticking to responsibilities, for pacing one's work, and for excellence at work may therefore be stronger in farm families.

For children participating in a joint enterprise, there are great gains to be realized from knowing more about what their parents do, from learning useful skills, and from knowing that they are contributing to the family. In many U.S. families there is, as a child grows up, a loss of what might be called *contact points.* The child may no longer be tucked in at night, no longer be awakened in the morning, no longer have help in dressing or in the preparation of food, no longer need an adult to provide transportation to the dentist or to a weekend activity. This reduction in the number of contact points may be necessary for a child to develop into an autonomous adult, but it also may be a source of problems. Although there is risk of tension whenever a parent monitors an offspring's chore doing (Kohl, 1976), farm parents may reduce the likelihood of some problems occurring by substituting contact points made through sharing of work or supervising the child's work for contact points that are eroded through ordinary child development. The higher level of parent-offspring contact is one explanation for the lower rates of delinquency in farm families (Economic Research Service, USDA, 1967).

The opportunity to see parents doing their daily work provides children with role models and opportunities to identify with parents (Stephens, 1979). Whereas a typical North American child may see role models primarily on television, in school, and in service occupations, a farm child is in a much better position to see what parents do and to use them as role models. This is, no doubt, among the reasons why a high proportion of farm children grow up to follow the occupation of their parents (Bratton and Berkowitz, 1976; Gasson, 1974; Hedlund and Berkowitz, 1978).

The average farm child may have many more opportunities than the average nonfarm child to feel responsible and useful (Bennett, 1969; Capener and Berkowitz, 1976; Stephens, 1979). Although farm modernization probably reduces the number of chores available for children (Stephens, 1979), for many farm children there are still clear-cut apprenticeship experiences extending over a long period of time. In fact, the training received by farm children in those areas allowed by safety and ability considerations is probably hard to duplicate in other occupations or in a school situation. Nonetheless, farm parents differ greatly in how much they encourage the development of independence and responsibility (Berkowitz and Capener, 1979).

Relationships between supervisor and the supervised have inherent sources of tension, and tension probably increases when one lives with the supervisor and when the supervisor sees the work requirement as open ended, as some farm parents do. Consequently, children growing up in farm families may have more need than children in most nonfarm families to find school or other interests to serve as "work" that can keep them legitimately apart from their parents. Such activities might also help compensate for any perceived deficiency in time with peers due to the heavy requirement for work at home. Farm children may also be more likely to establish private space—a bedroom or workshop—or to perform chores by themselves in order to minimize interaction with parents.

Grown Children

Kohl (1976) found that some farm and ranch children, particularly sons, went off to school or work and then returned to work on the family farm or ranch. This temporary separation from home is a way of establishing independence and distance. It also is a means of putting off decision making about where to live and about a possible lifetime occupation. The temporary separation also may allow the younger person to acquire some expertise and to return with more adult social skills, confidence, and autonomy.

Intergenerational contact can have particularly great potential for problems when adults of several generations farm together or share common concerns for the same farm, or when a farm is shifting from control by the older generation to control by the younger. The need for apartness tends to be especially great when there are such intergenerational relations. Coworking related adults of two generations have sources of relationship tension that they would never have were they working separately or as nonrelatives on the same enterprise. A younger person may be striving for feelings of self-respect, autonomy, and a fair share of responsibility. An older person may be striving to maintain decision making, for psychic and physical territory, and for the respect merited by greater experience and by precedence and investment in the enterprise.

The potential for intergenerational differences and tension exists in many aspects of farming, including methods of coping with external stressors; issues of authority and control (particularly between father and son); legal transfer of property and division of income; issues of obligation and indebtedness; in-law relations and conflict of loyalties; and changes in women's roles as children mature. These are discussed in more detail in the remainder of this section. Generational differences can also exist in methods of coping with external stressors; the older generation may be critical of the younger generation's involvement in farm strikes or price control disputes and the younger generation's financial liberalism and extensive use of credit may represent radical departures from the older generation's way of coping with money matters.

The issues of authority and control are the most obvious sources of tensions in a multigeneration operation. To some extent, criticisms of the younger generation by the older probably represent a wish by the latter to remain indispensible. Acceptance of everything the younger people did might imply that the elders had nothing to offer. In some cases, however, the younger adult may not have the necessary skills (Hedlund and Berkowitz, 1978). One way for the older person to retain some control is to resist passing on those skills.

Another aspect of the authority-control issues involves a paradox wherein farm offspring are socialized to cherish independence and the freedom to operate their own enterprise while being more or less controlled in their work in the family enterprise (Bennett, 1969; Kohl, 1976). This paradox might be a source of tension, especially since farm offspring are socialized to value family continuity in the operation of the enterprise and to value the passing of the enterprise from one generation to the next (Berkowitz and Capener, 1978; Bratton and Berkowitz, 1976; Bubloz and Eichorn, 1964; Capener and Berkowitz, 1976; Kohl, 1976; Salamon and Keim, 1979). The tension and the paradox are most galling when an adult offspring, possibly even well into middle age (Coughenar and Kowalski, 1977), is still operating under the supervision or at least partial control of parents. In many parts of the world, it is not unusual or even considered undesirable for adults to be under the control of their parents (for example, see LeVine, 1965, for some parts of sub-Saharan Africa; Wolf, 1968, for some Taiwanese families), but in North America, where independence is greatly valued, parental supervision of adult offspring has the potential to make the younger adults feel miserable and angry. This is surely one reason why the incorporation of an adult offspring into the family enterprise is a source of tension for so many families (Benedict, 1968; Bubloz and Eichorn, 1964). Kohl (1976) has suggested that in farm and ranch families in which there are several sons who might be incorporated into the enterprise, the son who gets along best with his father is most likely to be recruited into the enterprise even though that son's easy-goingness may be inconsistent with valuing of independence.

In family farms, the intergenerational tensions seem most often to exist between father and son. Noncommunication is alleged to be a problem in multigenerational operations (for example, see Bubloz and Eichorn, 1964). There is evidence, however, that these tensions are often reduced by the wife/mother working as peacemaker (Kohl, 1976), but use of a "neutral" peacemaker and relayer of communications can reduce communication to the point where crucial coordination is done poorly or not at all.

Another intergenerational issue is how to divide up the farm income fairly—how and when to decide that the younger generation gets a more equitable, equal, or greater share and is no longer of dependent offspring or "farmhand" status. Eventually this role and power shift may become the source of great tension.

It is not uncommon, particularly since more farm transfers or partial transfers now occur while the older farmer is still alive (Gasson, 1974, for

Great Britain), for multigeneration farm operations to be defined by legal agreement. This is partly a hedge against tax problems, particularly if one of the partners in the operation dies, but it is our impression that people too often believe that legal agreements are all that is necessary to solve inter-generation tension problems. As a result, they fail to develop the necessary system of mutual understanding, tolerance, and acceptance, and when tensions arise, they are even more upset because they thought the legal agreement would suffice.

Even when a farm operation involving a younger person is started without partnership arrangements with parents, often the operation is begun with help from the older generation (Bratton and Berkowitz, 1976). Research is needed on the felt and perceived obligations in such situations. For example, if the younger generation cannot afford to acknowledge the full debt to the older—perhaps because the debt is so great—the older may feel continually annoyed by the ingratitude of the younger. Or the younger generation may attempt to repay the debt to the older by doing favors or chores for the older that the older does not want done. The obligation to let someone do a favor one does not want may also be reversed, with younger adults feeling obliged to let retired parents and in-laws help with baby-sitting, cooking for a family event, or harvesting (Kohl, 1976).

In-law relations can also be a source of intergenerational differences and tension. There are feelings of conflict over loyalty and commitment in the younger person and fears of competition for loyalty and commitment by the older person. The in-marrying woman (see Kohl, 1976, and Saunders, 1979, for discussion of some of the problems of the in-marrying woman) sometimes remains a comparative outsider, while her husband is not. She may be subject to expectations placed on her by her husband or by his family and friends, or to conflicting pressures from husband and in-laws. Tension can center on her perceived or real lack of skills or lack of interest in the farm. If couples of two generations live together in a single dwelling, the re-sulting tension may cause them to move toward residential separation, for example, through purchase of a house trailer to put elsewhere on the farm-stead. But even residing in adjacent homes fails, for some, to provide adequate apartness.

As children mature, a woman's work changes. Not only is there less child-care work and more help with child care, but her children also tend to displace her from some farm work, particularly if they discontinue schooling at a com-paratively early age (Minge-Kallman, 1978). For some farm women, this displacement is a source of stress, possibly because the loss of roles leaves them with less to do, with less sense of being useful, with less contact with spouse, or with more sense of aging (Berkowitz and Hedlund, 1979; Hedlund and Berkowitz, 1978, 1979).

Retirement

Retirement is, for many farm families, a matter of intergenerational re-lationships and, as such, may be more stressful for farm families than for many other families. In farm families retirement tends to be delayed and taken on more gradually (Kohl, 1976; Rodgers and Burdge, 1972). Farming occupies so much of one's time, and so much of one's apartness is obtained through work, that farmers are often unusually ill-prepared or ill-disposed to retire (Kohl, 1976, who also emphasized a sex difference in her data). Many farmers were born and grew up on the land they farm—the homestead. Their identification with the farm and the land itself may seem inseparable from their identity otherwise, in which case retirement is especially traumatic. One advantage of an intergenerational arrangement that allows a gradual transition in work and responsibility from the older generation to the younger is that the older person can hang on to activities that give life meaning. Salamon (1978) found that in a German-American farm community in Illinois with a tendency for early retirements, "retirement" might at first be quite active, with only gradual withdrawal from the fields while the retiree continued to help the younger generation. The long process of withdrawal in that community generally involved a gradual takeover of management and ownership by a younger family member. Thus, retirement can be seen in some farm families as not an individual act but as an extended sequence of transitions in intergenerational relationships. And for the older generation in Salamon's sample, that perception seemed part of the motivation for retirement, to help younger family members.

Whenever a married man retires and spends more time at home, there is the potential for territorial battles between husband and wife. For farm couples who have had a traditional division of labor, with much of the household space being defined as the wife's, and particularly if the farm work has been a 365-day-per-year operation (as on a dairy farm), or if the man's principal apartness activity was to do farm work, the wife will have had little experience in coping with her husband's presence around the house, and the husband will have had little experience in finding niches for himself within the house. For such couples, stresses can be severe, and the husband may struggle to resume preretirement activities. Part of the intergenerational stress in relationship between a retiring farmer and a relative who is assuming operation of the farm may be a spillover from tensions in the retiring couple. Tension also arises when there is a question of whether the retired person is capable of continuing farm work, yet insists upon doing so. The younger generation may feel guilty, in the event of an accident, for having allowed the elder to attempt the work.

Retirement brings with it a shift in sources of gratifications that affect family relationships. A retired farmer or farm widow who maintains control of substantial assets may use those assets to obtain gratification from relatives. An older person may exchange the right to use those assets, particularly farmland, for deference and attention from relatives and the chance to control the lives of those relatives (Salamon and Keim, 1979, writing of a German-American community in Illinois). For a woman, the peak of power to obtain such gratification would typically come in widowhood (Salamon and Keim, 1979).

Inheritance

The issues surrounding inheritance are relatively often a source of intense, long-term tension in farm families (Titus, Rosenblatt, and Anderson, 1979). Cash values are high, and, for most people, inheriting land may be the only way to enter into farming. The experiences surviving offspring had with the parent whose death sets off a dispute often establish the grounds for conflicts over inheritance. Several offspring may have been socialized to value continuity in farm operation, perhaps particularly continuity in family ownership and in the surname of the persons working the farm. The other children may have been socialized to have farming skills. But the entire operation often is passed to one person; if passed to several there would not be continuity in the farm as the operation of a single nuclear family, and there might not be an economically viable operation. If the operation were passed to several people for joint ownership and operation, the independence value would be violated.

There are, of course, many other factors underlying inheritance disputes in farm families—particularly competing notions of fairness and the feelings of people who have married into the family. The operation of all these factors is often complicated by the expectations or lack of expectations established in intergenerational relationships that anteceded the death. If people do not discuss openly the eventual disposition of the farm, if they have only hints and innuendoes on which to base expectations, or if different family members have been told different things, the likelihood of bitter feelings over inheritance seems great.

Family Decision Making

Families that work together have the potential to extend their decision making into more areas than families that do not work together. Unless there is a strict division of labor that confines decision making concerning the joint economic enterprise to one person, family members will wrestle with decision making on enterprise issues as well as on domestic and social issues. Although rural sociology has provided more studies of enterprise decision making than of any other farm family dynamic, there are aspects of such decision making that remain to be researched. Postponing decisions about the farm operation may be difficult and can have very harmful consequences. Decisions about expansion or major financial moves need to be made with many variables being considered simultaneously, as well as with long-range goals or plans in mind. Decisions often must allow for unknowns such as weather and market fluctuations beyond the control of the farmer. All these factors help make decisions about the enterprise very stressful.

Decision making in the farm family involves a certain concreteness or rationality that masks the relationship complexities that are also involved when decisions are made. While it is possible to calculate specifics when looking at production costs for increased acreage, and even to estimate the yield range and profit, it is not so easy to talk about or even to be aware of the interpersonal difficulties that may be getting in the way of a decision. While difficulty in decision making is not unique to farm families, relationship factors that prevent consideration of all the necessary variables, that produce premature closure, or that lead to avoidance of a decision often have more serious consequences when the decision is enterprise related. The following are two examples of decision making processes on the farm that may be complicated by relationship issues.

1. Do farm families in which the adults have trouble making joint decisions differ from farm families that do not have decision-making problems in how and when they make decisions and in how these decisions are acted on? For example, if husband and wife do not trust one another, or if one of them has trouble keeping to commitments, do they put off making farm enterprise decisions? Or are decisions sometimes made unilaterally and then undermined by other members of the family? If a couple's joint decision processes typically lead to anger at one another, do they run a more conservative and unchanging enterprise?

2. The literature on families in treatment suggests that families often argue about issues that are not the real issues. For example, a couple might disagree about where to go on a Saturday night when the real issue is that A feels B is trying to be domineering, and B feels that A is discounting his or her feelings or that A cannot stand being with B, and B wants to force contact. Decision making about the enterprise may also have this quality. A family might, for example, discuss expansion of the enterprise when the underlying issue is how much affection the wife feels she is getting from the husband, how much attention the children feel they are getting, or how much the husband wants his wife and children to respect him. While such extension of conflict into the decision-making arena is not unique to farm families, it can have more critical results, in that the future well-being of the family finances may be involved.

Togetherness-Apartness

It can be argued that farm families have the opportunity for unusually great togetherness and for unusually great apartness (Rosenblatt, Nevaldine, and Titus, 1978). For members of farm families more than for members of nonfarm families, work life and home life tend to occur in the same or adjacent spaces.

Working together can produce great closeness, but there is a risk in that closeness, a risk of too much togetherness (Hagood, 1949). That risk is, however, limited. High levels of togetherness seem to produce tension only for some people (Rosenblatt, Titus, and Cunningham, 1979; Rosenblatt, Titus, Nevaldine, and Cunningham, 1979). Moreover, people who work together may find ways to work closely and yet be apart. In some farm families there is a clear-cut division of labor that enables even shared work to be done with minimal interaction (Beers, 1937; Kohl, 1976).

Farm families typically have ample outdoor space in which to gain apartness from one another. To one who has grown up on a farm, the availability of space may be taken for granted and can be an influential factor in preferences in physical living space and also in interpersonal relationships. Being accustomed to or needing a lot of outdoor space is also a potential source of stress in the family if for some reason (for example, bad weather, illness, long visits from relatives) family members are confined for a period of time to a smaller amount of space.

Although many urban commuters may envy the farmer who can walk out the door in the morning and be at work, there is a potential for problems that comes from working in proximity to one's residence. This proximity may produce either too much togetherness or too much apartness. For the farmer, it is always a temptation to be drawn to work; a person who works far from home will, when home, seldom be in a position to draw apart from family members in order to do more work. The opportunity for extra work hours in the farm family can create too much apartness in family relations. However, too much togetherness can also occur if somebody works in proximity to family members. Work at a task requiring concentration or continuity can be frustrating and relatively inefficient if interrupted. Although the proximity of work to home confers a possible advantage for togetherness, in that contacting another family member becomes relatively easy, it is probably harder to achieve a break from work and still maintain privacy. It is likely that many families must work out understandings about when a nearby family member is or is not available for interaction.

Many people develop interests in activities that help them to get apartness— reading, hobbies, television watching, and so on. For people on a farm, there may be less need to develop alternative activities; the farm work itself is always available to provide apartness and there is considerable pressure (from norms of respectability and success, from economic necessity, and from personal standards of excellence) to maximize production. Even if farm family members are together most nights, as are members of many nonfarm families, they may have less incentive for developing apartness activities since they still may have less time together than many nonfarm families, and, in some farm families, the time will be curtailed by early bedtimes. Consequently, some time put in on farm work may be done in part to just gain apartness.

Labor-saving and time-saving technological advances in farm and household equipment may increase the potential togetherness time of the farm family, and this may be a plus or a minus for them. There is evidence that full-time housewives in the United States have not reduced work time as a result of labor-saving inventions. These inventions have merely made it possible to do more housework and to meet higher standards. For farm operators in America the same may hold true—labor-saving milking machines, conveyor belt barn cleaners, and new devices for spraying, weeding, or harvesting, may merely increase the amount that is done in the time available and raise the standard of excellence the farmer attempts to meet. Farmers may expand the farm operation when they get new labor-saving equipment because they want to increase income, to buy even more machinery, to make full use of the new machinery, or to improve or expand buildings to house the new machinery. New equipment may replace the labor of somebody other than the farmer—for example, of a son who has gone off to college. However, machinery that cuts down a farmer's work time may bring about undesired increases in togetherness, particularly in families that deal with tensions by getting apart. Thus, in order to delimit tension, while at the same time increasing income, a farm operator with new machinery may merely work more land, add more animals to the herd, or add more fruit trees.

This perspective suggests that there are some noneconomic factors, such as togetherness-apartness, involved in economic decisions. It may not be a good economic risk to raise more animals or to plant on the farm's least productive acres, yet some farmers may take such risks because it maintains personal peace or peace in the family. An implicit risk in cutting down on herds or flocks or in planting less is that one may have an uncomfortably large amount of contact with family members.

Seasonal Variations in Work Requirements

Some North American farm families experience wide seasonal variations in requirements for farm work (Rosenblatt, Nevaldine, and Titus, 1978). There are times when most waking hours are invested, by at least some family members, in necessary farm work and other times when there is no pressing work. Both kinds of time expenditure may put stress on family relationships. During heavy work seasons family members may have insufficient contact, and the contact they have may be unrewarding because of fatigue, irritability over lack of contact, and tension over the work itself. During the off-season there is the risk of too much togetherness, of minor irritations being repeated so often that they become major problems, and of insufficient privacy.

Families may, however, have adaptations to the togetherness-apartness problems that accompany seasonal variations in work. They may routinize togetherness during heavy work seasons, so there are frequently times (for example, meal times) when family members can count on being together. Families may also routinize apartness during seasons of little work, for example, through separate visiting, through organizational involvements, through somebody taking a temporary job or a Cooperative Extension course, or through doing work saved up for the light season (equipment maintenance and repair, planning and preparation for the next work with crops, sewing, house painting, building repair). Routinization may provide valuable togetherness or apartness that otherwise might not be achieved.

Invariant Work Requirements

Daily work that is rarely or never interrupted by sabbath, holiday, or vacation—a condition particularly common to dairy farming—can be stressful. Family members find it difficult to do things they would like to do (for example, visit relatives or sleep late). Illnesses have to be ignored or tolerated despite discomfort or risk. When the need arises, some families may hire someone to do chores, swap time with another farm family, or seek help from retired relatives, but these options are not available for all people or every time the help is needed. For many farm families, the lack of flexibility in meeting needs for free time or for help, the lack of novelty, and the fatigue and boredom of the constant and heavy work routine only serve to augment family tension (Rosenblatt, Nevaldine, and Titus, 1978). These sorts of problems also exist for other families with constant heavy work requirements on at least one family member—for example, single-parent families or two-parent families with young children. Many families deal with tension by getting apart (Rosenblatt and Cunningham, 1976; Rosenblatt and Titus, 1976), and in farm families already separated by the daily work routine, even more separation may be sought by family members trying to cope with added tensions arising from that daily routine.

Unpredictable Weather as a Source of Tension

A conspicuous feature of the mass media in farming communities is the high priority given to weather reports and predictions. Weather is perhaps relatively unlikely to have a uniting effect on the family. Hailstorms, tornadoes, a too-early freeze, or extended periods of drought or rain can mean economic hardship or even financial ruin. Thus, fluctuations in the weather can easily result in increased stress in family relations. The stress may be aggravated by a sense that there are right or wrong things to do in order to minimize the economic effect of the weather. If a decision to plant a drought-resistant but low-profit crop, for example, turns out to have been wrong, family members may blame one another for the bad choice. Even if weather related decisions do not lead to recriminations and even if there is no clear economic stress resulting from bad weather, attempts to cope with weather problems are often stressful. Extremely long hours put in to "beat the rain," for example, add to the strain on family relations.

Cash-Flow Problems

Many farm families experience cash-flow problems (Keefe and Burk, 1967). Even though the farm assets may be valued at a very high level, there are times when there is no spare cash, when there have not been significant sales for some time, when loan payments are due, or when some other factor pushes the demand for cash up to or beyond the supply. There are also times when very large amounts of cash are at hand, particularly when a large sale has been made. These cash flow problems can have a wide range of impacts. One would expect that when little cash is available family disputes over how to spend what little money is available might arise. In anticipation of such times, some family members might be very frugal at other times, whereas other family members may want to spend at least a substantial fraction of a large amount of cash as soon as they get it. Thus, family conflict can occur both at times of low cash availability and at times of high cash availability. End of the year income-tax season is also a stressful time, both because of low cash availability and because it is a time of reckoning regarding the status of the farm (cf. Salamon, 1976). Internal Revenue Service requirements for farm tax returns may add to the burden.

Requirement of Substantial Cash Investments

Farming requires a very substantial cash investment. This means that many people who would like to farm and who have been socialized to farm cannot go into farming. No doubt some of those people—for example, those with many siblings—grow up with an orientation toward assuming a nonfarming occupation (Straus, 1964), but many farm offspring (even some who say they plan to do something other than farm), though oriented toward farming are unable to get into it full time. It seems important to us to investigate what happens to them and how their feelings of self-worth and their relations with relatives and friends who still can farm are affected by their inability to enter the family occupation.

Other people who are able to go into farming are able to do so only because of help from parents or other relatives or because of inherited land or money. When older family members hold so much financial power over younger ones, there is frequently additional stress in family relations. Younger family members may resent that power; many may be more careful in relations with the people who have so much power. Between young and old, there may be closer relations in some cases because of the financial bond, but in others there may be distance and loss of spontaneity.

Salamon and Keim (1979), studying a German-American community in which many widows had substantial land holdings, found that the landholding widows were in some cases "courted" by younger kin. Although some younger people in this situation might be insincere and nonconfrontive, the situation does seem to bind younger and older generations together and to minimize the isolation felt by the widows. In fact, some older female landowners distributed use of their land to young people in several different nuclear families, thus ensuring themselves of a wider range of contacts.

The cash requirements for farming lead many people to work extremely hard and to skimp for decades (Kohl, 1976). For people in that situation, any expenditure not absolutely necessary can be a source of tension. In many families, battles recur over expenditures (Kohl, 1976), with the farmer arguing that purchases for the enterprise (such as a tractor) should have precedence, and other family members arguing that many of the purchases for the enterprise are no more necessary than purchases they desire. Nonetheless, it seems clear that the success of the enterprise is dependent on all members being willing to forgo consumption for the sake of accumulating income-generating resources (Kohl, 1976).

High Rate of Industrial Accident

Farming is much riskier physically than many occupations. Farm families must have the capacity to care for injured family members and to cover the work their injuries prevent them from doing, but many families lack this capacity or have it only for short-run emergencies. There is no such thing as sick leave or sick-leave pay in farm families. Bubloz and Eichorn (1964) suggest that one can perhaps count on neighbors and friends in the short run but not in the long run. Hence, as can be expected, work injuries are more often a source of relationship tension in the typical farm family than in the typical nonfarm family.

In their study of farm families in which a farmer suffered from heart disease, Bubloz and Eichorn (1964) suggested that another issue arises when someone is injured or ill—control. A man who is ill is, to some extent, supposed to be cared for by his wife and perhaps by other family members. Yet if his work has dominated his life and if his apartness has been obtained primarily through work, it will be hard for him to stay away from work. In fact, many farmers may threaten health and life rather than give up valued work. Conflict in such cases arises over the man trying to get back to work while his wife or other caretakers try to keep him from overdoing things.

Alcohol use may also be associated with control battles, and of course the use of alcohol on the farm brings with it added risk in the operation of farm equipment. Alcoholism is not particularly uncommon on farms, and its effects in terms of injury are more common on farms than in work places in which errors rarely bring physical risk. More generally, tensions and responses to tension (such as alcohol consumption) add safety risks to farming; for farm families more so than for many nonfarm families, keeping family tensions minimal pays off in terms of minimizing work-related injuries.

High Economic Risks

For farm families, economic risks are also high. Income is unpredictably variable, dependent on a vast number of factors including weather, plant and animal diseases, changes in trade laws, regulations and agreements, and changes in the cost of petroleum. This unpredictability might be exciting to some, but for many it creates tension that affects family relations. Worries about economic conditions may lead to irritability; decisions that turned out to be wrong may lead to recriminations and defensiveness. Although we know of no research in the area, it does not seem unreasonable to expect a higher tension level in families with greater unpredictability of income and more opportunity to distribute blame when income is low.

It is possible, however, that since control is substantially in the hands of others, that decisions made in Washington or in the Middle East have enormous influence on one's own fate, families feel less responsible and less tense than we might think. In fact, the USDA, bankers, and other external human agencies that affect farm income may be seen as the enemy by many farm families, thus serving as a target for hostility and as an in-group-uniting factor, as enemy out-groups do for any in-group. Farmers have a substantial latitude to use and to manipulate these agencies (Bennett, 1967), and these agencies may be used as well as something to blame, to be angry at, and to unite against.

Isolation

Although the modern farm family is much less isolated than farm families were in the past, they are still relatively isolated, with some, like western ranch families, for example, quite remote geographically. This isolation can be measured in terms of the greater distance that has to be traveled to reach friends, relatives, shopping, or services; the paucity of public transportation; and the greater likelihood that roads may be temporarily impassable. There may also be greater dispersion of the places family members want to visit, so that for several people to be away from home simultaneously several cars or pickup trucks or a great deal of chauffeuring would be necessary. Farm family members may therefore spend more time together driving places, and for some that may help to meet togetherness needs. For others that may risk too much togetherness, though vehicle radios can help minimize interaction (cf. Rosenblatt and Russell, 1975). In addition, there is evidence from a German-American farm community that farm women tend to be more isolated than farm men (Salamon and Keim, 1979). This sex difference in isolation may vary among families, but it might be true of most when there are young children. Although telephones have, to a degree, lessened the isolation of a homebound person, the party-line system may preclude phone conversation about intimate issues (Salamon and Keim, 1979).

Isolation throws family members together and means that members are less likely to have accessible confidants. The relative isolation may also mean that fewer apartness activities are pursued away from home, thus reinforcing the pattern of turning to work for apartness (Rosenblatt, Nevaldine, and Titus, 1978). The comparative isolation might also reinforce children's focus on their parents as role models.

From a systems theory perspective, isolation of the farm family may be conducive to more enmeshed dynamics between members. Often the wife/mother maintains a powerful "switchboard" position in the family, managing much of the communication (Kohl, 1976). When such a communication pattern is coupled with comparative isolation, it has the potential to make things difficult for every family member. The central person can become the one who is blamed when things go wrong; the peripheral persons may feel controlled by the central one or may feel isolated from each other (cf. Saunders, 1979).

Relative isolation must be especially unpleasant when family relations are difficult. It is harder to find others to turn to for sympathy, human contact, or safety. Others will be less available to interfere or to provide gratuitous, but still possibly useful, advice. And turning to counseling agencies for help requires more energy and effort. Isolation can, however, serve as a strengthening factor, fostering a healthy reliance of family members on each other.

Physical isolation is probably a bigger problem for an elderly person living on a farmstead. Kivett (1978) found that elderly rural widows isolated by health and transportation problems reported being frequently lonely. Although urban widows might well give a similar view of things, the scarcity of public transportation might especially be a problem for farm elderly and might intensify health problems.

Conclusion

Although we have attempted to touch on all the relevant literature on tension and stress in farm families, much of what has been discussed is speculative. All topic areas would benefit from more research, and in many topic areas the next research that is done will in fact be the first.

We have argued that farm families have, when compared to nonfarm families, some unusual but potentially powerful relationship stressors. In addition, we have discussed various noteworthy characteristics of farm families that do not necessarily result in stress but that are important distinguishing components of farm life. Potential stressors include the likelihood of family members working together. In the short term, working together may produce tension from high amounts of togetherness, the necessity of mutual dependence, or problems with parent-child relations in a work setting. Over the long term, working together may become a problem in division of income and division of labor, decisions about when retirement is desirable or necessary, and how property will be divided. With family members working together there is ample opportunity for generational issues to emerge. Other sources of tension common to farm life include the invariant work requirements of some types of farming and the great seasonal variation in work load for other types of farming. Money flow can also be seasonal and, therefore, create money and relationship management problems. Decision making on the whole may be much more stressful for the farm family since decisions are often central to its livelihood. Weather, too, can be a source of stress in the farm family. The potential for accidents is greater on the farm, and high levels of family stress may be both a cause and an effect of farm accidents. Isolation from outside influences tends to be greater for the farm family and is also a possible source of stress.

There are, of course, many intervening variables that influence how each farm family handles its own stresses. Many of the noteworthy characteristics of farm families are also potential sources for coping with and utilizing their situation. Variation also exists in the availability of community resources to help them cope with stress.

Because of their differences from nonfarm families, farm families provide unusually rich opportunities for exploring theory in a number of areas—including togetherness-apartness theory; family system theory, particularly as it pertains to multigeneration relationships; household economics and power theories; and theories having to do with relationships in retirement and later years of the life cycle.

Note

1. For comments on an earlier draft of this chapter and for ideas we have included here, we are indebted to Steven Barta, Cheryl Buehler, Patricia A. Johnson, Bonnie Kamrath, and Sandra L. Titus.

References

Beers, H. W. "A Portrait of the Farm Family in Central New York State." *American Sociological Review*, 1937, 2, 591–600.

Bennett, J. W. Microcosm-Macrocosm Relationships in North American Agrarian Society." *American Anthropologist*, 1967, 69, 441–454.

___. *Northern Plainsmen*. Chicago: Aldine, 1969.

Berkowitz, A. D. and H. R. Capener. "The Human Dimension of Family Farming." *New York's Food and Life Sciences*, 1978, 11 (3), 16–19.

___. "Socialization and Transmission Patterns in the Farm Family." *New York's Food and Life Sciences*, 1979, 12.

Berkowitz, A. D. and D. F. Hedlund. "Psychological Stress and Role Congruence in Farm Families." *Cornell Journal of Social Relations*, 1979, 14.

Bratton, C. A. and A. D. Berkowitz. "Intergenerational Transfer of the Farm Business." *New York's Food and Life Sciences Quarterly*, 1976, 9 (2), 7–9.

Brown, D. L. "Recent Changes in the Demographic Structure of the Rural Family." In R. T. Coward (ed.), *Rural Families Across the Life Span: Implications for Community Programming*. West Lafayette, Indiana: Purdue University, 1977.

Bubloz, M. J. and R. L. Eichorn. "How Farm Families Cope with Heart Disease: A Study of Problems and Resources." *Journal of Marriage and the Family*. 1964, 26, 166–173.

Capener, H. R. and A. D. Berkowitz. "The Farm Family: A Unique Organization." *New York's Food and Life Sciences Quarterly*, 1976, 9 (3), 8–11.

Coppinger, R. M. and P. C. Rosenblatt. "Romantic Love and Subsistence Dependence of Spouses." *Southwestern Journal of Anthropology*, 1968, 24, 310–319.

Coughenour, C. M. and G. S. Kowalski. "Status and Role of Fathers and Sons on Partnership Farms." *Rural Sociology*, 1977, 42, 180–205.

Economic Research Service, United States Department of Agriculture. Supplement to *Age of Transition . . . Rural Youth in a Changing Society*. Supplement to Agricultural Handbook No. 347, 1967.

Gasson, R. "The Future of the Family Farm: Psychological and Social Aspects." *The Future of the Family Farm in Europe*. London: Centre for

European Agricultural Studies, Wye College, University of London, 1974.

Hagood, M. J. "The Farm Home and Family." In C. C. Taylor, A. F. Raper, D. Ensminger, M. J. Hagood, T. W. Longmore, W. C. McKain, Jr., L. J. Ducoff, and E. A. Schuler (eds.), *Rural Life in the United States.* New York: Knopf, 1949.

Hannan, D. F. and L. A. Katsiaouni. *Traditional Families? From Culturally Prescribed to Negotiated Roles in Farm Families.* Dublin: Economic and Social Research Institute, 1977.

Hedlund, D. E. and A. D. Berkowitz. "A Developmental Approach to Social-psychological Stress in Farm Families." Unpublished manuscript, Cornell University, 1978.

____. "The Incidence of Social Psychological Stress in Farm Families." *International Journal of Sociology of the Family,* 1979, 9.

Keefe, D. R. and M. C. Burk. "Interdisciplinary Analysis of Farm-Home Interrelationships in Decision-Making and Action on the Family Farm." *American Journal of Economics and Sociology,* 1967, 26, 33–46.

Kivett, V. R. "Loneliness and the Rural Widow." *Family Coordinator,* 1978, 27, 389–394.

Kohl, S. B. *Working Together: Women and Family in Southwestern Saskatchewan.* Toronto: Holt, Rinehart & Winston of Canada, 1976.

____. "The Making of a Community: The Role of Women in an Agricultural Setting." In A. J. Lichtman and J. R. Challinor (eds.), *Kin and Communities: Families in America.* Washington, D.C.: Smithsonian Institution, 1979.

LeVine, R. A. "Intergenerational Tensions and Extended Family Structures in Africa." In E. Shanas and G. F. Streib (eds.), *Social Structure and the Family: Generational Relations.* Englewood Cliffs, New Jersey: Prentice-Hall, 1965.

Minge-Kalman, W. "Household Economy During the Peasant-to-Worker Transition in the Swiss Alps." *Ethnology,* 1978, 17, 183–196.

Rogers, E. M. and R. J. Burdge. *Social Change in Rural Societies* (2nd ed.), New York: Meredith, 1972.

Rosenblatt, P. C. and M. R. Cunningham. "Television Watching and Family Tension." *Journal of Marriage and the Family,* 1976, 38, 105–111.

Rosenblatt, P. C., A. Nevaldine, and S. L. Titus. "Farm Families: Relation of Significant Aspects of Farming to Family Interaction." *International Journal of Sociology of the Family,* 1978, 8, 89–99.

Rosenblatt, P. C. and M. G. Russell. "The Social Psychology of Potential Problems in Family Vacation Travel." *Family Coordinator,* 1975, 24, 209–215.

Rosenblatt, P. C. and S. L. Titus. "Together and Apart in the Family." *Humanitas,* 1976, 12, 367–379.

Rosenblatt, P. C., S. L. Titus, and M. R. Cunningham. "Disrespect, Tension, and Togetherness-Apartness in Marriage." *Journal of Marriage and Family Counseling,* 1979, 5, 47–54.

Rosenblatt, P. C., S. L. Titus, A. Nevaldine, and M. R. Cunningham. "Marital

System Differences and Summer Long Vacations: Togetherness-Apartness and Tension." *American Journal of Family Therapy,* 1979, 7, 77–84.

Salamon, S. "Taxing the Family Off the Farm." Paper presented at the annual meeting of the American Anthropological Association, Washington, D.C., 1976.

____. "Farm Tenancy and Family Values in East Central Illinois." *Illinois Research,* 1978, 20, 6–7.

Salamon, S. and A. M. Keim. "Land Ownership and Women's Power in a Midwestern Farming Community." *Journal of Marriage and the Family,* 1979, 41, 109–119.

Salamon, S. and S. M. O'Reilly. "Family Land and Developmental Cycles among Illinois Farmers." *Rural Sociology,* 1979, 44, 525–542.

Saunders, G. R. "Social Change and Psychocultural Continuity in Alpine Italian Family Life." *Ethos,* 1979, 7, 206–231.

Sorokin, P. and C. C. Zimmerman. *Principles of Rural-Urban Sociology.* New York: Holt, 1929.

Stephens, W. N. *Our Children Should Be Working.* Springfield, Illinois: Thomas, 1979.

Straus, M. A. "Societal Needs and Personal Characteristics in the Choice of Farm, Blue Collar, and White Collar Occupations by Farmers' Sons." *Rural Sociology,* 1964, 29, 408–425.

Titus, S. L., P. C. Rosenblatt, and R. M. Anderson. "Family Conflict Over Inheritance of Property." *Family Coordinator,* 1979, 28, 337–346.

Wolf, M. *The House of Lim.* New York: Meredith, 1968.

Women's Division, Saskatchewan Department of Labor, *Farm Women.* 1977.

9

THE CHANGING ROLES AND STATUS OF RURAL WOMEN

Linda Bescher-Donnelly
and Leslie Whitener Smith

During the last two decades, social researchers have shown renewed concern over the changes in women's roles and increased female participation in the various societal institutions. However, within the rapidly expanding literature on sex roles, comparatively little attention has been given to the rural woman and her changing roles and status in society. While rural women must address many of the same conflicts and situations as urban women, their experiences are often complicated by the somewhat unusual nature of the rural value system, labor market structure, and community organizational patterns. Thus, generalizations that purport to explain the role behavior of all women may be inadequate for understanding changing sex roles in rural areas (Heaton and Martin, 1979; O'Leary, 1978). In addition, the stereotypic image used to describe all rural women as isolated farm wives who do little else but prepare meals, raise children, and help with the farm chores is misleading. "Farm wife" is not synonymous with "rural woman," and the roles and responsibilities of women in rural areas today are much more complex and diversified than this image suggests.

This chapter examines the increasing role diversity of rural women and focuses on their role behavior, functions, and responsibilities with respect to four major societal institutions: the family, the economy, the educational system, and the political structure. Use of this structural approach allows recognition of the importance of women's roles outside of the family and also draws attention to the continued existence of restrictive conditions and limited opportunities for many rural women. In this chapter we discuss some of the ideological and structural conditions that can restrict rural women from full and fair access to all of the various life sectors and conclude with suggested directions to help improve the status and lifestyle of rural women in the future.

Most of the data analyzed here refer to the role activities of all rural women and do not specifically focus on the individual farm and nonfarm components of the rural population. In 1980, approximately 27 million women aged 16 years and over lived in nonmetropolitan areas; less than 8 percent of them lived on farms (U.S. Bureau of the Census, 1980). Despite this figure, farm women constitute an important part of the rural population, and the reader is referred to other studies (Ferra, 1977a; Huffman, 1976) that examine the role activities of these women in greater detail.

Family Roles and Attitudes

Marriage, Divorce, and Sex-Role Ideology

Numerous economic, political, and social changes occurring in the United States over the last few decades have had a profound effect on the structure of the American family and on attitudes toward marriage, childbearing, and the roles of husbands and wives within the family. These changes have affected rural families as well, but recent evidence suggests that rural women continue to view marriage and family formation as desirable and normative social patterns.

As Brown notes in the opening chapter of this collection, rural people are more likely to marry earlier, have more children, and live in larger families than people in urban areas. While the divorce rate is increasing in both rural and urban areas, rural couples still experience less marital dissolution than their urban counterparts, and rural families are more often characterized by the traditional husband-wife family pattern. National public opinion data collected during the 1960s and 1970s provide further indications of the stability of rural marriage and report that rural people generally favored increasing the difficulty of obtaining a divorce and were less likely than others to approve of sexual experiences outside of marriage (Glenn and Hill, 1977; Larson, 1978). Another study of rural youth in Pennsylvania (Willits et al., 1973, p. 7) indicated that farm residents in 1947, 1960, and 1970 were less likely than residents of either nonfarm open country or towns to approve of divorce, even "when a man and his wife feel that they can no longer remain happily married."

The importance of marriage and family roles to rural people is also reflected in the more traditional sex-role ideology maintained by rural residents. Two innovative studies have attempted to use the lyrics of country music to describe the sexual ideology and normative role behavior of rural women (Flora and Johnson, 1978; Nietzke, 1975). These studies characterize rural women as loyal, understanding wives who forgive and forget, stick by their man, and honor the "double standard" of sexual conduct. Yet, Flora and Johnson (p. 170) suggest that "some relaxation of traditional sex norms is occurring for contemporary rural women . . . if popular music is at all faithful in mirroring the sentiments of its listeners."

There are serious questions as to whether or not popular country music accurately reflects the reality of rural society or can measure the extent of changing sex norms in rural areas. However, other studies based on different types of evidence do suggest that rural men and women will become more likely to accept nontraditional lifestyles and attitudes as greater individualism, male-female equality of status, and secularization of values become more prevalent in rural areas (Larson, 1978; Willits et al., 1973). Despite this perceived movement toward a more liberal sex-role ideology in rural areas, the extent to which these changes have occurred is still an open empirical question.

Both rural and urban women experience role conflicts between their family responsibilities and their participation in activities outside of the home, especially in the labor force. However, rural women appear to be maintaining a more traditional sex-role ideology, which could affect role selection and participation. One national sample (Glenn and Hill, 1977, p. 24), for example, indicated that 53 percent of all rural women interviewed in 1976 considered "being married with children, and no full-time job to be [the] ideal lifestyle" compared to only 38 percent of urban women in the larger cities (500,000 or more). Other studies examining the traditional breadwinner-homemaker dichotomy of sex-role attitudes suggest that rural women were more traditionally oriented than urban women on such items as women's employment outside of the home, marriage desires, participation in family decision making, and priority hiring of males over females (Stokes and Willits, 1974).[1] Roberts and Kowalski (1978, p. 7), using a scale of "modern feminism" that was based on attitudes toward such issues as sex equality of employment opportunities and earnings, sharing of household chores, and conflicts between children and career, concluded that "attitudes toward the key institution of the family continue to be more traditional or less modern for female farm residents." However, there is some evidence to suggest that, over time, as rural women continue to experience greater independence, financial security, and self-satisfaction from paid employment outside of the home, they will become more egalitarian and less conservative in their attitudes and lifestyles (Stokes and Willits, 1974; Rogers and Burdge, 1972). These more liberal values may well be passed on to the next generation through the socialization process.

Childbearing and Socialization

The total number of children borne by a woman is often used as an indicator of the degree to which women participate in the maternal role, and, traditionally, rural women have had more children than their urban counterparts. While both urban and rural fertility rates have been steadily declining since the late 1950s and the rural-urban differential has narrowed considerably, significant differences in fertility still exist, particularly among women under age 25 (Rindfuss and Sweet, 1975). In the future, the childbearing patterns of rural and urban women are expected to become more similar as women in rural areas increasingly adopt improved methods of birth control, modify their family size preferences, and take on additional activities outside of the home.

These changes do not mean that the rural mother is rejecting her traditional maternal role, but instead suggest that the nature of her family responsibilities is changing over time. Smaller families mean less time spent in childbearing and in child-rearing activities, and as rural children continue to enroll in school at a younger age and attend for longer periods of time, the educational system increasingly supplements the rural mother's socialization function.

However, the somewhat unusual nature of rural areas can also complicate the childbearing process of rural women, particularly those with large families and low incomes who live in geographically isolated regions of the country (Cochrane, 1977; Dunne, 1979). For those women who are family heads and almost solely responsible for the economic support of their children, the problems associated with child-rearing functions are even more severe. The greater social stigma attached to divorce or separation in rural places, limited job opportunities for women with few skills or inadequate education, transportation problems, and lack of child-care facilities complicate the social and economic responsibilities of the single parent in rural areas.

The rural wife continues to carry the major responsibilities for home care and child rearing. However, new patterns of marriage and family formation, greater educational attainment, and increased longevity have all contributed to changes in the life-cycle timing of rural women, and the manner in which they allocate their time to family-oriented functions. Rural women are no longer required to limit their outside activities to the periods prior to marriage or subsequent to their children leaving home. As the size of the rural family declines and the educational system and community structure assume more responsibility for teaching societal values to rural youth, many rural women are able to take on additional nonfamily activities during their childbearing years. Thus, changing family roles, responsibilities, and attitudes have served to push or pull many rural women into a variety of economic, political, and educational roles outside the family (Smith, 1979). Other rural women, however, especially those with low incomes and large families, living in the more isolated rural areas have been unable to take advantage of these changes, and many are still restricted in their role options.

The Economy: Labor Force, Occupations, and Earnings

Labor Force Participation

Since World War II, the level and patterns of women's labor force activities in the United States have changed drastically (Oppenheimer, 1973), and increasing numbers of women are seeking and finding employment in response to changing social and economic conditions. Changes in employment activity have occurred in the rural sector as well (Chenoweth and Maret-Havens, 1978; Brown and O'Leary, 1979). Between 1970 and 1980 alone, the number of nonmetropolitan women 16 years and over participating in the labor force increased by 4.5 million persons or 53 percent.[2] By 1980, 48 percent of all nonmetropolitan women were in the labor force (U.S. Bureau of the Census, 1980).

Labor force patterns of rural women vary by age, marital status, and presence of children and are closely related to progression through the various life-cycle stages—completion of schooling, leaving home, marriage, family formulation, and dissolution of family. Peterson (1979, p. 24) explains that "the transition to parenthood, to post parenthood, to post married, and the approach of retirement often triggers changes in patterns of labor force behavior, especially for women. At the same time, experiences in the labor force may affect the incidence and timing of these life-cycle transitions." These relationships are illustrated below.

Historically, if rural women worked at all, it was prior to marriage and childbearing. Now, women of all ages and marital status are entering or re-entering the labor market and remaining for longer periods of time. If present trends persist, rural women will continue to enter the labor force in increasing numbers, but may begin to enter at a later age as they remain in school longer. Increased investments in education and increasing economic and social returns to these investments will encourage these women to prolong their labor force activities, and once in the labor force they will be less likely to withdraw during the childbearing years. Of those who do drop out, however, many will return to their economic activities after their children enter school. Later age at marriage and the increasing rate of divorce both mean that more women will be required to enter the labor force in order to support themselves and their families. Also, policies encouraging early retirement may continue to reduce the labor-force participation of women over 40, although some recent data are now suggesting that concern with the effects of inflation on retirement income will encourage Americans to prolong their work lives as long as possible.

However, fluctuation in the traditional life-cycle progression is only one of the factors affecting changing work patterns of rural women. The development of a more liberal sex-role ideology, variations in family size and structure, modification in the use of time (especially in the household), and other changes in family roles and responsibilities noted previously have all contributed to the increased labor force activity of rural women. In addition, there are educational and economic incentives involved. As prices escalate and wages and educational levels continue to rise, women are increasingly drawn into the labor force. The price of remaining at home becomes a foregone wage, and as that wage increases women are encouraged to seek employment and find alternative means for child care and division of household chores. Women who have invested in higher education are now attempting to regain these costs over a lifetime in the form of a career. Thus employment allows many rural women the opportunity to supplement the family income and also provides them with some measure of financial independence and self-actualization in activities outside of the home (O'Leary, 1977).

These economic considerations have been accompanied by greater employment opportunities for women in rural areas, largely as a result of increasing industrialization and associated ancillary services. Between 1970 and 1980, the number employed in nonmetropolitan areas grew by over 7.3 million people (an increase of 32 percent), predominantly in the manufacturing, retail trade, and service sectors; women constituted over half of this growth (U.S. Bureau of the Census, 1980).

Occupational and Economic Status

Despite their increasing labor force participation, nonmetropolitan women continue to remain within a narrow range of occupations (mostly clerical and service jobs) that generally offer low wages, minimum levels of prestige, and little chance of advancement. Between 1970 and 1980, nonmetropolitan women made some gains among the higher paying professional and managerial occupations (making up 17 percent of women's total employment growth), but the major share of growth (58 percent) occurred among the lower status, lower-wage clerical and service jobs. Thus, in 1980, almost half of all nonmetropolitan women were in these occupations; only 16 percent were in professional and technical jobs—mostly teaching and nursing (Table 9.1).

This occupational distribution varied considerably from that of nonmetropolitan men who were more likely than their female counterparts to be

Table 9.1: Occupational Distribution of Employed Persons 16 Years and over in Nonmetropolitan Areas: 1970 and 1980[1]

Current Occupation	1970		1980	
	Male	Female	Male	Female
Total employed (thous.)	14,105	8,035	17,288	12,279
Professional, technical and kindred	10.3	15.0	11.9	15.8
Managers and administrators	10.2	3.9	12.6	6.3
Sales workers	5.2	6.7	4.8	5.9
Clerical and kindred	5.3	26.7	4.5	29.2
Craft and kindred	21.6	2.2	22.3	1.7
Operatives except transport	15.5	18.8	12.9	13.6
Transport equipment operators	6.4	0.6	6.2	1.0
Laborers, except farm	7.5	1.4	7.9	1.5
Farmers and farm managers	7.8	0.6	6.2	.9
Farm laborers and supervisors	3.9	1.2	3.3	1.4
Service workers, excluding private	6.3	17.8	7.3	19.9
Private household workers	--	5.2	--	2.8
Total percent	100.0	100.0	100.0	100.0

SOURCE: U.S. Bureau of the Census (1978a: table 13; 1980)
[1] The 1970-80 comparisons made here are based on figures from the 1970 Decennial Census of Population and the March 1980 Current Population Survey.

in higher paying managerial or crafts positions. These differences indicate a high degree of occupational segregation in nonmetropolitan areas suggesting that, for various reasons, nonmetropolitan women have been "restricted from full and fair access to the available positions in the labor market." (U.S. Commission on Civil Rights, 1978, p. 379.) Since occupations selected and wages paid help determine an individual's economic status, continued occupational segregation by sex can have serious implications for the improved economic status of nonmetropolitan women in the future.

Between 1969 and 1976, the earnings levels of nonmetropolitan males showed little improvement, largely as a result of the failure of wage increases to keep pace with inflation. However, the economic position of nonmetropolitan women actually deteriorated. The average annual earnings of nonmetropolitan women, after adjusting for changes in the cost of living, declined by $200—a decrease in real terms of almost 4 percent (U.S. Bureau of the Census 1978a). This decrease was due in large part to occupational shifts from generally higher-paying sales and operatives jobs into lower-paying service positions, as well as changes in part-time and temporary work status. Differences in education and work experience of new female labor force entrants may also be contributing to nonmetropolitan women's deteriorating economic situation. In addition, the gap in earnings between nonmetropolitan males and females did not diminish during the 1970s. In 1977, employed women averaged $5,120 in earnings, only 48 percent of the mean earnings for males; women employed full time (fifty to fifty-two weeks) received 54 percent of their male counterparts' earnings. Similar male-female differences were seen in almost all occupational groupings (Figure 9.1).

"Double Jeopardy" and Barriers to Improved Status

Rural women appear to be experiencing greater economic and occupational disadvantages than other groups and do not fare as well as urban women, urban men, or rural men on a variety of indicators. For example, the labor force participation rate of nonmetropolitan women remains consistently below that of other residence-sex groups and rural women are more likely to be concentrated among the lower-paying, lower-status occupational categories. In addition, Figure 9.1 shows that within almost every occupational grouping, nonmetropolitan women employed full time have lower average earnings than their nonmetropolitan male counterparts or males and females in metropolitan places.

These findings suggest that rural women encounter a situation of "double jeopardy"—a cumulative negative effect stemming from a combination of disadvantages associated with both their sex status and their place of residence (U.S. Commission on Civil Rights, 1978). Rural areas in general have been characterized by limited job opportunities and high rates of underemployment, which tend to impact heavily on the less experienced, less skilled rural women. Nonmetropolitan areas are less likely than metropolitan areas to receive funds for manpower and training programs to help upgrade the skills of the local labor pool, and small communities with limited economic bases

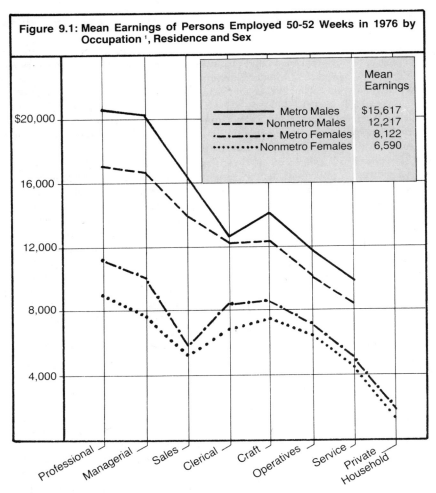

Figure 9.1: Mean Earnings of Persons Employed 50-52 Weeks in 1976 by Occupation [1], Residence and Sex

	Mean Earnings
Metro Males	$15,617
Nonmetro Males	12,217
Metro Females	8,122
Nonmetro Females	6,590

[1] Excludes occupational categories of transportation equipment operators, laborers, farmers and farm managers, and farm laborers and supervisors, since the base number for women in these categories was insufficient (less than 75,000) to calculate mean earnings.   Source: U.S. Bureau of Census (1978a: table 14).

DATA SHEET FOR FIGURE 9.1

	Metropolitan		Nonmetropolitan	
	Male	Female	Male	Female
Professional	$20,595	$11,307	$16,714	$9,190
Managerial	20,146	10,601	16,008	7,848
Sales	16,146	5,990	14,452	5,092
Clerical	12,662	8,015	12,453	6,861
Craft	14,437	8,073	12,412	7,015
Operatives	11,951	7,104	10,497	6,590
Service	10,086	5,424	8,535	4,571
Private Household	--	2,180	--	1,515
Total	15,617	8,122	12,217	6,590

are often unable to maintain needed social services. In addition, traditional values and beliefs concerning sex-role behavior can also influence rural women in their decision to seek work and in their occupational aspirations and selection. Unfortunately, for those rural women who occupy a third "negative status" and are also members of racial or ethnic minority groups, the differentials in occupational distribution and earnings are even greater (U.S. Bureau of the Census, 1978a).

Thus, various internal and external processes operate in rural areas to "cool out" or prevent women from entering the labor force or pursuing higher status occupational positions. Internalized barriers, for example, are learned as part of the definition of femininity. Childhood, adolescent, and adult socialization experiences that emphasize a traditional sex-role ideology for women and encourage acceptance of the "female traits" of noncompetitiveness, passivity, and vicarious achievement can influence the career aspirations and work attitudes of rural women. External or structural barriers, including discriminatory hiring and advancement policies, sex typing of jobs, lack of role models, and limited employment opportunities, also operate to discourage the economic advancement of rural women and restrict their role options.

Education of Rural Women

Limited education is perhaps one of the most effective barriers to labor force participation and occupational achievement. Recent research (Fratoe, 1978; 1979) indicates that rural people generally lag behind their urban counterparts in virtually all areas of educational attainment, and, in almost all cases where educational data are available by sex, rural women are more educationally disadvantaged than their urban counterparts. While the educational attainment levels of nonmetropolitan women are increasing over time, and greater proportions are finishing high school and continuing on in trade schools or colleges, these women still face serious educational problems. In 1979, about 4 percent of all nonmetropolitan women 25 years and over were classed as functionally illiterate (having less than 5 years of school); 38 percent had not completed high school, and only 23 percent had attended college (U.S. Bureau of the Census, 1979b). These data do not, of course, measure differences in quality of education, and rural students in general attend schools with fewer support staff and services, less revenue, and less per pupil funding.

Some researchers have suggested that women are less likely to invest their time in education because they generally participate in the labor force for only short periods of time. However, this rationale is now questionable in light of the increasing time that both rural and urban women are spending in the labor force. Because of their increased willingness to accept new economic roles outside of the family, rural women will be forced to realize the necessity for skill training and adequate levels of education in the future. While higher levels of education will encourage greater female labor force participation and perhaps help advance the occupational status of rural women, the relationship between education and economic improvement is more tenuous. Even when rural women do complete higher levels of education, the return on their investment is often much less than that of males. In 1977, the average earnings of nonmetropolitan females with a college degree were only 42 percent of the earnings of nonmetropolitan males (U.S. Bureau of the Census, 1978a). Thus, increased educational attainment will not provide the sole key to improving the economic position of rural women.

In addition, the educational needs of rural women cannot be adequately met by simply increasing the number of years spent in school. The educational requirements of rural women cover a wide variety of social issues, including personal growth and development, political participation, legal rights, health education, child care, counseling, and career development—subjects not necessarily learned through formal educational systems (Clarenbach, 1977; Dunne, 1979). Because of general isolation, inadequate transportation, prevailing behavior patterns, and numerous other factors common to rural areas, educational delivery systems designed to meet the varied needs of rural women must be innovatively developed.

Rural Women in the Political Structure

Politics has traditionally been viewed as part of the male domain, although in the past decade there has been evidence of women's increasing involvement in voting, public leadership, and community decision making. The gap in voting rates between men and women has narrowed considerably, and in the 1976 presidential election, women were as likely to vote as men (U.S. Bureau of the Census, 1965; 1969; 1973; and 1978b). While there is now near equality in voting between men and women, the female electorate continues to yield the greatest amount of voting power. More votes have been cast by women than men in every national election since 1964 (Krauss, 1974; Lansing, 1974; Lynn, 1975) and, in 1976, females accounted for 53 percent of all votes cast (U.S. Bureau of the Census, 1978b).

Little information has been reported on the voting patterns of men and women in rural areas. However, census data do indicate that nonmetropolitan people living on farms are more likely to vote in presidential elections than their counterparts; nonmetropolitan nonfarm residents are least likely to cast their votes. These reported residential voting differences actually appear to be increasing over time (U.S. Bureau of the Census, 1965; 1969; 1973; and 1978b). In addition, one statewide survey of voter participation in Illinois reported that more rural women voted in the 1976 presidential election than either rural males or urban females. Farm women had the highest voter participation rate of any residence-sex group surveyed (Burdge et al., 1978—reanalysis by the authors).

Women's involvement in politics has been most often expressed through voting and least often through holding state or national elected offices. The gains that women have been making in the past decade in obtaining elected positions have been in rural areas. Most women who have been elected to public office serve in county and local governments in smaller towns and sparsely populated counties of the United States (Diamond, 1977; Center for the American Woman and Politics, 1976). While rural women are more successful than urban women in being elected to local offices, neither group has made impressive gains in either state or national elections. Thus, while women in rural areas may stand a better chance of being elected to local positions than to state or national offices, these offices carry less prestige and power (Krauss, 1974).

Case studies of small American towns have documented an increase in political activities of rural women. Ethnographers in a Michigan community of 1,700 people noted an increase in the number of women running for village council, school board, and library board positions. However, opposition to women in politics was expressed by several community members who remarked that women were elected to office only because their husbands' families were prominent in the community. This suggests that competence and ability are not considered to be relevant criteria and that women cannot be elected on their own merits. A mother of young children was unable to gain election to the state legislature due to opposition from both men and women who remarked that she should stay at home with her children and run for local office in the community instead (Bescher-Donnelly and Donnelly, unpublished field notes, 1976).

In an ethnographic study in rural Bushler Bay, Washington, Colfer and Colfer (1978) reported that although the women were economically dependent on their husbands, they were highly organized in women-centered networks. Of the village's eighteen formal organizations, thirteen were either all female or female-dominated. Women were able to organize informal action groups and demonstrations as needed to deal with specific community issues, problems, or events.

Bokemeier and Tait (1978) found that women in rural communities are becoming politically active through the role of power actor—the interface between women's traditional role of homemaker and community volunteer and the "deviant" role of woman as an elected political leader. The community power actor role is one in which women's presence and involvement in community issues are given recognition in the decision-making process, rather than being regarded as subliminally present but irrelevant to the decision-making process. While this may presently be the actual situation of rural women, there is no reason why women should limit themselves to such secondary participation now or in the future.

Factors Affecting Political Participation of Rural Women

When it comes to running for elective office, rural women face many social-structural and internalized barriers to successful election. First, they are not socialized for political roles. There are few women in rural areas who serve as political role models for young girls and few female politicians to teach the necessary politicking skills to interested rural women. In addition, the sex-role socialization process teaches women that "the man is expected to be dominant in action directed toward the world outside the family; the woman is to accept his leadership passively." (Campbell et al., 1960, p. 490.) Rural women, in particular, hold to the more traditional sex-role ideology and more rural than urban women agree that "women should take care of running their homes and leave running the country up to the men" (Flora and Johnson, 1978, p. 179). The social pressure against women in politics is strong, and very often they do not have the confidence necessary to run for office. Second, when rural women do run for office, they tend to content themselves with local politics or low-level political offices (Flora and Lynn, 1974). Third, obtaining party backing and financial support can be especially difficult for rural women. At the state and local level, where rural women are participating most, male party leaders may oppose female candidates, and campaign contributions may be difficult to find. Finally, once elected, women face a type of discrimination by their male counterparts who effectively bar them from the informal "old boy" network by excluding them from "male only" organizations or poker clubs where votes are won and policies determined.

However, there are some positive factors that may help to increase the political participation of rural women. Paid employment outside the home, for example, may improve women's political participation by changing the focus of women from home and family to the outside world, by offering trade unions and professional organizations as bases for political activity, and by increasing their awareness of discrimination in work and the need for legislation to improve women's status (Anderson, 1975).

Education has been described as the most important variable in mediating voting and political participation (Jaquette, 1974). The higher the level of female education, the less the difference between men and women as measured by various indices of political involvement, voting, and stance on policy issues. In fact, better-educated women show higher voter turnout and greater political activism than men with equal education (Campbell et al., 1960; Lansing, 1974). However, improved education is not enough to eliminate differences in political participation. McCormack (1975, p. 13) notes that "Unless women perceive of political life as a place where they matter, where they are not just outsiders rounded up on election day, more education will not close the gap between the rates of male and female participation."

Rural women have not been socialized for political roles, and their sex-role ideology and behavior tend to be more traditional and conservative than those of urban women (Stokes and Willits, 1974). Such traditional attitudes are reflected in rural women's rejection of the women's liberation movement and failure to support the Equal Rights Amendment (ERA). The ERA has been an issue of much controversy for several years, and three more states are still needed in order to ratify the amendment.[3] A 1978 statewide survey of 9,892 Illinois residents revealed that more than half of the urban women and men supported passage of ERA, while rural residents were strongly opposed to ERA, regardless of employment status or educational attainment. Among rural nonfarm residents, 45 percent of women and 46 percent of men supported

ERA; among rural farm residents, 32 percent of women and 35 percent of men supported ERA (Burdge et al., 1978—reanalysis by the authors).

The rural woman's failure to support the ERA and the women's liberation movement may possibly be attributed to her apparent sense of satisfaction with women's equity. According to Larson (1978), rural women have the most positive perception of women's equality—nearly three-fourths of the rural women surveyed in a 1970 Gallup Opinion Poll believed that women get as good a break as men in the United States. In Gallup Opinion Polls of 1974 and 1975, barely a majority of rural women favored passage of the amendment (Larson, 1978). Rural women may be less in favor of ERA than other residential groups because they feel less need for legislated equity.

In addition, some rural women may feel that the women's movement and the ERA do not address the problems of rural women. In Iowa, rural farm women consider the women's movement to be a city-based phenomenon. They feel little rapport with a movement they say has ignored the particular problem farm women feel most acutely—the inequality in estate laws (Ogintz and Waterloo, 1977).

Problems of geographic and social isolation, poverty and underemployment characterize much of rural America. These problems affect men as well as women, but have more salience for women who feel the dilemma of balancing the traditional demands of rural culture with the need for economic security. As economic and social discontentment grows among rural women and as they see urban women increasingly entering politics, they will become more politically active.

Future Political Roles for Rural Women

Increasingly, rural women are becoming more political, as evidenced by the creation of new organizations, agencies, and projects to further rural women's needs. American Agri-Women (AAW) was established in 1974 to lobby for agricultural issues relating to women. AAW now has thirty-two state chapters, 3,000 individual members, and 30,000 members including affiliated women's organizations.

Rural American Women, Inc. (RAW), a national coalition of organizations and individuals, was created in 1977 to give women a voice in Washington and to make rural women's needs known to the nation. Its stated purpose is to involve rural women in the development and participation in those processes and structures that will enable them to participate effectively in strengthening their own communities. Today RAW has 22,000 members counting individuals and organizational memberships it represents.

In 1976, the National Advisory Council on Women's Educational Programs sponsored a series of hearings on the needs of rural women in the United States. The results of these hearings, published in the report, *Educational Needs of Rural Women and Girls* (Clarenbach, 1977), revealed that, in spite of both geographic spread and the great diversity of life situations represented by the rural women involved in the council's investigation, there was a striking similarity of perceived need. The message was clear:

> Rural women want to speak for themselves and have their voices solicited and listened to; they want to be recognized as significant and contributing members of their families and of society at large; they want to have the opportunity to become independent persons, to control their own lives, to have a role in the formulation of public policy, and to share somewhat equitably in the fruits of our society. (Clarenbach, 1977, p. 11.)

While achieving the right to vote had little impact on the social, economic, and legal quality of women's lives at the time, current social and economic changes seem to be propelling women into the political world. Rural women, as change agents, are in a position to determine their own lives by becoming more politically active as voters, power actors, and as elected officials. Gender roles, life cycles, and economic and legal factors are all independent variables related to the political participation of rural women and their impact on policy formation in the future.

Directions for the Future

The past few decades have seen remarkable changes in the roles and responsibilities of rural women as they increasingly seek new options and alternatives in family life, the employment sector, educational system, and political structure, and these trends are likely to persist as rural areas experience a population and employment growth unprecedented in recent years. Continued job growth, reduction of rural-urban income gaps, more adequate postsecondary education systems, and improvement in material conveniences all suggest that rural women will have increasing opportunities to improve their social and economic well-being in the future (Beale, 1977). However, many rural women have not participated in activities outside of the family. Additional efforts are still required to help establish a wide range of practical and socially acceptable alternatives for women, as well as to help improve their economic status, political power, and self-image.

Flora and Johnson (1978, p. 178) suggest that expansion of role options and improvements in self-definition will result from interrelated changes in all of women's role functions—sexuality, reproduction, socialization of children, and production. "Without changes in the production function (that is, the availability of work for decent wages), it is unlikely that the relative importance of the time-consuming functions of reproduction and socialization of children, as well as the production function of household care and maintenance, will change much in the lives of rural women." At the same time, unless traditional sex-role ideology and attitudes toward family formation and child rearing change, many rural women will not adopt additional role options outside of the family, even if opportunities exist.

Social policy designed to improve the social and economic conditions of rural women should be directed toward changing both the structural conditions and the traditional sex-role ideology that restrict both males and females in their life situations. Resocialization techniques and institutional restructuring procedures must be developed to permit both men and women to choose role options most appropriate to their needs, preferences, and ability, without inhibitions based on sex-role stereotypes. This by no means implies a complete reversal of roles. In fact, many rural women may choose to follow the traditional "feminine" behavior patterns and will be content in their roles as wives and mothers. Others, however, may wish to choose additional options or alternatives in some or all of the life sectors now limited almost exclusively to males. Still others, particularly farm women, wish to be recognized for the multiplicity of role positions they have traditionally held. In the future, new socialization models must be introduced to teach rural women to perceive, evaluate, and select the set of role options that best suits them.

These are long-range plans that can only be accomplished over time. However, the 1977 National Women's Conference in Houston identified more immediate goals and passed the following resolutions:

- The president and Congress should establish a federal rural education policy designed to overcome inequalities in opportunities available to rural women and girls.
- The Office of Management and Budget should set and enforce a policy that data collected on beneficiaries of all federal programs be reported by sex, minority status, and by urban-rural or metropolitan-nonmetropolitan areas, based on a standard definition.
- Data on employment of women and on public programs on behalf of working women should include in their definitions farm wives and widows who perform the many tasks essential to the farm operations.
- A farm wife should have the same ownership rights as her spouse under state inheritance and federal estate laws. Tax law should recognize that the labor of a farm wife gives her an equitable interest in the property.
- All programs developed on behalf of rural women should include Blacks, migrants, Native Americans, Alaskans, Asians, and Hispanics, and all isolated minorities, and affirmative action programs should be extended to include all disenfranchised groups.

Unfortunately, the "state of the art" on rural women suffers from many data gaps and research limitations, and several recent bibliographies (Ferra, 1977b; Joyce and Leadley, 1977; Women's Educational Equity, 1978) and a research agenda (Clarenbach, 1977) have signaled the need for additional and comprehensive research on rural women. A systematic basis of knowledge that permits a more detailed and accurate view of the demographic, sex-role, and sexual behavior changes of rural women and recognizes the somewhat unusual aspects of rural culture and society is vitally important for developing policies, programs, and legislation to improve the status and lifestyle of women in rural areas.

Notes

1. However, it should be noted that these rural and urban women expressed similar attitudes on items related to equality of earnings and employment outside the home. In addition, there was some ambivalence and ambiguity in the findings, since rural women apparently adhered to traditional attitudes concerning "women's place" in the home but recognized the importance of a college education and indicated a strong belief in equal pay for equal work.

2. The 1970–80 comparisons made here and elsewhere in the chapter are based on figures from the 1970 Decennial Census of Population and the March 1980 Current Population Survey (CPS). While these figures are not strictly comparable because of differences in the size of the sample population, they provide an indication of the relative changes that have occurred over time. See Bureau of Census (1978a) for additional details on comparability of Census and CPS data.

3. There are fifteen states (Alabama, Arizona, Arkansas, Florida, Georgia, Illinois, Louisiana, Mississippi, Missouri, Nevada, North Carolina, Oklahoma, South Carolina, Utah, and Virginia) that have not ratified the ERA as of June 1980.

References

Anderson, K. "Working Women and Political Participation." *American Journal of Political Science,* 1975, 19, 439–454.

Beale, C. "The Recent Shift of U.S. Population to Nonmetropolitan Areas, 1970–75." *International Regional Science Review,* 1977, 2 (2), 113–122.

Bescher-Donnelly, L. A. and W. L. Donnelly. Unpublished field notes, Contract No. OEC-0-72-5245, National Institute of Education, U.S. Department of Health, Education and Welfare, 1976.

Bokemeier, J. L. and J. L. Tait. "Women as Power Actors: A New Trend in Rural Communities." Paper presented at the annual meeting of Rural Sociology Society, San Francisco, California, August 1978.

Brown, D. L. and J. M. O'Leary. "Labor Force Activity in Metropolitan and Nonmetropolitan America." Washington, D.C.: Economics, Statistics, and Cooperatives Service, U.S. Department of Agriculture, 1979.

Burdge, R., R. M. Kelly, and H. J. Schweitzer. "Illinois: Today and Tomorrow." Urbana, Illinois: University of Illinois, 1978.

Campbell, A., P. E. Converse, W. E. Miller, and D. E. Stokes. *The American Voter.* New York: Wiley and Sons, 1960.

Center for the American Woman and Politics. *Women in Public Office: A Biographical Directory and Statistical Analysis.* New York: R. R. Borcher, 1976.

Chenoweth, L. and E. Maret-Havens. "Women's Labor Force Participation— A Look at Some Residential Patterns." *Monthly Labor Review.* 1978, 101, 38–41.

Clarenbach, K. F. *Educational Needs of Rural Women and Girls.* Washington, D.C.: National Advisory Council on Women's Educational Programs, 1977.

Cochrane, H. S. "The Plight of Rural Women in Upstate New York." Geneseo, New York: State University of New York at Geneseo, 1977.

Colfer, C.J.P. and M. Colfer. "Inside Bushler Bay: Lifeways that Counterpoint." *Rural Sociology,* 1978, 43, 204–220.

Constantini, E. and K. H. Craik. "Women as Politicians: The Social Background, Personality, and Political Careers of Female Party Leaders." *Journal of Social Issues,* 1972, 28 (2), 217–236.

Diamond, I. *Sex Roles in the State House.* New Haven: Yale University Press, 1977.

Dunne, F. "Traditional Values/Contemporary Pressures: The Conflicting Needs of America's Rural Women." Paper presented at the Rural Education Seminar, College Park, Maryland, May 1979.

Ferra, D. "Women in Agriculture: A Review of the Literature." *Associates NAL Today,* 1977, 2, 28–32 (a).

____. *Women in American Agriculture: A Select Bibliography List 103.* Washington, D.C.: Economic Research Service and National Agricultural Library, U.S. Department of Agriculture, 1977 (b).

Flora, C. B. "Rural Women." *Associates NAL Today,* 1977, 2, 16–21.

Flora, C. B. and S. Johnson. "Discarding the Distaff: New Roles for Rural Women." In T. R. Ford (ed.), *Rural U.S.A.: Persistence and Change.* Ames, Iowa: Iowa State University Press, 1978, 168–241.

Flora, C. B. and N. Lynn. "Women and Political Socialization: Consideration of the Roles of Motherhood." In J. S. Jaquette (ed.), *Women in Politics.* New York: John Wiley and Sons, 1974, 37–53.

Fratoe, F. *Rural Education and Rural Labor Force in the Seventies.* Rural Development Research Report No. 5. Washington, D.C.: Economics, Statistics, and Cooperative Service, U.S. Department of Agriculture, 1978.

____. *The Educational Level of Farm Residents and Workers.* Rural Development Research Report No. 8. Washington, D.C.: Economics, Statistics, and Cooperative Service, U.S. Department of Agriculture, 1979.

Glenn, N. O. and L. Hill, Jr. "Rural-Urban Differences in Attitudes and Behavior in the United States." *The Annals of the American Academy,* 1977, 429, 36–50.

Heaton, C. and P. Martin. "Labor Force Participation Differs Significantly for the Rural Women." *Monthly Labor Review,* 1979, 102, 71–73.

Huffman, W. E. "The Value of the Productive Time of Farm Wives. Iowa, North Carolina, and Oklahoma." *American Journal of Agricultural Economics,* December 1976, 836–841.

Jaquette, J. S. (ed.), *Women in Politics.* New York: John Wiley and Sons, 1974.

Joyce, L. M. and S. M. Leadley. *An Assessment of Research Needs of Women in the Rural United States: Literature Review and Annotated Bibliography.* University Park, Pennsylvania: The Pennsylvania State University, 1977.

Krauss, W. R. "Political Implications of Gender Roles: A Review of the Literature." *American Political Science Review,* 1974, 68, 1706–1723.

Lansing, M. "The American Woman: Voter and Activist." In J. S. Jaquette (ed.), *Women in Politics.* New York: John Wiley and Sons, 1974, 5–24.

Larson, O. F. "Values and Beliefs of Rural People." In T. R. Ford (ed.), *Rural U.S.A.: Persistence and Change.* Ames, Iowa: Iowa State University Press, 1978, 91–112.

Lynn, N. "Women in American Politics: An Overview," In J. Freeman (ed.), *Women: A Feminist Perspective.* Palo Alto, California: Mayfield Publishing Company, 1975, 364–385.

McCormack, T. "Toward a Nonsexist Perspective on Social and Political Change." In M. Millman and R. M. Kanter (eds.), *Another Voice.* New York: Anchor Book, 1975, 1–33.

Nietzke, A. "The Media . . . Doin' Somebody Wrong." *Human Behavior,* 1975, 4, 66–68.

Ogintz, E. and C. Waterloo. "Feminism Comes to Iowa Farms." *Des Moines Sunday Register,* October 30, 1977.

O'Leary, J. M. "Labor Force Characteristics of Nonmetropolitan Women." *Associates NAL Today,* 1977, 2, 22–27.

____. "Effects of the Recent Recession on the Labor Force Participation of Nonmetropolitan Women." Paper presented at the annual meeting of Rural Sociological Society, San Francisco, California, August 1978.

Oppenheimer, V. K. "Demographic Influence on Female Employment and the Status of Women." In J. Huber (ed.), Changing Women in a Changing Society, special issue of *American Journal of Sociology,* 1973, 78, 946–961.

Peterson, J. L. "Work and Socioeconomic Life Cycles: An Agenda for Longitudinal Research." *Monthly Labor Review,* 1979, 102, 23–27.

Rindfuss, R. R. and J. A. Sweet. "Rural Fertility Trends and Differentials." *Family Planning Perspectives,* 1975, 7, 264–269.

Roberts, A. E. and G. S. Kowalski. "Farm Residence or Background and Women's Sex Role Attitudes." Paper presented at annual meeting of Rural Sociological Society, San Francisco, California, August 1978.

Rogers, E. M. and R. J. Burdge. *Social Change in Rural Societies.* New York: Appleton-Century-Crofts, 1972.

Smith, L. W. "Changing Family Roles of Rural Women." Paper presented at Rural Sociological Society meetings, Burlington, Vermont, August 1979.

Stokes, C. S. and F. K. Willits. "A Preliminary Analysis of Factors Related to Sex Role Ideology among Rural-origin Females." Paper presented at Rural Sociological Society Meetings, Montreal, Canada, 1974.

Stuart, N. G. and J. C. van Es. "Women in Local Politics." *Journal of Community Development Society of America,* 1978, 9, 43–51.

U.S. Bureau of the Census. "Voting Participation in the National Election, November 1964." *Current Population Reports, Population Characteristics.* Series P-20, No. 143, October 1965.

____. "Voting and Registration in the Election of November 1968." *Current Population Reports, Population Characteristics.* Series P-20, No. 253, October 1969.

____. "Voting and Registration in the Election of November 1972." *Current Population Reports, Population Characteristics.* Series P-20, No. 253, October 1973.

____. "Social and Economic Characteristics of the Metropolitan and Non-metropolitan Population: 1977 and 1970." *Current Population Reports, Special Studies.* Series P-23, No. 75, November, 1978 (a).

____. "Voting and Registration in the Election of 1976." *Current Population Reports, Population Characteristics.* Series P-20, No. 322, March 1978 (b).

____. "Voting and Registration in the Election of 1978" *Current Population Reports, Population Characteristics.* Series P-20, 1979 (a).

____. Current Population Survey. Unpublished data, March 1979 (b).

____. Current Population Survey. Unpublished data. March 1980.

U.S. Commission on Civil Rights. *Social Indicators of Equality for Minorities and Women.* Washington, D.C.: U.S. Commission on Civil Rights, 1978.

Willits, F. K., R. C. Bealer, and D. M. Crider. "Leveling of Attitudes in Mass Society: Rurality and Traditional Morality in America." *Rural Sociology,* 1973, 38, 36–45.

Women's Educational Equity Communications Network. *Rural Women and Education.* San Francisco, California: Women's Educational Equity Communications Network, 1978.

10

MIDDLE AGE IN RURAL AMERICA: ADAPTING TO CHANGE[1]

Dena B. Targ

There is a growing recognition that the experience of middle age is not an unchanging *fact* for all times, all places, and all individuals. Despite this awareness, most research findings currently available focus on predictable patterns of development for white, middle-class, urban adults (Elder, 1977; Neugarten and Datan, 1973; Schram, 1979; Troll, 1975). This chapter begins with a brief summary of the extant research findings about men, women, and marriage in middle age. Then, additional areas of important concern—especially to women—at middle age are discussed. Finally consideration is given to a number of factors associated with rural as compared with urban residence that may change or modify the experience of middle age.[2]

Middle Age in Urban America

In order to study middle age in America it is first necessary to define it. No single definition is used throughout the theoretical, empirical, statistical, and popular work on the subject. Three major ways in which the term is used refer to chronological age, family stage, and work stage. The most specific definition of middle age is that of the United States Census Bureau, which generally uses the chronological ages 45 through 64 as its criterion. In terms of family development, middle age is usually considered as synonymous with the "empty-nest period," or the time between when children leave home and the husband retires (Lowenthal et al., 1975; Lowenthal and Chiriboga, 1972). Middle age has also been studied as a stage in work development primarily for men (Barnett and Baruch, 1977; Levinson et al., 1978). The summary of findings on middle age that follows is based on these three definitions.

Chronological Age

One set of central findings on middle age includes a chronological, a biological, or an age referent. For example, researchers note among people in middle age a sense of bodily decline and a recognition of one's mortality. There is a sense of aging, of being old rather than young; emphasis shifts from the "time since birth" to the "time left to live" (Levinson et al., 1976; Neugarten, 1968; 1976).

Family Stage

In terms of family development, the empty-nest stage is considered to be synonymous with middle age. Several empirical studies have investigated life satisfaction in general as well as marital happiness specifically at this stage. Results of these studies indicate that for women, the empty-nest stage, compared with earlier stages, represents an increased or at least an unchanged level of life satisfaction (Glenn, 1975; Lowenthal and Chiriboga, 1972; Neugarten, 1976). As to men in this stage of family development, Glenn (1975) found that some loss of overall happiness was likely when children left home. However, other studies report findings parallel to those concerning women—increased or unchanged levels of life satisfaction at this stage in comparison to other stages (Cohen, 1979; Glenn, 1975).

Finally, research investigating marriage at this time does not provide uniform results. Glenn (1975) found marital happiness generally higher for both men and women at this stage. Lowenthal and Chiriboga (1972) presented more mixed findings in terms of husbands' and wives' appraisals of each other. While men were twice as likely to give positive evaluations of their wives, wives were twice as likely to evaluate negatively. Rollins and Cannon (1974) reanalyzed studies of marital satisfaction across the fmaily life cycle. They concluded that life-cycle stage is too global a variable to be an important independent variable relative to marital happiness for either men or women.

Role reversal in middle age—or at least less differentiation between roles—appears common among middle-aged married couples. Men become less aggressive, more affiliative, less dominant in the marital relationship (Lowenthal and Chiriboga, 1972; Neugarten, 1968). This lessening of sex-role differentiation has been interpreted as a result of the woman facing the empty nest and the man facing retirement. "It may be that the apparent reversal of sex differences at this stage reflects an attempt at compensation or substitution among those women facing the empty nest. Conversely, the expressive concerns of men may be a kind of anticipatory adjustment to their pending retirement, which several expect to occur in the not too distant future." (Lowenthal and Chiriboga, 1972, p. 11.)

Work Stage

The period preceding mid-life or mid-life transition is characterized as the time for thinking through youthful aspirations and later achievements and reconsidering aspirations, whether achieved or not (Levinson et al., 1976). Lowenthal and Chiriboga (1972) found that most men in their sample (average age, 51) did not find work to be a current source of satisfaction. However, this lack of satisfaction does not appear to be linked with middle age. Most do not report that their work was a source of satisfaction in the past. Additionally, Lowenthal et al. (1975) reported that these same middle-aged men were disappointed that work was not more important to them. They entered the labor force with the expectation that hard work would be rewarded with success. They had now reached a plateau in their careers and were beginning to question whether or not they were responsible for their own lack of achievement.

Work development relates to life-cycle stage in terms of economic attainment as well as occupational achievement (the two are, of course, related). Economic needs vary and peak at different stages of the life cycle. One high point of need occurs during the middle-age years for men (the decade of their 40s and early 50s). However, only in high-level professional jobs do peaks of earnings coincide with peaks of demand. For families in which the principal wage earner is middle-aged and is not a high-level professional, middle age is likely to be a time at which standard of living falls unless an additional worker enters the labor force (Oppenheimer, 1974).

Crisis or Transition

Another set of findings concerns the question of whether middle age offers a crisis or a transition. While middle age has been, and is still, considered a crisis, both in popular and in academic work (Feldman and Feldman, 1975; LeShan, 1974; Levinson et al., 1978; Sheehy, 1974), it has been found empirically to be a transition or a stable stage rather than a time of crisis (Brim, 1976; Lowenthal et al., 1975; Neugarten, 1976).

Several authors, recognizing that mid-life crisis is not inevitable, have suggested the conditions under which such a crisis will occur. At the individual level, Brim (1976, p. 8) contends that middle age will be a crisis if several problems occur at once: "If, for instance, during the same month or year the man throws off his last illusions about great success; accepts his children for what they are; buries his father and mother and yields to the truth of his mortality; recognizes that his sexual vigor and indeed interest, are declining and even finds relief in that fact."

A more sociological perspective sees the timing of events, rather than the number, as central. An event that is "off-time" in terms of age-status norms is more likely to cause problems than an event which is "on-time." In addition to the distinction between events that are "on-time" and "off-time," the distinction between anticipated and unanticipated events is also important. For example, divorce for middle-aged women is more likely to be traumatic than widowhood in old age (Neugarten, 1976).

Critique

Even this brief summary of what is known about American men, women, and marriage in middle age indicates a number of shortcomings in our knowledge. Three primary deficiencies place limitations on our understanding of this developmental stage. The first is that the literature focuses on what are considered the "regular," "inevitable," or "predictable" transitions or stages in the adult life cycle, and thus does not consider the "unanticipated" or "off-time" occurrences, such as divorce, widowhood, or employment for women. The second is that the empty-nest literature focuses on parental-postparental differences rather than on differences within each group. The third is that relevant sociological variables, such as urban versus rural residence, are either ignored or findings are assumed to be generalizable to all causes.

Unanticipated and Off-Time Changes

Divorce. The study of inevitable changes that occur across the life course precludes looking at unanticipated events—for example, divorce and widow-hood at middle age. While these events may be unanticipated or off-time, they are not uncommon, especially for women. Seventy-six percent of women aged 45 to 54 are married with husband present; only 67 percent of women aged 55 to 64 are still married. Fifteen percent of women aged 45 to 54 are widowed or divorced. Twenty-five percent of women 55 to 64 are widowed or divorced (U.S. Bureau of the Census, 1979).

Women who have been full-time homemakers and who become divorced or widowed during middle age face a plethora of problems centered around becoming both economically and emotionally self-sufficient. This group has been labelled "displaced homemakers." There is no unemployment insurance for displaced homemakers. They are often too young for Social Security benefits. At the local level there are more than 150 programs providing services to this group of women. At the national level, legislation was introduced into Congress in 1977 to establish model displaced homemaker centers in each state to offer training and counseling services. In 1978, this legislation was modified and absorbed into the CETA (Comprehensive Education and Training Administration) Act. Many legislators resisted stipulating a minimum age requirement for use of services; consequently, constituent groups are monitoring delivery of services under this act to ensure consideration of the special needs of middle-aged women.[3]

Women and Work. The concentration of predictable patterns of adult development as well as the tendency to define women according to family functions has led at best to a cursory consideration of women and work at middle age or to a mention of its effect on men (Barnett and Baruch, 1977; Levinson et al., 1976). An examination of the patterns of labor force participation among middle-aged women shows that it is substantial, it is higher among women aged 45 to 54 than among women 55 to 64, and it varies according to marital status. Of those 45 to 54 years of age, single women have a labor force participation rate of 76 percent, divorced women 69 percent, and married women 50 percent. Among those 55 to 64 years of age, single women have a labor force participation rate of 60 percent, divorced women 53 percent, and married women 36 percent (U.S. Department of Labor, 1976). Until recent years, the largest increases in the labor force participation of married women were among the middle aged.

One important question regarding married women and work concerns the effect on men, women, and marriage of women's entry or reentry into the labor force at middle age. Work may be an important factor for women in making a successful transition to the empty-nest stage. Work may be a factor in the lessening of sex-role differentiation between husbands and wives discussed earlier. Whether this lessening of sex role differentiation has positive or negative consequences is still subject to interpretation. One view suggests that the personality changes that a female experiences in mid-life toward independence and away from emotional reinforcement of her husband will undermine an important source of his feelings of self-worth (Brim, 1976). An alternative view posits that increased marital satisfaction observed during the middle years is a result of increases in the time women spend away from home, especially in work roles and the concomitant decrease in sole financial responsibility for husbands and decrease in housework for wives (Schram, 1979). Whether positive or negative, the observed modification of the affective and instrumental dimensions of sex roles at middle age may be as much a result of women entering the labor force as it is the result of anticipatory socialization for retirement (Targ, 1979).

Empty Nest: Positive or Negative?

Current research on women in the empty-nest stage emphasizes comparisons with prior or future life-cycle stages. Findings indicate that many—but not all—women experience this as a positive period in their lives. Perhaps because prior research, often based on psychiatric patients or a problem approach, placed so much emphasis on the difficulties of the empty-nest stage, attention has been drawn to these new positive findings. Three reasons given for this adjustment are the difficulties in living with teenagers, on-time arrival of the empty nest, and involvement in alternatives.

One factor positively affecting women's adjustment to the empty nest is that it is often difficult to live with teenagers. Many women may therefore be relieved when their children leave home (Neugarten, 1976; Schram, 1979). A second reason for transition rather than trauma relates to the fact that the empty nest is anticipated. When the empty nest is on-time rather than early, it arrives slowly rather than coming as a surprise. Women, therefore, have time to consider and plan for the next phase of their lives. There is also evidence that late arrival of the empty nest carries negative consequences for the psychological well-being of women (Harkins, 1978). An additional factor assumed to influence women who experience few difficulties in the empty-nest stage is their involvement in education, paid work, or volunteer work (Schram, 1979; Troll, 1971).[4]

One methodological factor affecting the positive generalizations reported by so much research is inherent in the composition of the populations sampled. The women under consideration in the samples are married (or at least living with another adult) and thus are not being left alone at the postparental period (Glenn, 1975).[5]

While problems at the postparental stage are not as prevalent for women as previously thought, there are, however, women who do have problems caused by or associated with their children's leaving home. Research tells us this; attendance at programs for women facing decisions at mid-life tells us this; personal experience tells us this. In order to solve these problems, it is important to locate their exact nature and sources.

Middle Age in Rural America

The experience of middle-aged men and women is not uniform but rather is the result of a number of factors. Some of these factors, especially as they affect women, have been examined in the preceding section. The remainder of this chapter will consider the effect of rural versus urban residence on the middle-aged period in the life cycle (for a discussion of other factors affecting the experience of middle age see Troll, 1975).

As reflected in census data, changes have occurred in *both* rural and urban areas in family-related characteristics of the population: age at first marriage has declined; the divorce rate has grown; labor force participation of women, including mothers, has increased. However, differences in these demographic characteristics persist between rural and urban areas. Rural people, in comparison to their urban counterparts, marry earlier and have more children. Rural marriages are less likely than urban marriages to end in divorce. The labor force participation rate continues to be lower among rural than urban wives and mothers (Brown, 1977).

Rural Women at Middle Age

The discussion above provides some indication of the climate of change and persistence in which rural middle-aged people live their lives and suggests aspects of the empty-nest period and divorce in middle age that have the potential of being more traumatic for rural women than for urban women. Middle-aged rural women have been married longer, have more children, and are less likely to be in the labor force than their urban counterparts. It is women who have accepted the traditional feminine role, who have invested themselves in their children, and who have not created alternatives for themselves who are likely to experience troubles facing the empty nest (Perrucci and Targ, 1974; Schram, 1979). This generalization is likely to apply equally to rural nonfarm and urban women. It would at first seem that the farm wife who has responsibilities in connection with the farm, for example, taking care of the books, making business decisions, and working in the field would avoid problems because of this involvement. However, she is subject to two sources of role loss at middle age—family and work. She is likely to see her children gain adult status and at the same time take over portions of her farm responsibilities (see Chapter 8 by Rosenblatt and Anderson).

Divorce at middle age is more traumatic for rural than urban women. Although the divorce rate is increasing in rural areas, it is still lower than that in urban areas. In addition to the problems her urban counterpart faces, a rural woman divorced at middle age would be likely to experience stronger negative evaluations of divorce—from within herself as well as from family, friends, and the surrounding community (Lowe and Peek, 1974; Marano, 1980).

In addition, it is more difficult for her to find and meet with other women experiencing similar situations.

Rural postparental and divorced women who are seeking alternatives in education, job training, and employment as well as additional or new sources of emotional support, are likely to have problems locating assistance.[6] First, rural women, by definition, live in sparsely settled or isolated areas and are thus faced with constant transportation problems in good and bad weather that hinder them or prevent them from taking advantage of the few available educational alternatives (Clarenbach, 1977; Joyce and Leadley, 1977). In a sample of mature women students, 50 percent stated they would not have been enrolled if a college had not been within easy commuting distance (Westervelt, 1975).

The distance factor leads to a related problem. There are fewer educational programs for rural women than for urban women in general and for middle-aged rural women in particular. One of the reasons is that there are fewer students available to enroll in specialized courses or programs. Programs that receive federal funds often set prerequisites for minimum enrollment. These guidelines need to take into account the number of women within reasonable commuting distance who need and take advantage of the program rather than an absolute number requirement (Clarenbach, 1977).

Another problem for rural displaced homemakers, in particular, is that although many may need support from human service professionals, they are reluctant to seek help. Many middle-aged rural women feel that they and their families should be self-sufficient. Furthermore, they may be distrustful of new programs, such as displaced homemakers centers, in their community (Marano, 1980).

As can be seen from the above, attention needs to be focused on educational delivery in rural areas as well as on content. The programs should be brought to the audience rather than centralized as in densely populated areas. In addition, many programs will have to create or build on local credibility. One solution to the distance problem alone is the innovative use of television to overcome the high cost of education in rural areas. Another more general solution is credit and noncredit courses and workshops designed and provided by appropriate combinations of continuing education departments, women's studies programs, and the Cooperative Extension Service, which includes university-based expertise, locally based credibility, and a statewide delivery system.

Rural Men at Middle Age

There are little or no data that focus specifically on rural men at middle age. Therefore, brief speculations will be based on multiage studies of rural in comparison with urban men as well as data on farm families. Schumm and Bollman (see Chapter 7) have reported that rural husbands, in comparison with urban husbands, see themselves as giving in more often to their spouses in reference to their obtaining paid employment. This would suggest a problem area for middle-aged rural men who are more likely than younger men to hold to traditional sex roles and, therefore, to object to their wives working.

Middle-aged rural men who are farmers are likely to have a number of problems at this time because their families and their work are so intertwined. Status and career questions will be closely related to parent-child relationships, although there may be no empty nest, since children often remain on the farm or live nearby. The middle-aged farmer involved in a multigeneration farm may be working through problems of taking over increasing responsibility from his father at the same time that he deals with how to achieve equity in sharing farm responsibility and proceeds with his progeny (Rosenblatt and Anderson, Chapter 8).

Rural Marriages at Middle Age

Data reported in this volume indicate that there is no statistically significant difference between rural and urban couples in terms of satisfaction with spouse or with marriage.[7] That is, when all other sources of satisfaction or dissatisfaction are taken into account, rural residence versus urban residence is not an important factor. This does not necessarily mean that there is no difference between rural and urban areas in the proportion of people who are satisfied with their marriages, because factors that affect marital satisfaction may be differentially located in rural and urban areas. For example, there is a difference in marital satisfaction as size of family increases. A greater proportion of rural than urban families have large families. Therefore, more rural couples than urban couples are likely to be unhappy. How will this particular situation affect middle age? If the association of lower marital satisfaction with larger families is the result of problems with children, financial pressures caused by children, and couples spending more time with child-centered activities rather than with each other, then satisfaction with the marriage should increase when the children leave home. If, however, dissatisfaction derives from other factors, or if it seriously separates the couple emotionally, dissatisfaction could increase. Evidence from studies of middle-aged urban residents indicates that more of the couples will be in the former than the latter category. As more rural couples have fewer children, this particular factor may be less important in the future.

Not all correlates of marital satisfaction are differentially distributed between rural and urban areas. For example, couples from both areas see themselves as equally empathetic and congruent on self-disclosure. Moreover, joint decision making and open communication are associated with marital satisfaction in both rural and urban samples. In the future, rural couples who are not satisfied with the level of communication in their marriages will be more likely to divorce, contributing to the number of people in rural areas who will have been divorced by middle age. In the near future, dissatisfaction will affect the divorce rate among middle-aged couples—but not as much as among younger couples, who are more likely to expect higher levels of marital satisfaction and to accept the possibility of divorce if those levels are not achieved.

Conclusion

Despite the recognition that being middle-aged is not an abstract experience, there has been little attempt to explore the differences between being middle-aged in rural as compared to urban America. This chapter contributes to such an exploration by positing some general differences between urban and rural America as well as some demographic changes within rural America that affect this period in the life cycle. It should be noted that this chapter, as prior work on middle age, makes many generalizations, albeit about rural Americans—and they are not a homogeneous group. Further research is needed to specify the effect of other important variables, especially race and class, upon the experience of middle age, in rural as well as in urban America.

In many aspects of marital and family happiness, research has shown little or no difference between rural and urban individuals and families. However, further research is needed to explore the effect of traditional family and work norms on those who are caught in the transition between the old and the new. For example, as noted before, the divorce rate is rising in rural areas, although it is not as high as it is in urban areas, and public opinion continues to be more negative about divorce in rural as compared to urban areas. What is the specific effect on a displaced homemaker, divorced in middle age, of her own attitudes, those of friends and family, as well as the community in general? How does the differential in approval or disapproval of divorce in rural versus urban areas affect the resources available to the divorcee and ultimately her ability to cope with the situation?

Finally, the experience of middle age is conditioned by the historical period in which people live as well as by the particular situation of individuals. To be middle-aged in rural America today is not the same as it was in 1960, nor the same as it will be in 2000. Once we have developed an understanding of middle age as it is lived by various groups of people in rural America during the next decade, we will need to turn our sights to the future and consider such questions as these: What issues will continue to divide rural and urban areas? What problems will confront men in rural areas—farm and nonfarm—who are 25 today, as they become middle aged in 2000? How will the difficult economic times in the next decade affect the middle-aged marriages of the future? What options will be available in rural areas in the year 2000 for women who have been working from ages 25 to 45? One thing is certain, middle age will continue to be experienced in the context of personal and social change.

Notes

1. An earlier version of this paper was presented at the Family in Rural Society Session, Rural Sociological Society Annual meetings, San Francisco, August 1978. An earlier version of the material focusing on urban women was published in "Toward a Reassessment of Women's Experience at Middle

Age," *The Family Coordinator,* 28 July 1979, 377–382.

2. I recognize that this sets the urban experience as the standard. However, the available literature is based on urban samples. In addition, there is evidence that norms and values do spread from urban centers to rural communities. Therefore, the rural future can, to some extent, be seen in the urban present and past.

3. For information on many aspects of the situation of displaced homemakers, see the *Journal of Home Economics,* 71, Summer 1979.

4. The empirical evidence on this point is sparse, based on different populations, and contradictory. See Birnbaum (1975) and Harkins (1978).

5. For additional comments on methodological factors affecting results of studies of marital satisfaction over the life cycle, see Schram (1979).

6. The following discussion on alternatives focuses on education. Problems in finding suitable alternatives in job training, employment, or volunteer work, while not identical, are likely to be equally difficult. For a discussion of displaced homemakers centers in rural areas, see Marano (1980). For a discussion of the educational and economic situation of rural women of all ages, see Chapter 9 of this volume by Bescher-Donnelly and Smith.

7. The material in this section is based on Chapter 7 of this volume by Schumm and Bollman.

References

Barnett, R. and G. K. Baruch. "Women in the Middle Years: An Overview." Paper presented at the meeting of the Society for Research in Child Development, New Orleans, Louisiana, March 1977.

Birnbaum, J. A. "Life Patterns and Self-Esteem in Gifted Family-Oriented and Career-Committed Women." In M. T. Schuck Mednick, S. Schwartz Tangri, and L. Wladis Hoffman (eds.), *Women and Achievement: Social and Motivational Analysis.* New York: Halsted Press, 1975, 396–419.

Brim, O. G., Jr. "Theories of the Male Mid-life Crisis." *The Counseling Psychologist,* 1976, 6 (1), 2–9.

Brown, D. L. "Recent Changes in the Demographic Structure of the Rural Family." In R. T. Coward (ed.), *Rural Families Across the Life Span: Implications for Community Programming.* West Lafayette, Indiana: Indiana Cooperative Extension Service, 1977, 18–41.

Clarenbach, K. *Educational Needs of Rural Women and Girls.* Washington, D.C.: The National Advisory Council on Women's Educational Programs, 1977.

Cohen, J. F. "Male Roles in Mid-Life." *The Family Coordinator,* 1979, 2, 465–471.

Elder, G. H. "Family History and the Life Course." *Journal of Family History,* 1977, 2, 279–304.

Feldman, H. and M. Feldman. "The Family Life Cycle: Some Suggestions for Recycling." *Journal of Marriage and the Family,* 1975, 37, 277–284.

Glenn, N. O. "Psychological Well-being in the Postparental Stage: Some Evidence from National Surveys." *Journal of Marriage and the Family*, 1975, 37, 105–110.

Harkins, E. B. "Effects of Empty Nest Transition on Self-report of Psychological and Physical Well-being." *Journal of Marriage and the Family*, 1978, 40, 549–556.

Joyce, L. M. and S. M. Leadley. *An Assessment of Research Needs of Women in the Rural United States: Literature Review and Annotated Bibliography*. University Park, Pennsylvania: Department of Agricultural Economics and Rural Sociology, Agricultural Experiment Station, The Pennsylvania State University, 1977.

Journal of Home Economics, 1979, 71.

LeShan, E. *The Wonderful Crisis of Middle Age*. New York: Warner Books, 1974.

Levinson, D. J., C. M. Darrow, E. B. Klein, M. H. Levinson, and B. McKee. "Periods in the Adult Development of Men: Ages 18–45." *The Counseling Psychologist*, 1976, 6, 21–25.

Levinson, D. J., C. M. Darrow, E. B. Klein, M. H. Levinson, and B. McKee. *The Seasons of a Man's Life*. New York: Knopf, 1978.

Lowe, G. D. and C. W. Peek. "Location and Lifestyle: The Comparative Explanatory Ability of Urbanism and Rurality." *Rural Sociology*, 1974, 39, 392–420.

Lowenthal, M. F. and D. Chiriboga. "Transition to the Empty Nest." *Archives of General Psychiatry*, 1972, 26, 8–14.

Lowenthal, M. F., M. Thurner, and D. Chiriboga. *Four Stages of Life: A Comparative Study of Women and Men Facing Transitions*. San Francisco: Jossey-Bass, 1975.

Marano, C. E. "Displaced Homemakers: Critical Needs and Trends (A Summary Report with Special Emphasis on the Rural Displaced Homemaker)." Speech delivered at the 1980 Agricultural Outlook Conference, Session 18, Washington, D.C., November 7, 1979.

Neugarten, B. L. "Adaptation and the Life Cycle." *Counseling Psychologist*, 1976, 6 (1), 16–20.

____. "Adult Personality: Toward a Psychology of the Life Cycle." In B. L. Neugarten (ed.), *Middle Age and Aging*. Chicago: University of Chicago Press, 1968, 137–147.

____. "The Awareness of Middle Age." In B. L. Neugarten (ed.), *Middle Age and Aging*. Chicago: University of Chicago Press, 1968, 93–98.

Neugarten, B. L., and N. Datan. "Sociological Perspectives on the Life Cycle." In P. B. Baltes and K. W. Schaie (eds.), *Life-span Developmental Psychology: Personality and Socialization*. New York: Academic Press, 1973, 53–69.

Oppenheimer, V. K. "The Life Cycle Squeeze: The Interaction of Men's Occupational and Family Life Cycles." *Demography*, 1974, 11 (2), 227–245.

Perrucci, C. C., and D. B. Targ (eds.). *Marriage and the Family: A Critical*

Analysis and Proposals for Change. New York: David McKay Company, 1974.

Rollins, B. C. and K. L. Cannon. "Marital Satisfaction Over the Family Life Cycle: A Reevaluation." *Journal of Marriage and the Family,* 1974, 36, 271–282.

Schram, R. W. "Marital Satisfaction Over the Family Life Cycle: A Critique and Proposal." *Journal of Marriage and the Family,* 1979, 41, 7–12.

Sheehy, G. *Passages: Predictable Crises of Adult Life.* New York: E. P. Dutton, 1974.

Targ, D. B. "Toward a Reassessment of Women's Experience at Middle Age." *The Family Coordinator,* 1979, 28, 377–382.

Troll, L. *Early and Middle Adulthood: The Best is Yet to Be—Maybe.* Monterey, California: Brooks/Cole, 1975.

_____. "The Family of Later Life: A Decade Review." In C. Broderick (ed.), *A Decade of Family Research and Action.* Minneapolis: National Council on Family Relations, 1971, 187–214.

U.S. Bureau of the Census, "Marital Status and Living Arrangements: March 1978." *Current Population Reports.* Series P-20, No. 338. Washington, D.C.: U.S. Government Printing Office, 1979.

U.S. Department of Labor. *Mature Women Workers: A Profile.* Washington, D.C.: U.S. Department of Labor, Employment Standards Administration, Women's Bureau, 1976.

Westervelt, Esther M. *Barriers to Women's Participation in Postsecondary Education: A Review of Research and Commentary as of 1973-74.* Washington, D.C.: U.S. Government Printing Office, 1975.

11

FAMILY NETWORKS
OF THE RURAL AGED[1]

Edward A. Powers, Patricia M. Keith,
and Willis J. Goudy

In 1962, Sussman and Burchinal commented that most sociologists investigating family patterns had used urban samples, confining research to the WUMP—white, urban, middle-class Protestants. The field has not changed greatly in the last decade. Of the fifteen major studies on aged families published in the 1960s, only two (Youmans, 1963; Shanas et al., 1968) presented data on the aged in rural settings.

Perhaps it has been assumed that work on the rural aged would be conducted by rural sociologists. In the judgment of Smith and Zopf (1970), however, few studies of rural family life have been conducted since mid-century; this observation is supported by Payne and Bailey (1967) and Anderson (1957). In nearly forty years, only two articles in *Rural Sociology,* the official journal of the Rural Sociological Society, were concerned with family patterns of the rural aged.

We are starting from the assumption that the family patterns and friendships of the rural aged are not *necessarily* the same as those of the urban aged. We do not automatically subscribe to what may be an artificial rural-urban distinction, but instead suggest that not enough is known about rural patterns or rural-urban differences to assume that data on urban patterns are generalizable to rural settings. The few comparisons of rural-urban patterns that exist (Bultena, 1969; Bultena et al., 1971; Shanas et al., 1968; Youmans, 1963) suggest there are differences in family interactions and, indeed, that many aspects of rural patterns run counter to extant myths of the integrated rural setting. Such myths reflect the long-standing assumption that the disintegration of the family has proceeded further in the city and that the heterogeneous nature of the city has a deleterious effect on primary groups and undermines intrafamilial activities (for example, Bossard, 1948; Burgess and Locke, 1945; Loomis and Beegle, 1950; Martindale and Monachesi, 1951; Mirande, 1970).

What, then, is known about the rural aged? What has been demonstrated about the family patterns of the older individual in rural settings?

Family Patterns

Residence

The maintenance of independence is a major goal of most older persons. Few rural aged want to live with children even after retirement (Bauder et al., 1962; McKain and Baldwin, 1953; Sewell et al., 1953). No doubt being able to maintain independence is a source of considerable satisfaction, while the threatened loss of independence from financial difficulty or health problems is a major source of worry. To many, moving in with relatives must be visible proof of increasing dependency. In a rural Pennsylvania community (Britton et al., 1961), most residents felt that it was admirable to live alone and, further, either disapproving or at least neutral toward the idea of older persons living with family. Many qualified their responses by suggesting that it would be acceptable for older persons to live with relatives if they could no longer care for themselves. But, when the question of shared residence was asked of older persons in an Iowa study (Martel and Morris, 1960), there was considerable resistance to the idea of living with relatives, even if circumstances might require a change in residence. The least acceptable alternative to living independently was residing with a sibling or with a child. Persons in rural settings were less willing to live with a relative than were urban residents.

When a number of these individuals in Iowa were reinterviewed ten years later (all were more than 70 years of age when interviewed the second time), there was even greater resistance to the suggestion of moving in with relatives (Bultena et al., 1971). Indeed, respondents were as willing to move into a nursing home as they were to live with children or other close relatives.

But what are actual residence patterns? The rather gradual retirement process and transfer of property in rural areas (Bauder et al., 1962; Heady et al., 1953; Kaplan and Taietz, 1958; McKain and Baldwin, 1953) would suggest that there is a large number of three generation households. Certainly this fits stereotypes of the close-knit rural family.

The census gives only general categories of household composition but does contain several pertinent facts for 1970. It has been suggested that the aged in the open country, particularly upon the death of a spouse, move into small towns, and in fact the rural aged in towns of under 1,000 or in the open country were more likely to be living alone than were urban aged. But the percentage of the aged in central cities who were living alone was greater than in other urban areas (U.S. Bureau of the Census, 1971).

Perhaps the best sample providing information on the rural aged is that of Shanas and her associates (1968) who obtained nearly 2,500 interviews in the United States in a stratified multistage probability design. Among other things, they compared the family characteristics and behaviors of three occupational groups—white collar, blue collar (including service workers) and agricultural workers.[2] They found that aged persons in rural areas were more likely to be living with relatives, which they argued was a result of the greater number of children in rural families and the larger proportion of low incomes forcing joint residence.[3]

Overall, the data suggest that, in general, the rural aged are most likely to live with a spouse. The next most frequent pattern is to live alone. When rural aged live with others, it is usually with children. The number who live with children may well have changed in recent decades. Koller (1954) estimated that 25 years ago one-quarter of the rural households in Ohio were three generation. But less than one-tenth of the rural aged were living with children in 1970 (U.S. Bureau of the Census, 1971). Women were more likely to be living with children, and the child with whom parents were living was more likely to be a daughter (Shanas et al., 1968).

Proximity and Contact with Children

Nowhere is the mobility of the young more obvious than with the children of the rural aged. Only 19 percent of the children of rural Iowa aged (Bultena et al., 1971) and 26 percent of the children of Wisconsin rural aged (Bultena, 1969) lived in the same community as their parents. Contrariwise, 34 percent of the children of urban aged in Iowa and 51 percent in Wisconsin were in the same community as their parents. Despite the high outmigration of children, most rural elderly had at least one child who was readily accessible. In three separate studies, over two-thirds of the parents had at least one child within a half-hour drive or so (Bultena, 1969; Shanas et al., 1968; Youmans, 1963). In fact, more than half of the aged in each study had at least one child within a few minutes. However, in a study of rural Missouri communities (Rosencranz et al., 1968) a relatively large proportion of older persons did not have living children (20 percent). One-fifth of their respondents were over 80 and, thus, were experiencing an increasingly common problem of many aged—outliving their children. Nevertheless, more than half of the total sample had a child living within 15 miles.

The location of the nearest child is important for familial contact and assistance. The amount of help received and the extent of personal contact will be affected by changes in the proximity of children. It could be argued that with increasing age there is likely to be geographic convergence between aged parents and at least one of the children; that is, one child becomes more accessible through the residential mobility of either the parents or a child. This has been tested with ten-year longitudinal data in Iowa (Bultena et al., 1971). For most, there had been no change in the accessibility of the nearest child. Sixteen percent did have their nearest child within the community, but for 12 percent the nearest child was farther away.

Although it seemed that rural aged were more likely to have seen at least one child recently (Shanas et al., 1968), the urban aged visited with their children more frequently (Bultena, 1969; Youmans, 1963). No doubt this reflects, in part, the urban proximity of children, but only to a degree. Among the urban aged in Kentucky (Youmans, 1963), a greater proportion had weekly contact with children within 9 miles, as well as with children within a 10- to 49-mile radius. Thus, even at greater distances, the aged in urban settings maintained contact with their children.

Several factors seem to affect parent-child contact. Age, especially for men

(Britton and Britton, 1972), and occupation (Bauder and Doerflinger, undated) were related to the frequency of contact with children. But contrary to the assumption that the contact and care of aged parents usually falls to daughters, beyond a slight difference in residence patterns, there was little sexual differentiation in the amount of contact rural men and women had with either sons or daughters (Pihlblad and Adams, 1972; Shanas et al., 1968).

Most attention to kinship ties has been limited to investigations of face-to-face contact. Yet, most contact between the aged in rural settings and their children is by telephone. In rural Iowa (Powers and Liston, 1971) only a third of the total interaction with children was face to face, but more than half was by telephone. Considering all sources of interaction—phone, face to face, and mail—94 percent had at least one child contact a week and 63 percent had two or more child contacts a week.

Proximity and Contact with Siblings

Little is known about the location of the brothers and sisters of the rural aged. Youmans (1963) found that Kentucky rural aged actually lived closer to siblings than to children (the median distance to children was 47 miles and the median distance to siblings was 37 miles). Sixty percent of the aged in Casey County (rural) were within 9 miles of at least one brother or sister, but only 41 percent of the aged in Lexington lived that close to a sibling.

Certainly, brothers and sisters play an important role in the social world of the rural aged. Yet, the frequency of contact with siblings is less than that with children (Bultena, 1969; Shanas et al., 1968; Youmans, 1963). Proximity is important in the extent of contact. Youmans (1963) found that 75 percent of the siblings who lived within a 9-mile radius were seen at least monthly, compared with only 30 percent who lived within a 10- to 50-mile area. At greater distances sibling contact was effectively terminated; half the brothers and sisters living more than 50 miles away were not seen once a year.

Contact with Family

With the exception of Adams's (1964) work in a southeastern urban setting, there has been little attention to the more qualitative nature of kinship ties. Bultena et al. (1971) have some indirect evidence of the changing nature of family contact for a sample of rural aged. In both 1960 and 1970, their respondents were asked about activities that provided the greatest satisfaction in life. Over the decade, there was a considerable decrease (from an average of five, to two) in the number of activities mentioned. In 1960, most activity centered on social contacts and the home. In 1970, only home-centered activities were still sources of greatest satisfaction. Hobbies were the only activity that were satisfying to an increasing number of persons, although TV and radio still were important to a large number of persons. The percentage of persons who received greatest satisfaction from contact with children had decreased from 64 to 5 percent. Those who received greatest satisfaction from contact with other relatives decreased from 51 to 1 percent. Thus, a considerable number of persons evidenced emotional withdrawal from family contacts.

Despite a change in the importance of contact with relatives, there is little suggestion that the rural aged are isolated. In one county in Iowa (Fuller et al., 1963) only 17 percent in rural communities and 12 percent in the open country had not seen a "blood relative" within the last month. Britton and Britton (1967) suggested that the large number of rural aged who had not had contact with relatives in the Iowa study may have resulted from interviews being conducted in February. Only 8 percent of the rural aged in a national sample had not seen at least one child (let alone relative) within the last month (Shanas et al., 1968). Further, 4 percent of the elderly in south-western Iowa had not had contact with a child—face to face, by mail, or by telephone—during the last week, and only one-third had less than daily contact with a child (Powers and Liston, 1971).

Assistance

The norm of intergenerational reciprocity still is strong in the United States. An exchange of aid between generations is both expected and frequently observed in areas such as baby-sitting, aid during illness, housework, transportation, shopping, advice, money, or money equivalents (Adams, 1964; Aldous and Hill, 1965; Christopherson et al., 1960; Sharp and Axelrod, 1956; Sussman, 1953). The pattern in intergenerational assistance is for aid to flow from the old to the young and from the middle generation to parents and children (Adams, 1964; Aldous and Hill, 1965). It is these assistance patterns that have led to the rejection of the concept of the "isolated nuclear family" so long assumed to best describe the American family.[4]

Despite intergenerational help, there are verbal norms of noninterference. To establish and maintain independence is an important goal in American society. Yet, for most persons, the later stages of the life cycle produce the threat of, if not actual, dependency.

Helping Patterns

Information on rural-urban differences in assistance to older persons is somewhat contradictory. A national sample (Shanas et al., 1968) and a study in small Missouri towns (Rosencranz et al., 1968) found that three-fifths of the rural aged were receiving *some* form of help from children. Yet, only two-fifths of older persons in both rural Iowa (Bultena et al., 1971) and in two small communities in Pennsylvania (Montgomery, 1965) received *regular* assistance from all sources of help, including children. The regularity of assistance may be a crucial factor in determining the extent of assistance to the rural aged.

In an Iowa study (Bultena et al., 1971), most help was provided in nonpersonal areas, particularly housework, shopping, transportation, and yard work. These four activities accounted for over two-thirds of all help received. Less than one-fifth of the daily assistance was in personal areas—getting in and out of bed, climbing stairs, medical care, etc. Most assistance was provided by the friend-kin network with children and their families providing more than half of all assistance. Similar helping patterns were observed in Missouri (Rosencranz et al., 1968). In the only reported study of Blacks, the rural aged in

Georgia desired and received a different type of assistance from children than did urban Blacks (Jackson, 1970).

Widowhood

Almost 40 percent of the rural aged are widowed and, of course, women are more likely than men to be without spouses (U.S. Bureau of the Census, 1971). From the little that is known about rural widowhood, it seems that it is an especially isolating experience for males. In an investigation of more than 1,500 rural elderly in Missouri (Pihlblad and Adams, 1972; Pihlblad et al., 1972) most men and women continued to live alone, maintained independence, and kept contact with children and other relatives. But there were a number, particularly men, whose lives were seriously disrupted. After the initial years of adjusting to widowhood, men were more likely to experience a significant decline in contact with children and other relatives and in formal organization and religious-group memberships. Similar sex differences in the isolation of the widowed aged have been observed in rural Washington (Berardo, 1967). By using a social-isolation index consisting of measures of residence patterns, family and friend visiting, employment, and attitudes, it was found that widows were twice as likely, and widowers four times as likely, as married persons to be isolated. Rural-urban differences in social isolation were insignificant for widowed individuals.

The rural widowed are more dependent on relatives than are married individuals. Montgomery (1965) found that the widowed aged in rural Pennsylvania were twice as likely to receive regular assistance and more likely to take the advice of relatives and others in areas such as finances, food, and buying habits. Again, the situation seemed more extreme for men than women. Men in rural Missouri (Pihlblad and Adams, 1972) were more likely to turn to others for housekeeping services and transportation. Except for a change in whether a member of the immediate family drives the car, widowhood did not seem to cause similar disruptions for most women. Adjustments in social contacts and household activities occurred, but were less extreme and more gradual.

The Iowa Older Workers Panel Study

In the research that we have reviewed, little attention has been given to family patterns of the aged in rural settings as they relate to occupational categories or work status. In the analysis that follows, we examine change in the social networks of older men in terms of occupation and work status.

Methodology and Sample

In 1964, interviews were conducted with a sample of fully employed males 50 years of age and older. The 1,870 Iowans were living in or near communities of from 2,500 to 10,000 population. Respondents were sampled from five occupational categories: self-employed professionals, salaried professionals, proprietors of small businesses, factory workers, and farmers. The occupational classes studied did not represent all occupational groups in nonmetropolitan midwestern communities, nor were they necessarily the most important. They did include, however, the self-employed and the salaried or wage worker, the professional and the nonprofessional, and the agricultural and nonagricultural worker. For each occupational category, sampling rates within the communities were determined so that a uniform statewide sampling rate was maintained. Surviving respondents were reinterviewed in 1974 (N = 1,332). Of the initial 1,870 respondents, 71 percent were reinterviewed, 22 percent were deceased, 4 percent refused to be reinterviewed, 2 percent were never recontacted, and 1 percent were too ill or senile. Thus, more than 91 percent of those eligible for the second interview cooperated in completing the 1974 survey instrument.

The data reported below are from both sets of interviews. Change over the decade in each of the following categories is considered: marital status, household composition, and interaction with children, grandchildren, and siblings. Helping patterns also are examined in relation to occupation and work status.

Marital Status in 1964 and 1974

When first interviewed in 1964, almost all of the men (94 percent) were married but there was variation among occupational groups. Professionals were most likely to be married (97 percent), while factory workers were least likely (87 percent). Only twenty men in the sample were widowed, the largest proportion of which were factory workers. Only eighteen persons were divorced or separated. Three percent of the men had never been married and most of these were farmers and factory workers. Thus marriage was the dominant pattern, although it was somewhat related to occupation.

Ten years later, most of the men still were married. Now businessmen reported the highest incidence of marriage (93 percent) followed by farmers and professionals (approximately 90 percent each), and finally factory workers (83 percent). Only 131 of the total sample of 1,332 were not married, and most of them were widowers. As in the first interview, widowerhood was most prevalent among factory workers.

Households in 1964 and 1974

For most people, the household is an important center of social interaction and, in fact, is the primary location of interactants for many (Powers and Bultena, 1976). It therefore was important to examine the household composition of this sample as well as the amount of time spent with household members.

As might be expected, when first interviewed most men lived in households that included a wife and were usually one- or two-generation households (Table 11.1). Businessmen and both groups of professionals were likely to live in single-generation homes, while factory workers and farmers were more likely to be in two-generation households. Few men in any occupational category lived alone, although the largest number with no one else in the house were factory workers.

Table 11.1: Household Composition in 1964 and 1974, by Occupation

Occupation	Respondent Only		Single Generation (husband & wife)		Two Generation (husband, wife and children)		Three Generation (husband, wife children & grandchildren)		Incomplete Family Unit (husband & children; husband, wife, grand-children; husband, wife & other relative)		Non-Familial Household (respondent & a non-relative)	
	1964	1974	1964	1974	1964	1974	1964	1974	1964	1974	1964	1974
Farmers	3.7%	6.1%	47.7%	72.9%	42.3%	12.7%	.4%	.4%	4.5%	6.9%	.8%	.8%
Factory Workers	8.1%	13.1%	35.8%	67.1%	47.2%	11.8%	2.1%	.8%	4.6%	4.2%	.4%	2.1%
Businessmen	2.8%	6.6%	53.5%	79.5%	38.7%	7.9%	.9%	.3%	4.0%	8.0%	-	.6%
Salaried Professionals	.7%	4.2%	51.2%	82.9%	43.6%	7.7%	.3%	-	1.3%	3.1%	2.8%	1.7%
Self-Employed Professionals	2.5%	6.1%	57.2%	82.0%	36.3%	7.0%	.4%	-	2.4%	3.6%	.8%	.8%

Since most of the men were married when reinterviewed, it was not surprising that most were still living with a spouse in 1974. At that time the majority of households in each occupational grouping was a single-generation unit, particularly for businessmen and professionals (Table 11.1). Factory workers and farmers were most likely to have children at home, although factory workers were also twice as likely as any other occupational grouping to live alone or reside in a nonfamilial setting.

But household composition does not necessarily indicate much about interaction. Therefore we asked our sample how much time they spent with members of their household in nonwork situations (such as eating, talking, watching TV, reading, and playing games). When first interviewed in 1964, few men in any occupational group spent much time with household members (Table 11.2). Since all were fully employed at the time, this is not very surprising. Weekends, however, were different. In each occupation there was a marked increase in the amount of time spent with family on Saturdays that increased even more on Sundays. Farmers were the only exception, spending less time with household members than any other occupational group. Interestingly, farmers with the lowest rates of divorce and separation spent the least amount of nonworking time with family members. Ten years later the amount of time spent with family had increased for all days of the week. Farmers again were still least likely to spend time with household members, even if retired.

The amount of time spent with family was also related to work status, at least during the work week (Table 11.3). Fully employed men spent the least amount of time with family members, followed by partly employed men. Work status differences also were observed on Saturdays, although to a lesser degree. But the increase in nonwork time spent with family was not totally a function of retirement patterns. Fully employed men in every occupational category averaged more time with family members in 1974 than had occurred ten years earlier.

1974 Familial Interaction

When reinterviewed, more exact information was obtained on the amount of contact these men had with three types of relatives—children, grandchildren, and siblings. There was a marked difference in the amount of contact occupational groups had with children (Table 11.4); farmers and factory workers had the highest rate of contact with each child, businessmen were about average, and professionals, particularly salaried, had the lowest. In fact, farmers and factory workers had twice the contact with each of their children as did salaried professionals. Contrary to the common belief that once a person withdraws from work there is time to spend with others, we found that men who were working full time had a higher rate of contact per child than did either partly employed or retired men.

As might be expected given their number of children, farmers and factory workers reported the largest number of grandchildren. Nearly a fifth of the farmers and factory workers had at least thirteen grandchildren, compared

Table 11.2: Average (Mean) Number of Hours Spent with Family in Non-Work Activities, by Occupation, 1964 and 1974

☐ 1964 ☐ 1974

Occupation	Weekdays		Saturday		Sunday	
Farmers	4.1	7.3	7.3	9.0	8.4	9.3
Factory workers	4.9	7.4	9.9	10.3	11.0	10.7
Businessmen	4.2	7.8	7.5	9.8	10.2	11.4
Salaried Professionals	4.7	7.7	8.8	10.8	9.9	10.4
Self-Employed Professionals	4.8	7.7	8.5	10.9	10.1	12.2

Table 11.3: Average (Mean) Number of Hours Spent with Family in Non-Work Activities by Worker Status, 1974			
Work Status	Day of Week		
	Weekdays	Saturday	Sunday
Working Full-time	5.9	9.4	10.7
Working Part-time	7.5	10.4	11.3
Retired	9.7	11.2	11.4

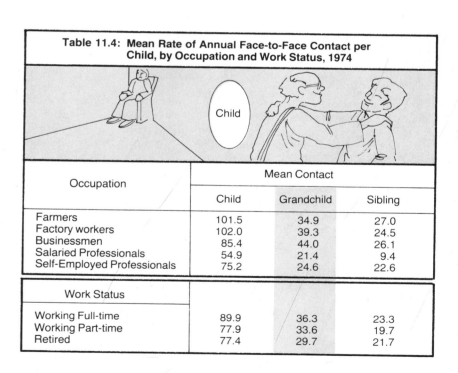

Table 11.4: Mean Rate of Annual Face-to-Face Contact per Child, by Occupation and Work Status, 1974			
Occupation	Mean Contact		
	Child	Grandchild	Sibling
Farmers	101.5	34.9	27.0
Factory workers	102.0	39.3	24.5
Businessmen	85.4	44.0	26.1
Salaried Professionals	54.9	21.4	9.4
Self-Employed Professionals	75.2	24.6	22.6
Work Status			
Working Full-time	89.9	36.3	23.3
Working Part-time	77.9	33.6	19.7
Retired	77.4	29.7	21.7

with only 4 percent of professionals. Although differences were not as extreme as with child contact, the amount of interaction these men had with grandchildren was related to occupation (Table 11.4). This time, businessmen had the most frequent contact, followed by factory workers and farmers and, finally, professionals. Once again salaried professionals had the lowest rate of contact of any occupation; half that of businessmen. Work status again was related to the amount of contact. Men working full time had greater contact with grandchildren than did partly employed or retired men.

Siblings were not nearly as important for interaction patterns as were children or grandchildren. The size of the family of orientation was related to occupation (mean number of brothers or sisters: farmers, 3.4; factory workers, 3.3; businessmen, 2.6; salaried professionals, 2.3; self-employed professionals, 2.0). Yet, with the exception of salaried professionals, there was little difference in the amount of contact with siblings, either by occupational grouping or work status (Table 11.4).

Clearly farmers and factory workers had the largest number of close relatives with whom to interact and, for the most part, had the highest rate of contact per interactant. Professionals, particularly salaried professionals, had the least amount of family contact. Nonetheless, family roles were important in the lives of most men; children, grandchildren, and siblings appear to provide opportunity for regular contact. In short, few of our men reported family interaction patterns that suggested social isolation.

Dependency Patterns

It is clear that old age is not considered by many to be the most desirable time of life. Americans tend to venerate youth and virility, and being defined as "old" brings predominantly negative evaluations. It should, therefore, be expected that persons will resist such definitions of themselves. In conceding they are "old," they must acknowledge that they now occupy a highly devalued status in American society. The maintenance of independence, however, allows persons to resist definitions of themselves as old. What would happen if these men no longer could consider themselves to be independent?

We were concerned with who the respondents felt should provide assistance if there was need. In the area of health, the vast majority of men in each occupational category felt the family was responsible for such assistance (Table 11.5); at least four-fifths of each occupation ranked the family as the institution most responsible to provide help. Few felt other groups—government, church, neighbors—should assume a major responsibility for health-related assistance. But this was not the case if there were to be financial need. The government was felt to have primary responsibility for money problems by a large proportion of the men, particularly businessmen, farmers, and factory workers (Table 11.5). Among both groups of professionals, a majority felt the family was most responsible in case of financial need, although a sizable number also considered the government to have a major obligation in this area. Together, the family and the government accounted for at least 95 percent of the responses of each occupational group. In areas of both

Table 11.5: First Ranked Source of Assistance if Physically or Financially Dependent, by Occupation

Occupational Category	Physically Dependent Type of Assistance				Financially Dependent Type of Assistance			
	Govt	Family	Neighbor	Church	Govt	Family	Neighbor	Church
Farmers	7.4%*	86.9%*	2.9%*	2.0%*	59.7%*	38.2%*	-*	.4%*
Factory workers	11.4%	81.0%	6.8%	.4%	61.9%	36.8%	.4%	.4%
Businessmen	9.5%	84.9%	3.8%	.3%	51.4%	46.5%	.3%	1.6%
Salaried Professionals	9.5%	81.3%	2.8%	4.6%	46.8%	49.3%	.4%	1.8%
Self-Employed Professionals	6.2%	86.4%	3.3%	.8%	37.8%	58.8%	—	—

*Percents do not sum 100% because not all men answered all questions.

financial and physical need, employment status was not related to the responses of the men.

Summary

The men in this study, for the most part, were socially engaged and fairly independent. Most were married and living in a household that included at least a spouse, although factory workers and retired men were more likely to be widowed and alone. Both occupation and work status were related to the amount of contact the men had with family members. When first interviewed in 1964, the amount of contact the men had with family members was low and continued to be low for men who were still employed in 1974. Family contact on weekends and in retirement was much higher. There were also occupational differences in family contact. Farmers had the lowest contact within the household in both 1964 and 1974, while factory workers had the highest in 1964 and professionals the highest in 1974. Nevertheless, there was a trend toward more family contact, despite occupation or work status.

Data obtained only in 1974 provided a glimpse of three roles of our men— as a father, grandfather, and brother. Factory workers and farmers had the largest number of relatives and greatest amount of contact with each type of interactants, while professionals, particularly salaried men, had the lowest.

We also were concerned with the extent to which the men had been able to maintain independence. Scarcely a tenth of any occupation or work status considered themselves dependent. If there were physical needs, almost all men felt help should be provided by the family and help should be given by either the family or government if there were financial needs.

Thus, this group of men, despite employment status or occupational grouping, appeared to have extensive social networks. The common stereotype that retirement living is associated with major social disruption was not observed.

Policy Implications and Research Needs

With fully one-third of the aged living in rural settings, it seems natural that policy should be based on research conducted on the rural aged. We do not suggest research attempting to fill minute gaps in the literature; rather, comprehensive longitudinal studies of the rural family, which would be of greatest utility. Because such studies are seldom attempted, articles purporting to add to the literature will continue. Until replication and longitudinal efforts are completed, such efforts, although helpful, offer only a temporary solution.

Comprehensive studies should include both interregional and rural-urban samples. Differences in patterns of friendship and family interaction between aged in rural and urban settings seem to reflect variation in both proximity and the mobility of the aged. Residential propinquity is important for social networks, particularly with close relatives (Klatzky, 1972). The rural aged are likely to live alone and to have a number of children who have migrated.

Consequently it was anticipated that the rural aged would have less overall parent-child contact and interact regularly with fewer children. Even though relatives are less available to the rural aged, they usually have some access to these family members. Even so, these relationships are more limited than those of their urban counterparts, suggesting that propinquity is very important for contact, especially with the increasing age-related mobility problems of older siblings.

In addition to obtaining help from family and friends, rural aged families benefit from a variety of public and private agencies. Because of great physical separation in rural areas and the attendant low visibility, cooperation among service agencies becomes an important concern. Thus, interorganizational relationships should be encouraged and examined. Providing services without duplication mandates a system based on agency cooperation. Fostering interagency cooperation should be general policy. Such relationships are usually claimed to exist. Yet, the increasing number of organizations working with rural aged families makes cooperation difficult. Studies of both interorganizational relations in rural areas and techniques for building these ties are needed.

A related problem concerns the failure of aged rural residents to use the organizational resources provided (Powers and Bultena, 1974). Although the elderly do not want to use relatives or friends, they usually depend upon informal linkages for assistance. Research could indicate methods to increase the use of formal agencies without the loss of independence and self-respect. Religious institutions may be the most appropriate organizations around which programs acceptable to the aged could be structured (Pihlblad and Rosencranz, 1969; Stojanovic, 1972).

Public and private agencies, however, often stress assisting the individual rather than the family unit. Service delivery systems provide excellent aid to individuals living alone, but often treat families as if they were composed of nonintegrated groupings of individuals. Powers and Bultena (1974) suggest family-directed assistance for some aged. Although their data and argument provide support for useful policy recommendations, the difficulties of program change plus the potential impact of family-related assistance in rural areas are not known. For example, in most discussions of the aged, children are assumed to be in the prime of life and fully capable of financial, social, and psychological support of older relatives. The current aged, however, may have offspring who also are in the later stages of the life cycle. Parent and offspring both may be classified as aged, fully retired, and in need of public and/or private agency assistance. If the retirement age continues to be lowered, the number of such family units will increase dramatically. The implications of this are difficult to predict, but the nature of the questions that must be answered is evident. For example, when the offspring leave the work force, what changes take place in various parental ties? Are offspring more likely to use available agency services than are parents? Do offspring increase their interaction with parents when all are aged?

To set policy accurately, research should be conducted by applied social scientists who can attempt alternative small-scale demonstration programs on the basis of research findings. After program evaluation is completed, the most appropriate course of action should be apparent. Existing state cooperative extension services provide a delivery system useful in training assistance personnel and evaluating program impact; this system strongly identifies with rural areas and provides accredited entry to most rural families. Without initial research, demonstration programs, evaluation, and cooperative interorganizational relationships, attempts to assist the rural aged family will continue to represent an effort so diversified as to contribute negligibly and sometimes even negatively to those who need help. Although it should seem obvious after recent federal efforts to reduce poverty, researchers and agency personnel too often continue to protect their own fiefdoms rather than cooperate in meaningful attempts to develop comprehensive studies and programs related to aged rural family patterns.

Notes

1. A revision of a portion of this chapter appears in E. A. Powers, P. M. Keith, and W. J. Goudy, "Family Relationships and Friendships among the Rural Aged," in T. O. Byerts, S. C. Howell, and L. A. Pastalan (eds.), *Environmental Context of Aging.* New York: Garland STPM Press, 1979.

2. Although they believe that the three occupations reflect rural and urban populations, they provided no definition of rural, and not all white collar and blue collar workers were in urban areas.

3. Rural-urban differences in 1970 in the number of children ever born per 1,000 women 65 years of age or older ever married were 3.4 and 2.6 respectively. Rural-urban differences in the percentage of persons 65 or older below poverty levels were 28 and 13 percent respectively (U.S. Bureau of the Census, 1971).

4. There are scores of studies addressed to this issue. To attempt to be exhaustive would do little more than overlook a number of excellent studies. To many, however, the turning point in this debate was the interdisciplinary volume on intergenerational relations edited by Shanas and Streib (1965). For a discussion of the literature on urbanism and kinship, see Sussman and Burchinal (1962).

References

Adams, B. "Structural Factors Affecting Parental Aid to Married Children." *Journal of Marriage and the Family,* 1964, 26, 327–331.

Aldous, J. and R. Hill. "Social Cohesion, Lineage Type and Intergenerational Transmission." *Social Forces,* 1965, 43, 471–482.

Anderson, W. *Bibliography of Researches in Rural Sociology.* Ithaca, New York: Cornell University, 1957.

Bauder, W. and J. Doerflinger. "Patterns of the Withdrawal from Occupational

Roles Among Older Men." Unpublished final report of the Cooperative Research and Demonstration Grants Program, U.S. Department of Health, Education and Welfare, undated.

Bauder, W., O. Duncan, and J. Tarver. "The Social Security and Retirement Program of Oklahoma Farm Operators and Farm Landlords." Stillwater, Oklahoma: Agricultural Experiment Station Research Bulletin B-592, 1962.

Berardo, F. M. "Social Adaptation to Widowhood Among a Rural-Urban Aged Population." Pullman, Washington: Agricultural Experiment Station Bulletin 689. College of Agriculture, Washington State University, 1967.

Bossard, J. *The Sociology of Child Development.* New York: Harpers, 1948.

Britton, J. and J. Britton. "Expectations for Older Persons in a Rural Community." *Geriatrics,* 1962, 17, 602–608.

_____. "The Middle-Aged and Older Rural Person and His Family." In E. Youmans (ed.), *Older Rural Americans.* Lexington: University of Kentucky Press, 1967.

_____. *Personality Changes in Aging.* New York: Springer Publishing Company, 1972.

Britton, J., W. Mather, and A. Lansing. "Expectations for Older Persons in a Rural Community: Living Arrangements and Family Relationships." *Journal of Gerontology,* 1961, 16, 156–162.

Bultena, G. "Rural-Urban Differences in the Familial Interaction of the Aged." *Rural Sociology,* 1969, 34, 5–15.

Bultena, G., E. Powers, P. Falkman, and D. Frederick. "Life After 70 in Iowa." Ames, Iowa: Sociology Report 95, 1971. (Most of the data of this study presented in this paper does not appear in the report. Further analysis of the data was necessary to present rural-urban distinctions.)

Burgess, E. and H. Locke. *The Family.* New York: American Book Company, 1945.

Christopherson, V., J. Vandiver, and M. Krueger. "The Married College Student." *Marriage and Family Living,* 1960, 22, 122–128.

Fuller, W., R. Wakeley, W. Lunden, P. Swenson, and E. Willis. "Characteristics of Persons 60 Years of Age and Older in Linn County Iowa." Ames, Iowa: Agricultural and Home Economics Experiment Station Special Report 33, 1963.

Heady, E., W. Back, and E. Peterson. "Interdependence Between the Farm Business and the Farm Household with Implications on Economic Efficiency." Ames, Iowa: Agricultural Experiment Station Research Bulletin 398, 1953.

Jackson, J. "Aged Negroes: Their Cultural Departures from Statistical Stereotypes and Rural-Urban Differences." *The Gerontologist,* 1970, 10, 140–145.

Kaplan, J. and P. Taietz. "The Rural Aged." *Geriatrics,* 1958, 13, 752–757.

Klatzky, S. "Patterns of Contact with Relatives." Washington, D.C., American Sociological Association, 1972.

Koller, M. "Studies of Three-Generation Households." *Marriage and Family Living,* 1954, 16, 205–206.

Loomis, C. and J. A. Beegle. *Rural Social Systems*. New York: Prentice-Hall, 1950.

Martel, M. and W. W. Morris. *Life After Sixty in Iowa*. Iowa City, Iowa: Institute of Gerontology, 1960.

Martindale, D. and E. Monachesi. *Elements of Sociology*, New York: Harpers, 1951.

McKain, W. and E. Baldwin. "Old Age and Retirement in Rural Connecticut." Storrs, Connecticut: Agricultural Experiment Station Bulletin 299, 1953.

Mirande, A. M. "Extended Kinship Ties, Friendship Relations, and Community Size: An Exploratory Inquiry." *Rural Sociology*, 1970, 35 (2), 261–266.

Montgomery, J. "Social Characteristics of the Aged in a Small Pennsylvania Community." University Park, Pennsylvania: College of Home Economics Research Publication 233, 1965.

Payne, R. and W. Bailey. *The Community: A Classified, Annotated Bibliography*. University of Georgia, Athens, Georgia, 1967.

Pihlblad, C. T. and D. Adams. "Widowhood, Social Participation and Life Satisfaction." *Aging and Human Development*, 1972, 3, 323–330.

Pihlblad, C. T., D. Adams, and H. Rosencranz. "Social-Economics Adjustment to Widowhood." *Omega*, 1972, 3, 295–305.

Pihlblad, C. T. and H. Rosencranz. "Older People in the Small Town: A Final Report." Columbia, Missouri: Department of Sociology, 1969.

Powers, E. and G. Bultena. "Correspondence Between Anticipated and Actual Use of Public Services by the Aged." *The Social Service Review*, 1974, 48, 245–254.

____. "Sex Differences in Intimate Friendships of Old Age." *Journal of Marriage and the Family*, 1976.

Powers, R. and M. Liston. "A Study of the Patterns of Living of the Elderly in Iowa Non-Urban Population Centers." Ames, Iowa: Home Economics Research Institute No. 65, 1971.

Rosencranz, H., C. T. Pihlblad, and T. McNevin. "Social Participation of Older People in the Small Town." Columbia, Missouri: Department of Sociology, 1968.

Sewell, W., C. Ramsey, and L. Ducoff. "Farmers' Conceptions and Plans for Economic Security in Old Age." Madison, Wisconsin Agricultural Experiment Station Bulletin 182, 1953.

Shanas, E. and G. Streib. *Social Structure and the Family: Generational Relations*. Englewood Cliffs, New Jersey: Prentice-Hall, 1965.

Shanas, E., P. Townsend, D. Wedderburn, H. Frits, P. Milhj, and J. Stehorwer. *Old People in Three Industrial Societies*. New York: Atherton Press, 1968.

Sharp, H. and M. Axelrod. "Mutual Aid among Relatives in an Urban Population." In R. Freedman, A. Hawley, W. Landecker, G. Lenski, and H. Mines (eds.), *Principles of Sociology*. New York: Holt, Rinehart and Winston, 1956.

Smith, T. L. and P. Zopf. *Principles of Inductive Rural Sociology*. Philadelphia: F. A. Davis Company, 1970.

Stojanovic, E. "The Dissemination of Information About Medicare to Low-Income Rural Residents." *Rural Sociology,* 1972, 37, 253–260.

Sussman, M. "The Help Pattern in the Middle Class Family." *American Sociological Review,* 1953, 18, 22–28.

Sussman, M. and L. Burchinal. "Kin Family Network: Unheralded Structure in Current Conceptualization of Family Functioning." *Marriage and Family Living,* 1962, 24, 231–240.

U.S. Bureau of the Census. "General Population Characteristics: 1970." Washington, D.C., 1971.

Youmans, E. "Aging Patterns in a Rura! and an Urban Area of Kentucky." Agricultural Experiment Station Bulletin 681, Lexington, Kentucky, 1963.

PART 4

PROSPECTS AND PERSPECTIVES ON RURAL FAMILIES

12
THE FAMILY IN RURAL SOCIETY: IMAGES OF THE FUTURE

William M. Smith, Jr.,
and Raymond T. Coward

The family is a unit of interacting persons, the source and seedbed of human personality, the wellspring of affection, emotional support, and life-long security. Families determine the kinds of persons who grow up in any generation, time, or place; and the kinds of persons they become determine the nature of their community, nation, or world. The nuclear family is one of the most fragile of all human relationships, overloaded with the tensions, stresses, frustrations, and fatigue of a complex and changing world. It is vulnerable in part because persons enter it with unrealistic expectations and distorted goals and with less preparation or orientation than is given for a driver's or hunter's license.

During the decade of the 1970s, prophets and would-be prophets predicted the deterioration, decline, and demise of the family. Assorted shreds of evidence were quoted and misquoted to support whatever position the writer or speaker upheld. An increasing divorce rate, lower birth rates, increases in family violence and in the numbers of single-parent households, and experimental forms of the family were all cited as indicators of illness or impending death. Yet, for the most part, these predictions were overstatements and, to paraphrase Mark Twain, the notice of the demise of the American family was greatly exaggerated (Coward and Smith, 1981).

Memories and nostalgia, sermons and stereotypes, and the paucity of research data all combine to distort our conception of what families are like or what they ever have been. This may be especially true in relationship to families in rural society, where stereotypes abound and data are scarce.

The image of the family in rural society must not be frozen in "still life" forms, like a Grandma Moses painting or a Currier and Ives print. The family in rural society would be more accurately characterized as the "family-in-process" or the "family-becoming." As the chapters of this volume have repeatedly emphasized, the family in rural society has undergone significant modifications. Simultaneously, the society in which these families live has been remarkably altered in the last quarter of a century.

Rural America is characterized currently by both persistence and change (Ford, 1978). Certain features of the rural environment have remained stable and have precipitated continuity in the family as well as in other rural groups and institutions (for example, less population density, fewer governmental services, and greater integration of work and family). At the same time, dimensions of the rural community have dramatically changed and have been associated with significant positive and negative shifts in the quality of life (for example, increases in industrialization, continued declines in the numbers of family-owned and operated farms, energy costs, and increased environmental consciousness). These concurrent changes in both families *and* the rural United States have rendered many of the popularly held images of rural families obsolete, outdated, or at best, suspect. It is apparent that a changing rural society has important ramifications for the family and that the changing family is also affecting the nature of rural society (Coward, 1980).

Given this pervading atmosphere of change and evolution, it is perhaps foolhardy to attempt to extract generalizations about the future. Yet, certain salient trends are so apparent that it is relatively safe to consider their impact on the future of rural families. The details presented in the preceding chapters provide a base from which we can speculate about the balance between stability and change that families in rural society are likely to strike in the future. We can use this base to consider the prospects of families entwined in a rural society characterized by both persistence and change. And finally, we can use this base to construct a research agenda that, if completed, would provide the empirical data necessary to better understand this expanding segment of our American culture.

Rural Families: Changes and Choices

Below are discussed those trends that are most salient when attempting to understand the rural family of today *and* tomorrow.

Rural Family Diversity

Many of the widely held beliefs and stereotypes about what the rural family was "in the olden days," "might be," or "ought to be" are based on mental images about fictional *farm* families. Many continue to equate farm with rural, and the traditional virtues of farm families (individual sacrifice, hard work for common goals, etc.) are often generalized to all of rural America. In the 1980s, however, farm families will constitute a minority of the families in rural society. It is, therefore, a gross distortion to characterize the family in rural society as only the farm family.

Similarly, it is inaccurate to portray the family in rural society as only the traditional, intact nuclear family, amply supplied with homemade help in the form of live-in relatives or hired hands nearby. As the preceding chapters have illustrated, families in rural society reflect a variety of alternative living arrangements. Nor is the rural family the urban family in a more placid setting. Rural families cope with environments (physical and social-psychological) that are different from those of urban families. Such factors as space, isolation, interaction between occupation and other family roles, or the dependence on seasons, weather, and climate are constantly in the foreground for rural families living in open country, remote homesteads, or small towns and villages. At the same time, it must not be assumed that the family in rural society reflects a single ethnic heritage. Patterns of family life developed in "cultural islands" by Blacks, Mexican Americans, Amish, Scandinavians, French-Canadians and other ethnic groups reflect social adaptations in marginal and rapidly changing environments as well as responses to the power or authority of a controlling elite.

Mobility and migration have also contributed to diversity. The traditional rural family was assumed to have "roots" in one place, one farm, one village. Yet, in this century the rural United States has already experienced both a widespread out-migration of families as well as a reversed in-migration (Beale, 1975). The current influx of outsiders, flatlanders, city folk, and easterners has added to an existing pluralistic mosaic in rural America. It is still impossible to predict how long this reverse movement will last or how far the streams will flow from the metropolitan centers; however, the effects on rural life, including the family life of in-migrants and of those who never moved, have already been observed, although not yet adequately studied. The in-migrants themselves are not a homogeneous group. They include, as characterized by Ploch (Chapter 3), the "scruffy" and the "baronial," propelled by various goals and values, some rejecting metropolitan lifestyles, some returning home, most seeking emotional and physical security and wishing for greater control over their own welfare and that of their children.

In addition to these residential shifts, thousands of families continue to crisscross the rural United States annually as "migrants" in search of a livelihood. The major fact of their lives is economic hardship. Their lifestyles are quite different from those of the hired hands or tenant farmers of the turn of the century who saw a step-by-step progression up the ladder of success feasible if they worked hard enough and if they "stayed put."

In short, many of the descriptions of family life contained in the previous chapters have illuminated the diversity that has developed or has recently been exacerbated in the family in rural society. Diversity is, therefore, a central and critical characteristic of the rural family of today and of the near future. This diversity must be recognized by service providers, community planners, and policymakers. It must be taken into account and integrated into the future projections for the rural United States. From the standpoint of research, there must be a greater understanding of the implications of this diversity for community development, individual expectations, and family interactions.

Family Roles

Families perform an infinite variety of functions, some shared with other groups and agencies, others divided among family members or shared by family members. When changes occur in society, the functions performed by different groups shift, some by design, others by default. Along with other groups and institutions in rural society the family has been moving from a horse-and-buggy organization to the computerized age. Changing roles can result in problems, especially when the process occurs rapidly or when individuals are unprepared for new role behavior. However, in spite of considerable popular mythology, changing roles do not automatically indicate a breakup or disintegration of the family or of any other group. Indeed, it may signal a more rational, more competent designing and playing of roles.

The social problems of geographic and social isolation, poverty, and underemployment—all characteristics of much of rural America—limit the range of role options available for many men and women. But, as Bescher-Donnelly and Smith (Chapter 9) have reminded us, these problems often have more salience for women. While rural women continue to view marriage and family as desirable and normative patterns, they are increasingly aware of the achievements and status of their urban sisters and of the changing nature of responsibilities required to maintain a family. Several influences have operated, and will continue to operate, to modify the scenario and timing of roles of rural women (for example, increased education, changing expectations, increased longevity, and new patterns of marriage and family formation).

Inflation has also contributed to the increased attraction of women into the labor force and in turn to an increased price for remaining at home. At the same time, the skills of a homemaker in such areas as clothing construction, preparing and preserving food, or even child care reflect a higher dollar value when the inflated costs of purchasing substitutes in the rural marketplace are considered. The economic conditions of the rural labor force may also lead to intensified stress within the family as husbands feel their status and functions jeopardized by loss of employment, temporary layoffs, or obsolescence of their skills.

Part-time farmers are also an example of the changing roles in rural society. Their numbers are increasing. Off-farm work can provide supplemental income, may moderate the impact of seasonal fluctuations, can build liaisons between farm and nonfarm residents in an area, and often makes it possible for families who could not otherwise begin farming or remain in farming to do so and support a family. Concurrently, such work may alter the dynamics of the family system and holds the potential for increased stress and tension. Unfortunately, little is known of the familial ramifications of this phenomenon.

Considerable public attention is being called to one-parent families, which are increasing in numbers and burdened with problems that, in most instances, are too complex to solve without outside help. Little or no attention has been paid to the special needs of these children in small schools or other rural community settings. In rural areas, the problem is compounded to the extent that divorce and separation are frowned upon. If assistance is not available through the extended kinship system, new supports for one-parent families must be created in rural communities, as they have been in many metropolitan centers.

Of those persons maintaining families without a spouse, the overwhelming majority are women. The greater incidence of poverty and its associated problems is closely related to whether the head is male or female. Moreover, the incidence of poverty among female-headed households is even greater in rural than in metropolitan areas. As with other problems derivative from poverty, there can be a tendency to "blame the victim" rather than to ferret out the cause and design a remedy. Since one-parent families do not fit the traditional stereotype of a "good family" in a rural setting, it is relatively easy to keep them invisible, along with other signs of rural poverty.

The last members of the nuclear-family triad—the children—have also experienced changes in their traditional roles and family circumstances as rural families have evolved and diversified. Fertility is on the decline in non-metropolitan families, and thus rural children today are growing up with fewer siblings. Rising divorce rates and births out of wedlock mean that many rural children are reared in single-parent homes or reconstituted families. Changes in the structure of the rural labor market have reduced the norm of father and son working together on chores. We know little about the adaptations of children whose parents have suddenly decided to move back to the country. Indeed, such moves are often motivated in large part because of a perceived positive influence on the child's growing years; yet, we have no evidence exploring the quality of the parent-child relationship following such moves or the consequences for the child's life of the shift in residence. In fact, although we know that growing up in rural America in the 1980s is different from what it was at the turn of the century, we are unable to precisely define the immediate effect of those differences or to predict the consequences of the differences for later adult development. There is much to know, and much to be done, before we understand the influence of rural environments on children and child rearing.

Rural and Urban: Merging or Diverging?

Although geographical isolation has been, and still is, a factor that influences organization participation and family interaction in rural society, the effects of isolation may be diminishing. Mass-media news and advertising bring metropolitan standards, lifestyles, attitudes, expectations, and activities into every home—and barn! Although the exact impact of this influence is still being debated, there is little doubt that some amount of "spillover" of metropollyana has occurred.

The immediate effects of the near environment of rurality clearly both pose limitations and provide resources in the process of family or community development. Coping with *space* relationships alone creates, and will continue to create, differences between families in metropolitan and nonmetropolitan areas. Distances between family, friends, and kin; distances to needed services; distances to markets; distances to social or religious centers; distances to schools—how distance is perceived and how it is used affects relationships within and between families. In the same vein, attitudes toward the relationship between people and the land is another cluster of attitudes and values found throughout rural society that sets it apart from urban America. Perhaps most consistently and logically integrated into the totality of life by Native Americans, some expression of the man-land relationship colors many rural family transactions. There is more than a grain of truth in the simplistic statement, "The land shapes the people and the people shape the land" (Kramer, 1980, p. 67).

Other features of the rural environment also call for unique cultural responses from those who live outside cities. Special occupations demand differences in pace. For the dairy farmer, for example, there is no hurrying the cows at milking time, and every day of the year the family and work routine is fixed by a bovine schedule. Rural families have been described as "steadfast," that is, they stay at home and work hard. On the well-kept farm, homestead, or small business there is a dedication of family members to "husbandry." Individuals not only care *for* resources but they care *about* them in the sense that they try to leave their place in better condition than they found it. Today both farms and these traditional rural values are under siege. The seemingly pervasive urge to get bigger as fast as possible is often inconsistent with stewardship, entrepreneurship, and other requisites of a people-land alliance.

With respect to families, the debate about how much merging there has been on the rural-urban continuum has centered for the most part on the question of whether rural families are becoming more like urban families. Those who argue that a merging is occurring give emphasis to nonmetropolitan statistics indicating increased rates of divorce, decreases in fertility rates, and increases in the numbers of rural women who work outside the home. Since these trends have become characteristic of urban families, proponents conclude that the two environments are becoming more alike.

In contrast, others propose that the rural-urban distinction continues to be useful and that rural families are indeed significantly different from their urban counterparts. To support their position they point to the younger ages at marriage of rural couples, the larger rural family sizes, the lower labor force participation of rural women, and smaller divorce percentages.

Both sides are correct. Many of the changes that have been witnessed in urban families have their parallels in families who reside in small towns and rural communities. It is as if the two are riding on parallel but different roads—going in the same direction but remaining on distinctly separate paths (Coward, 1980).

Supportive Services

American society has at times, and in certain places, been plagued by too many organizations and too little organization. As we have indicated, changes in the family may lead to *improved* functioning and stimulate development. But when changes happen too quickly, when persons are caught up in changes or changing situations that they can not handle alone, some outside support or assistance must be provided. Organizing to help families be more resourceful, to "help them help themselves," involves analysis, setting priorities, planning, action, evaluation, and accountability. The absence of a coordinated federal policy for rural America *or* one for American families (Coward, 1980; Coward and Smith, 1981) probably means that governmental support for the family in rural society will lag behind the need for help.

Although few empirical studies of rural family life have been conducted since mid-century, families in rural areas have been designated by some laws as "targets" for public programs, have been "involved" as putative consumers of such programs, and have seen personnel come and go with changing programs. Programs have been projected and carried out with little or no attempt to precisely determine the lifestyles, situations, goals, needs, or problems of rural families. To compound the errors, programs have been evaluated with no attention to what effect they may have had on family interaction or family continuity. Community development projects have been planned and carried out with little or no regard for their impact on the family or how family or kinship systems might support or retard the developmental process. "Accountability" to the "donor" often seems more important than "accountability" to the "recipient." Our society acknowledges that competence in performing family roles is closely intertwined with achieving success in roles in other systems such as work, but we drag our collective feet in asking what families need for defining quality family life or in providing for those needs when they are demonstrated.

The preceding chapters have indicated several "critical need points" for the family in rural society—today and in the immediate future. Some of the situations that create these needs are shared with families in urban society (such as, the quality of public schooling, leaving home, marriage, parenthood, and family dissolution); others are unique to rural society or are more critical under rural conditions. For example, the changing roles for rural women will require innovative programs in adult education and counseling. Similarly, as more rural mothers spend greater amounts of time outside the home in the labor force, and as more young families move into rural areas, the need for planned, supervised child-care alternatives will become increasingly critical. Additionally, as long as poverty plagues rural society, there will be a need for outside support for the family.

Finally, public and private agencies often stress assisting the individual rather than the family unit. Some service delivery systems treat families as if they were composed of nonintegrated groupings of individuals. Agency functionaries sometimes forget that the family may directly and indirectly assist or block any outside efforts to bring about change in a family member. Mother may collect all sorts of recipes and good ideas about nutrition, but father may hold a veto on applying them, especially if he buys the groceries.

To the Future

Any attempt to project what the family in rural society will be like at any future period is blocked by a shortage of data about the present and past situation of rural families. The persistent unique aspects of rural society and of the rural environment must be recognized. The need for more detailed and accurate statements of demographic data, family patterns, sex roles, lifestyles, and changes in family coping behaviors is critical. Such data are vital for developing policies, fashioning or discarding programs, and producing legislation to improve the day-to-day living of families in rural society. There must be some insurance that the family is not remolded, sacrificed, disenfranchised simply for the sake of "progress"—however that may be defined.

Will the family have a place or a function in the future rural society? Will it increase in importance as a means for helping individuals maintain their wholeness in a complex society? Or will it be relegated to the social scrap heap along with the small-town post office, the general store, and the livery stable?

Despite the sobering list of "crises" that confront the family in rural society, it would be wrong to think that rural families are in a shambles. Rural families, like other families, have many strengths, and we are only recently experiencing a renewed interest in delineating more precisely the inherent qualities of strength in families (Stinnett, Chesser, and DeFrain, 1979). At the same time, the popular romantic images of rural families must be reshaped to reflect more accurately the reality of the 1980s. Family scholars must direct their attentions to illuminating the antecedents of familial changes that have been documented in rural society and identifying the consequences of these changes on the quality of rural family life.

This should not be misconstrued as a plea to repeat in rural America every piece of research ever completed on urban or suburban families. Certain areas of family research would not appear to be significantly changed by examining the intervening effects of the macroenvironment. In contrast, there are other areas where a sensitivity to the rural environment and the changing nature of that environment would lead social scientists to be interested in certain styles of family functioning or particular stages of family development.

Elsewhere we have discussed in greater detail what we believe to be the research priorities for the 1980s for scholars of the family in rural society (Coward and Smith, 1981). Within each of the three categories we identified there is much to do and much to understand. Briefly, the priorities are:

- a better and more comprehensive understanding of internal family dynamics and the family life cycle as it is manifested in rural society;
- a more comprehensive exploration of the relationships of rural families to major external institutions (schools, churches, health systems, governments, banks, and labor and production markets, etc.); and
- a need to identify strategies that are effective for developing and delivering human services in rural environments.

Delineating the research priorities and marshalling the resources necessary to address the issues are clearly two distinct achievements. The first will not automatically lead to the second. The chapters of this volume have repeatedly concluded that additional research is needed. Such pleas are often shallow attempts by academicians to disguise self-serving rhetoric. We *do not* believe that is the case here. To the contrary, we believe that there are legitimate, and urgent, reasons for requesting that families in rural society become a social science research priority. For this to happen, however, rural issues must be given increased visibility and we must foster a more accurate perception of family life in rural America among service providers, scholars, and policymakers. In summary, let us state our case as follows:

- We *know* that the nonmetropolitan population in America is growing.
- We *know* that rural America has undergone significant and rapid changes in the last quarter of a century and that these changes can affect the quality of family life.
- We *know* that many families in rural society are experiencing severe and critical problems of an economic, interpersonal, individual, and familial nature.
- We *know* that supportive services for families are fewer and narrower in range in nonmetropolitan America.
- Yet, we continue to have an *inadequate understanding* of the impact of all of the above, and other unlisted trends, on sustaining and enhancing the quality of life for families in rural America.

References

Beale, C. L. *The Revival of Population Growth in Nonmetropolitan America.* Washington, D.C.: Economic Development Division, Economic Research Service, U.S. Department of Agriculture, 1975, ERS-605.

Coward, R. T. "Rural Families Changing, But Retain Distinctiveness." *Rural Development Perspectives, 1980,* 3, 4–8.

Coward, R. T. and W. M. Smith. "The Family in Rural Society." In D. A. Dillman and D. Hobbs (eds.), *Rural Society: Research Issues for the 1980s.* Boulder, Colorado: Westview Press, 1981, forthcoming.

Ford, T. R. (ed.). *Rural U.S.A.: Persistence and Change.* Ames, Iowa: Iowa State University Press, 1978.

Kramer, M. *Three Farms.* Boston, Massachusetts: Little, Brown and Company, 1980.

Stinnett, N., B. Chesser, and J. DeFrain (eds.). *Building Family Strengths: Blueprints for Action.* Lincoln, Nebraska: University of Nebraska Press, 1979.

INDEX

SAD. *See* School Administrative
    District
Salamon, S., 154, 160
San Antonio (Texas), 97-98
San Joaquin Valley, 101
Saskatchewan (Canada), 149
Satisfaction, 188, 189, 200. *See also*
    Rural families, satisfaction in
Schneider, D. M., 98
School Administrative District (SAD)
    (Maine), 48
Schumm, Walter R., 4, 193
Shanas, E., 60, 200
Shepardson, M., 106
Shimkin, D., 94
Simmel, Georg, 57
Skitikuk School, 45
Slesinger, D. P., 18
Smith, F. E., 52
Smith, Leslie Whitener, 4, 224
Smith, R. T., 98
Smith, T. L., 131, 135, 136, 139, 199
SMSA. *See* Standard Metropolitan
    Statistical Area
Social isolates. *See* Back-to-the-land
    social isolates
Social networks, 57, 61, 212
    women-centered, 177
    See also Iowa, older workers study
South, 64, 89, 94, 95
Southeast, 66, 76
Southwest, 96
Spanier, G. B., 139
Standard Metropolitan Statistical Area
    (SMSA), 20
Sterilization. *See* Contraception
Stolzenberg, R. M., 15
Straus, M. A., 33, 60-61, 68
Sussman, M. B., 58, 130, 199
Sweet, J. A., 9, 14, 131

Tagalog, 119
Tait, J. L., 177
Targ, Dena B., 4, 5
Tax law and women, 181
Teenagers, 105-106
Tenant farms, 30-31, 223
Tennessee, 95
Texas, 89, 90, 91, 92, 93, 94, 96, 97, 99,

    102, 103, 104
Thornton-Stahura, B., 138
Toledo (Ohio), 132-133
Tracking, 48
Tweeten, L., 40

Urban families, 9, 57, 58-68, 129, 169
    Black, 95
    Filipino American, 113
    Mexican American, 96, 100, 101
    See also Divorce; Fertility; Marriage;
        Urban society
Urbanization, 57, 58, 59, 60-61, 63, 68,
    96, 101
Urban society, 16
    and rural society compared, 17-20,
        130-133, 135-138, 173-175, 176-177,
        192-195, 199, 200, 201, 203-204,
        214 n3, 226
Utang na loob. See Obligation
Uxorilocal residence, 101

Vegetable farms, 31
Virginia, 79-82, 83
Virilocal residence, 101
Voluntary associations, 116

Waite, L. J., 15
Walang hiya (shameless), 119
Warland, R. H., 89, 92
Warner, Lyle G., 3
Warrior role, 110-111
Washington, 112, 177, 204
Weber, Max, 57
Wells, Miriam J., 4
West, 31, 58, 64, 75, 76
Western American Kinship System, 75
Westoff, C., 15
White collar workers, 60, 63, 200. *See
    also* Iowa, older workers study
White, urban, middle-class Protestants
    (WUMP), 199
WUMP. *See* White, urban, middle-class
    Protestants
Widowers. *See* Iowa, older workers
    study; Widowhood
Widowhood, 189, 190, 204
WIFE. *See* Women Involved in Farm
    Economics